D1572829

◆ THE OTHER MARILYN

ALSO BY WARREN G. HARRIS

GABLE AND LOMBARD

Marilyn in Hollywood (1930).

THE OTHER MARILYN

A BIOGRAPHY OF

MARILYN MILLER

WARREN G. HARRIS

 ARBOR HOUSE · *NEW YORK*

Manufactured in the United States of America

10 9 8 7 6 5 4 3 2 1

This book is printed on acid-free paper. The paper in this book meets the guidelines for permanence and durability of the Committee on Production Guidelines for Book Longevity of the Council on Library Resources.

Library of Congress Cataloging in Publication Data

Harris, Warren G.
   The other Marilyn.

     Bibliography: p.
     Includes index.
     1. Miller, Marilyn, 1898–1936. 2. Entertainers—United States—Biography. I. Title.
PN2287.M643H3   1985   792.2′.092′4 [B]   84-18515
ISBN 0-87795-584-0 (alk. paper)

FOR ANOTHER MARILYN
AND HER AUNT MAUDE.

CONTENTS

Illustrations follow page 134

CHAPTER ONE

MISS MILLER, YOU'RE ON!

THERE WAS A TIME, in the roaring, topsy-turvy decades between the First and Second World Wars, when the name Marilyn and the initials MM signified only one luminary—Marilyn Miller. She was Broadway's premiere musical comedy star, the prized creation of the Great Glorifier, Florenz Ziegfeld. Theater critic John Mason Brown crowned her the "Titania of the Jazz Age."

The great performers have a natural spark, a personal incandescence, that cannot be acquired or imitated. Petite, doll-like Marilyn Miller was one such performer. Something magical happened when she appeared on stage. She had rivals who may have been better dancers, singers, actresses, or mimics, but no one individual could equal her when it came to combining all those talents. Her golden blond beauty was as fresh and delicate as a flower petal. She seemed to radiate happiness with an unfading smile that was unforgettable. She always looked as if she were getting as much enjoyment from her work as the audience was.

Marilyn Miller had been entertaining the public continually from the age of five, when she joined her family's vaudeville act under the moniker "Mademoiselle Sugarlump." She first gained prominence at sixteen in *The Passing Show of 1914* and became a head-liner in the *Ziegfeld Follies of 1918*. But her period of greatest popularity occurred between 1920 and 1933, when she starred in such long-running hits as *Sally, Sunny, Rosalie,* and *As Thousands Cheer*.

Jerome Kern, Irving Berlin, George Gershwin, Vincent You-mans, Sigmund Romberg, and Victor Herbert composed music for her. P. G. Wodehouse, Guy Bolton, Ring Lardner, Ira Gershwin, Otto Harbach, Oscar Hammerstein II, and Moss Hart were among her lyricists and writers. At James M. Barrie's choosing, she was the first person to play the role of Peter Pan in the United States after the aging Maude Adams relinquished her monopoly on it.

Unless evidence can be produced to the contrary, it was Marilyn Miller who introduced the name Marilyn into American nomen-clature. Young courting couples went to her shows and fell in love with her and the type of delicate beauty that she personified; when they married, they named their firstborn daughters after her. There was even a nickel cigar called the "Marilyn," sold in boxes decorated with an enchanting hand-tinted photograph of its namesake.

As a cover girl and model for many of the leading magazines, she was a great influence on fashion. Women bobbed their hair and made up their faces to look like her; they copied her frilly frocks and fanciful hats. In a rare demonstration of its affection for Marilyn Miller, the public purchased $1,250,000 worth of World War I Liberty Bonds from her in a single evening.

Off stage as well as on, Marilyn Miller was always beaming. She seemed so happy, and yet her life was shadowed by physical and mental torment. She suffered from chronic sinusitis and blinding migraine headaches. The pain was excruciating, but an unyielding willpower kept her going.

She had three disastrous marriages. Her first husband was killed in a car crash less than a year after their wedding. Her second was addicted to drugs and alcohol. The third was an eager chorus boy eleven years her junior.

Marilyn was a victim of changing times and tastes. Although she was revered on Broadway, her attempts at becoming a Hollywood star were a crushing failure. And the Great Depression spelled an end to the type of "Cinderella" stage musicals that were her specialty throughout the twenties.

"It may sound strange, but I never want to grow old. I never want to see the day when I cannot sing and dance as I can now," Marilyn Miller said in 1922, when she was only twenty-four. "I cannot bear to think of being middle-aged, with all my success behind me. The picture of a dear, gray-haired old lady by the fireside doesn't appeal to me."

The statement was prophetic. She died fourteen years later, five months before her thirty-eighth birthday. Toward the end of her life she grew fearful that she was losing her beauty, and she rarely showed her face in public in daylight. She rested behind drawn curtains all day, saving herself for the night, when she would emerge, exquisitely dressed, covered with jewels, glowing with vitality.

Nobody who saw Marilyn's entrance into nightclubs or theatrical premieres could guess what agonies she was going through. She and her much younger husband were finding it harder and harder to get along. Her horrible migraine headaches were a daily occurrence. Friends saw her in such pain that she would stand and beat her head against the wall until they had to pull her away.

It was a time of profound despair. How could she compete any longer with the newer crop of stars? How could she impose her aging face on roles that called for younger beauty?

In the end, she may have just given up. Carrie Wallace, Marilyn Miller's personal maid and confidante for many years, once said: "She wasn't too bright about many things. That spot in your head that's soft when you're a baby, it didn't never harden up. She kind of thought that life would be like the shows she was in. When the story was nice and everything came out fine in the end and it was lovely and everybody was happy. That's the way she thought it was going to be. And when it wasn't like that, she just kind of cried a little and then she died."

Ten years after Marilyn Miller's death, another celebrated Marilyn emerged. Already twenty years old by then, she was a peroxide blonde with the name of Norma Jean Dougherty when she signed a one-year, $125-a-week contract with 20th Century-Fox Film Corporation on August 26, 1946.

Norma Jean was quite a looker, but her potential as a movie star was questionable. As a first step, her name would have to be changed. Production chief Darryl F. Zanuck wanted something glamorous and easy to remember, yet distinct from those of the studio's current leading ladies, who included Betty Grable, Gene Tierney, Linda Darnell and Maureen O'Hara.

Marilyn Miller's spirit may have been floating over Hollywood that day. Her former sweetheart and fiancé Ben Lyon, who'd retired from acting to become a Fox talent scout, spotted something of Marilyn's luminous qualities in Norma Jean and told the new contractee that she'd find no more magical name than that.

And since it seemed to have brought Marilyn Miller good fortune, why not an alliterative last name that would give Norma Jean the same initials as her forebear? Without wasting any time, Norma Jean herself came up with Monroe, which was her mother's maiden name.

Did anyone ever notice that the names Marilyn Miller and Marilyn Monroe each contain the same number of letters—an unlucky thirteen? The name Marilyn and the monogram may have been a curse rather than a good-luck charm.

Not until Marilyn Monroe died, sixteen years after she assumed her new name, could the eerie parallels between the two Marilyns be noticed. Marilyn Monroe also had three unsuccessful marriages—including one in which her name actually became Marilyn Miller—and her last years were a similar study in decline. At her passing, Marilyn Monroe was thirty-six, a year younger than Marilyn Miller when she died.

Marilyn Monroe's story has been told a million times. Now it's the original Marilyn's turn.

$\mathbf{M}$ADEMOISELLE SUGARLUMP

HER REAL NAME WAS Marilynn Reynolds. Her first name paid tribute to her maternal grandparents, Mary and Lynn Thompson (the second "n" was dropped in the early 1920s). She was born on September 1, 1898, in Evansville, Indiana, a port city on the Ohio river that was a link between the unhurried Old South and the bustling, industrial North. It was the year of the 112-day Spanish-American War, Marie and Pierre Curie's discovery of radium, and the publication of Henry James's *The Turn of the Screw*. More relevant to Marilyn Miller's subsequent career, 1898 not only brought the very first photographs taken by artificial "flash" light, but also marked the birth of George Gershwin and Vincent You-mans, who would compose songs for her, and of Gertrude Lawrence and Adele Astaire, who would become her personal friends and professional rivals.

Marilyn was the fourth and last child born to Edwin D. Reynolds and the former Ada Thompson, both then in their early thirties. The other Reynolds children were Ruth, the eldest, then nine; Claire, seven; and Edwin, Jr., three. Marilyn was the first member of her immediate family to be born outside the state of Tennessee;

both sides were descended from Irish and Scottish immigrants who had settled there at the end of the eighteenth century.

A lineman for the Cumberland Telephone Company, Edwin Reynolds helped to install some of the first phone systems in the rural South and the Midwest. Since his job kept him traveling much of the time, home for the rest of the family was his mother-in-law's house in Memphis. It was intended for Marilyn to be born in Memphis, but when the time was approaching, yellow fever broke out in the city. Ada Reynolds fled in panic with the three children to Evansville, almost three hundred miles to the north, where her husband was working.

Under less urgent circumstances, Ada Reynolds would have chosen to sail on one of the steamships that connected Memphis and Evansville via the Mississippi and Ohio rivers. But the circuitous voyage took four days and she couldn't risk giving birth on board. As it was, she arrived in Evansville by train just in time. Several hours later, in Edwin Reynolds's temporary lodgings above a corner grocery store, Marilyn was delivered by the hastily summoned neighborhood doctor.

Legend had it that Marilyn was born with her incandescent smile permanently engraved on her face. She was a beautiful baby, small and delicately formed. When she grew into full bloom, her porcelainlike complexion, golden blond hair, and greenish blue eyes were attributed to her father and the Reynolds lineage.

That Marilyn bore slight physical resemblance to her mother didn't mean that Ada Reynolds was unattractive. She was handsome rather than beautiful, a brunette with strong features and a magisteral bearing. In her youth, Ada was the singing and dancing darling of the Thompson family; her considerable talent seemed to be passed on to all four of her children. As soon as they could walk and talk, Ada did everything to encourage their musical development. By the time Marilyn was born, Claire had become an accomplished pianist who did not read music but could play anything from the classics to ragtime after one hearing. Ruth and young Edwin were versatile singers and dancers.

Ada Reynolds was a prime example of that show business phenomenon known as the stage mother. Thwarted from becoming a professional entertainer herself by early marriage and parenthood, she transferred her ambitions to her offspring. Unfortunately, Edwin Reynolds did not share his wife's dreams of turning their children into entertainers; in fact, he threatened to leave her if she ever dared let them perform. In the God-fearing heartland of America at the end of the nineteenth century, show people were considered vagrants and social outcasts. For a woman especially, entering the theatrical life was almost as terrible a fate as becoming a prostitute.

Her husband's opposition only made Ada Reynolds more determined to succeed. She started to assemble an "act" for Ruth and Claire, designating herself their manager, choreographer, costume designer, and makeup artist. Replying to ads in *The Billboard* and other trade papers, she was able to secure a few scattered bookings in amusement parks and beer gardens, which stressed the range of the talents they presented over the quality, and weren't too particular about hiring inexperienced newcomers as long as they worked cheap.

At about this time, Edwin Reynolds was coming up for a promotion in his job with the Cumberland Telephone Company. When he was reassigned to Nashville on what was to be a permanent basis, Ada did not want to make the move. That was the end of the marriage. No compromise was attempted; Reynolds cleared out and Ada and the children never saw him again. She eventually obtained a divorce on grounds of desertion.

Without Edwin Reynolds's financial support, his family's welfare now depended wholly on the success of the act featuring Claire, who was billed as "the phenomenal doll pianist," and Ruth, "the dainty little vocalist and dancer." The Reynolds Sisters' first engagement landed them on a nine-act variety program at the Glenwood Park Summer Theatre in Little Rock, Arkansas. Within a few days, little Master Edwin Reynolds, Jr., was worked into the routines as a "coonshouter," performing black dialect songs that were much in vogue then, despite (or due to) their sometimes racist implications.

Baby Marilyn was still too young to take part. She was looked after backstage by whomever happened to be handy while her mother was taking care of business; her crib was really the top drawer of the family's wardrobe trunk. Marilyn Miller didn't qualify as one of those entertainers "born in a trunk," but she certainly was raised in one.

Although it would never make a headline attraction, the Reynolds family act was well received. Audiences, comprised mainly of parents and their children, found much to identify with in the three gifted Reynolds youngsters. But as one booking led to another, it became apparent that the theatrical life wasn't going to be as glamorous or as high paying as Ada Reynolds had dreamed. Earnings barely equaled expenses, and living conditions were terrible—an endless succession of overcrowded dressing rooms, third-class railway coaches, and dingy boardinghouses.

Ada Reynolds soon realized that something would have to be done about Marilyn. Once she started to toddle, she was in everyone's way. And though Ada didn't enjoy appraising her youngest child in monetary terms, she was the only member of the group who wasn't paying his or her own way. Marilyn's minimal food and clothing expenses were still enough to cause a deficit in Ada's accounts book.

The only solution was to send Marilyn to Memphis to stay with her grandmother and namesake, Mary Thompson. Ada's twin brother, Leon Thompson, a printer by trade, and his wife, Louise, lived with Mrs. Thompson. The couple had no children of their own, so they offered to share the responsibility of caring for Marilyn.

Marilyn lived with her relatives in Memphis for about four years. As a result, she blossomed into something of a southern belle; there was a distinct trace of a Dixie drawl to Marilyn Miller's speech, especially in her frequent use of the expression "Yes, suh!" But there was nothing of the southern bigot about her. On the Memphis street where Marilyn lived, there were only blacks for playmates, the children of servants who worked for the neighbors and her own relatives. The difference in color was meaningless to a little girl seeking companionship; that attitude never changed in adult life.

If it hadn't been for one of those black friends, there might never have been a Marilyn Miller. When she became famous, she always credited a black youth who used to bring coal into the house for fires in the wintertime as her first rhythmic inspiration. Instead of walking into a room, he danced—shuffling, tapping, and buck-and-winging in a way that was magical to the wide-eyed girl. Marilyn started to imitate him and before long she could match him step for step.

Meanwhile, an event took place that was of equal importance in shaping Marilyn's future. Somewhere in her travels around the vaudeville circuits, Ada Reynolds acquired another husband—Caro Miller. Once a letter carrier in Findlay, Ohio, his patrician good looks and magnetic personality had so impressed the people along his postal route that they encouraged him to abandon the job in favor of a theatrical career. By the time he married Ada Reynolds, Caro Miller had acted, sung, danced, and performed acrobatics in everything from vaudeville and circuses to minstrel shows and Gilbert and Sullivan operettas.

Caro Miller was three years younger than Ada Reynolds. They seemed to be made for each other. She needed a father for her children as well as someone to take over the management of the act, which was proving too difficult for her to handle in a male-dominated business. Miller had been floundering as a solo artist and could see a good future for himself in combination with the Reynolds children.

In keeping with the patriotic fervor of the times, Caro Miller created a new act called the Four Columbians. To give the impression that they were a blood-related unit, the children started to use the name Miller rather than Reynolds. But that was only for the sake of appearances. Although Miller was, by definition, their stepfather, no legal steps were taken to change their surname or to make him their guardian.

The grandson of a fire-and-brimstone preacher of the Civil War era, Caro Miller tended to be a puritanical taskmaster. During rehearsals with the children, he used an ebony walking stick as a teacher would a pointer; and laggards were apt to get a whack or two across their backsides. Caro terrified Claire and Ruth into obedience, but their younger brother was more rebellious and finally had to be removed from the routines.

The act was temporarily renamed the Columbian Trio. With everybody dressed in red, white, and blue satin costumes that looked as if they were cut from the American flag, Caro Miller and the two girls did fifteen minutes of singing and dancing, plus tributes to some of the top stars of the era.

When the relationship between Caro Miller and his stepson continued to deteriorate, it was decided that the only place for the boy was with Marilyn and the Thompson family back in Memphis. When Ada Miller took him there, she made a surprising discovery. As she was about to walk into the dining room one morning, she saw Marilyn heading for the sideboard, upon which sat a huge bowl of grapes. Since they were just out of her reach, Marilyn raised herself up and stood on her toes like a ballet dancer.

Ada rushed over and asked her to do it again. Marilyn not only obliged, but also demonstrated some of the dance steps that she'd learned from her black friends. Although Ada had neglected Marilyn in favor of the three older children, she suddenly had to consider her from a new perspective. Now four years old, Marilyn was an adorable wisp of a thing, only two feet tall and weighing thirty-eight pounds. Her Uncle Len delighted in comparing her to the child in Sir Joshua Reynolds's painting *The Age of Innocence*, a copy of which hung in the Thompsons' front parlor for that very reason.

It didn't take Ada Miller long to realize that with the right training and encouragement, Marilyn could replace her brother as one of the Columbians. So instead of merely depositing Edwin in the care of his Memphis relatives, a swap was made and Marilyn was toted back to join the Millers' gypsylike wanderings. In this new existence, Marilyn would have no permanent home. Her address changed overnight or by the week, depending on the length of the engagements that Caro Miller was able to secure.

In the beginning, her stepfather suspected that Marilyn might be as troublesome as her brother, but she quickly won "Papa Gig" over with her sunny disposition and eagerness to be accepted as an equal in her new family unit. There were no immediate plans to put Marilyn into the act. She was still too young: Miller believed that no one should let a child loose on stage before the ripe old age of five! And if he'd learned anything from his experience with Edwin, it was that he'd been too severe with the boy. Marilyn was to be allowed to develop at her own pace.

There couldn't have been a better time for Marilyn to start a career. The years 1905–13 were gold rush days for vaudeville, which had the highest revenues and paid the biggest salaries of any branch of show business. A frenzied bidding war for talent was being waged between the dominant Keith-Albee empire and such challengers as William Morris, Klaw and Erlanger, the Shuberts, Martin Beck, and Marcus Loew. Wooed with larger and more comfortable theaters, lavish productions and star-studded bills, the public changed its attendance habits from a Saturday night event to two or three times a week. There were more than two thousand vaudeville theaters in the United States; for an act to play each one without repeats would have taken six years.

The circuits distinguished between "big time" and "small time." Every vaudevillian aimed for the big time of the large cities, where the best theaters, salaries, and working conditions prevailed; this usually meant two performances a day, in the afternoon and evening. Small time could mean anything from three to a dozen shows a day, in second- or third-rate theaters in urban neighborhoods, towns, and the remote villages of the "boondocks."

Although the Columbian Trio was then unquestionably small time, there were enough engagements to keep the Miller family continually busy. One summer afternoon in 1903, while they were making a tour of amusement park theaters in Ohio and Illinois, the one nonperforming member had an unforgettable experience. Marilyn's nursemaid took her on her first visit to that new entertainment wonder, the nickelodeon. Marilyn was dazzled. The pictures not only moved, but for a minute or two showed a beautiful ballerina pirouetting across a vast stage. Marilyn insisted on sitting through the entire program again and again just to see that brief sequence.

When she met her family that evening, Marilyn was still ecstatic. In her babyish way, she rhapsodized about the film and twirled around on her toes in hopeful imitation of the images still flickering through her mind. "If I had a costume that would bounce up and down, I could be just like that pretty lady," she told her mother.

To indulge the child, Ada Miller cut up some old skirts and petticoats and assembled them into a reasonable facsimile of a ballet dress. Marilyn was such a picture of sweetness when she put it on that her sister Ruth couldn't resist comparing her to a lump of sugar. From that evolved Marilyn Miller's lifelong nickname, "Lumpy."

Now that she had the beginnings of a stage wardrobe, Marilyn wanted to join the Columbians. Caro Miller was vehemently against it, but not wishing to discourage her too much, he allowed her to dress up and watch from the wings. During the evening show, when the Columbians were taking their final bows, Marilyn rushed out to congratulate them—and was caught center stage by another rise of the curtain. As the surprised audience started to laugh at the unannounced addition to the cast, the tiny girl, not the least bit flustered, curtsied demurely and launched into her charming ballerina imitation. The crowd applauded in surprise and pleasure.

That date, August 20, 1903, was entered into the family records as Marilyn's professional debut. Henceforth she would be known as Marilyn Miller. Two weeks later, a few days after her fifth birthday, she was belatedly baptized under that name at St. John's Episcopal Church in Cuyahoga Falls, Ohio.

For the time being, the Columbians continued to call themselves a trio, with Marilyn as a surprise guest artist identified only as "Mademoiselle Sugarlump." At first, she was on and offstage in a flash, but as her confidence grew she insisted on being given more to do. She brought such sparkle to the act that Caro Miller couldn't refuse. Every morning, after he put all three girls through an hour of rigorous exercise and practice, he gave Marilyn an additional hour all to herself. Very quickly, she added clog dancing (a sort of tap in wooden shoes), singing, and impersonations to her repertoire.

Most difficult for Marilyn to master was a routine that became one of her specialties, "The Dancing Doll." Taking her cue from a cranking sound made by her mother, Marilyn would march stiffly onstage from the wings like a mechanical toy. Caro Miller would pretend to sprinkle her with magic dust and then she slowly came "alive" and danced about with thistle-down grace. It required enormous concentration and control for a five-year-old, and in learning the routine Marilyn also had her first lesson in how to deal with Caro Miller's violent temper. She tried to heed his every criticism, but when he was displeased with her, there was no way that Marilyn could escape a spanking or a swipe of his cane. The trick was to let him strike where the bruises wouldn't show.

In later years, Marilyn Miller tended to paint a very pleasant picture of her childhood on the vaudeville stage. "How I loved it all—the contrast between backstage and the glory of being out behind the footlights, with kindly audiences in front of me who always seemed to have a warm place in their hearts for Mademoiselle Sugarlump," she once said. "It was not work at all for me, but the most fascinating kind of play.

"People often express a great deal of pity for children of the stage. So far as my own experience goes, I say without hesitation that my sisters and I were anything but proper objects of pity. We were as happy as the day is long. More pains were taken over our education than is devoted to that of most children; we had better clothes, better food, and constant parental care and supervision. We were treated as very important young ladies! And our childhood was natural, healthy and wholesome, while we learned at the same time many valuable lessons in discipline and responsibility."

Marilyn was always reticent about the brutality that she suffered at the hands of her stepfather. If she recalled the unhappier moments of those early years at all, it was in a detached way, without casting blame on anyone in particular: "I didn't choose to go on the stage. I was put on the stage because a living had to be earned. It's not a very pleasant childhood to look back on. I remember three small children, my sisters and myself, catching trains at unearthly hours of the night, getting out of trains in wan, gray dawns, dressing and undressing in the cellars of dusty old theaters. I practiced and practiced until I was too tired to know what I was doing, or why."

Apart from Caro Miller, if anyone deserved to be called the villain of Marilyn Miller's childhood, it was probably the social reformer named Elbridge T. Gerry, whom she once described as "the greatest of all possible nuisances." Gerry's Society for the Prevention of Cruelty to Children set all kinds of rules for the employment of minors. In the big cities especially, children under a certain age (usually five or six) were prevented from appearing on a stage in any capacity whatsoever. The situation was further complicated by separate standards that seemed to favor the dramatic theater over the less serious forms of entertainment. In Chicago, for example, a child of six was permitted to "act" in a straight play, but forbidden to "perform" in vaudeville or musical comedy.

Marilyn Miller described that period in her life as "ten years of evasions and hair-breadth escapes, hounded by child labor officers. Many a time we could play only small towns along the boundaries of a state so that we could pack up in an instant and dash across the border in case of trouble."

Those occasions when the law prevented Marilyn from appearing on stage with the Columbians were the unhappiest of her young life. She insisted on dressing up in her little costume anyway and would stand tearfully in the wings. There, like Peri at the Gates of Paradise, she gazed with longing toward her own particular heaven behind the footlights.

Since New York was the headquarters of the Gerry Society, Marilyn and the Columbians never worked on Broadway. The capital of the big time, it was the ultimate goal of all vaudevillians. The closest the Millers came was a Masonic Lodge benefit show at the Hotel Astor, which was supposed to be outside the jurisdiction of the Gerry Society but proved otherwise. Caro Miller was hauled into court and fined fifty dollars.

On that trip, Marilyn Miller saw Times Square for the first time. Awestruck by all the gaudy excitement, she told her mother that she'd be back one day: "I'll dance to Broadway on my toes and they'll put my name in electric lights."

To avoid problems with the Gerry Society, Caro Miller sought bookings outside the United States, where child labor laws were less restrictive or didn't exist at all. American entertainers were in vogue overseas, on the theory that anything imported was better than domestic. It was easy to line up tours lasting two or three years because of the great distances that had to be covered. At least half of Marilyn's youth was passed outside her own country. She and the Columbians worked all over the world—in Canada, Mexico, Cuba, the West Indies, England, France, Germany, Austria, Turkey, Russia, the Hawaiian Islands, and even China, where they stocked up on exquisite backdrops and embroidered costumes that would serve them for years.

Marilyn made her first trip abroad when she was five, shortly after joining the Columbians. She had two unforgettable experiences that she talked about for the rest of her life. In Birmingham, England, the family appeared on the same bill with Lillie Langtry, who gave Marilyn her first lesson in how a star should behave by insisting that a red carpet be laid from her dressing room to the stage for her entrances and exits.

A few weeks later, Marilyn had the lucky coincidence of meeting

Langtry's former lover and main claim to fame, King Edward VII, who was staying at the Duke of Devonshire's Chatsworth Manor while the Columbians were appearing in nearby Sheffield. One evening, the duke arranged for the complete bill at the Empire Theatre to come over after dinner to entertain. Marilyn danced on her toes before King Edward and was rewarded with a gold sovereign bearing his likeness.

All during those early years, Ada Miller carefully documented the progress of what she called "the Tribe" in a series of scrapbooks. Filled with press clippings, programs, photographs, and other personal mementos, the volumes unintentionally became a record of Marilyn's gradual rise from bit player to "star" of the family. Page after page showed her receiving the major share of attention, whether it was as the Little Japanese Premier in a Christmas pantomime of *Aladdin*, a diminutive Seminole Indian chief doing a war dance, or Little Eva to Caro Miller's Uncle Tom when the family briefly joined a summer stock company.

After serving her apprenticeship as Mademoiselle Sugarlump, Marilyn was made a full-fledged member of the act, which then became known as The Five Columbians (with Ada Miller also joining in the singing and dancing). They advertised themselves as "The Acme of Refined Novelty Entertainers—The Most Handsomely Costumed Act in America."

In 1907, a reviewer for *The Billboard* praised their "gorgeous scenery, a trellis of gold and silver entwined with gloriously hued flowers, scintillating in all the colors of a prismatic rainbow. Each member is introduced in various versatile selections until the grand finale, when the four ripest of the Columbians assemble in elegant jeweled costumes of the fifteenth century period and execute a graceful minuet. Then comes the transformation to the 'Fairy Grotto of Roses' where Miss Marilyn Miller is discovered perched upon the petals of a huge rose. Leaping daintily to the ground, she executes her marvelous dance of the French *premiere danseuse* with all the grace and art of one many years her senior."

Like her little poker-faced friend Buster Keaton, whose family of knockabout comedians sometimes shared the same bill with the Five Columbians, Marilyn was becoming well known in her own right. Caro Miller seized every opportunity to use Marilyn for publicity purposes. At the end of Saturday matinee performances, Marilyn would host a party on stage for the children in the audience and dole out free candy, cookies, and pink lemonade. During a booking in Kansas City, she made a surprise appearance at the annual banquet of the fraternal organization known as the Order of Ancient Eggs, where she was "hatched" from a huge papier-mâché egg and danced on the dais table.

But the high point of these promotional activities took place in the summer of 1908, when Caro Miller heard that the management of an amusement park in Ohio was offering $5 in gold to the first child to swim the full 550-foot length of its new bathing pond on opening day. Although Marilyn had never taken a swimming lesson in all of her nearly ten years, Caro Miller developed her into a champion in less than three weeks time. Marilyn not only won the prize, but also reams and reams of valuable press coverage throughout the United States.

The press often described Marilyn in terms of powder puffs, bon-bons, jeweled stickpins, matchboxes, and pen nibs. As child performers often do, she became very sensitive about her size, especially when anyone insinuated, jokingly or otherwise, that she was really a thirty-year-old midget. More than once, Caro Miller tried to persuade Marilyn to pretend to be one of the little people in order to avoid problems with the Gerry Society, but she refused.

If Marilyn wanted to be anyone, it was Adeline Genée, the Danish ballerina who was enjoying immense popularity in America under the auspices of an up-and-coming impresario named Florenz Ziegfeld. Known as "poetry in motion," Genée whirled, skipped, and soared through the air with an ethereal lightness that was the envy of all her contemporaries. Marilyn was treated to a Genée performance in Chicago on her eleventh birthday and instantly fell under her spell. Adeline Genée not only became her role model, but also the dancer who Marilyn Miller was most compared to by critics in later years.

In homage to her new idol, Marilyn asked her stepfather to arrange a routine for her based on Genée's wonderful and daringly sensual "Soul Kiss." In Genée's original version, the ballerina tempted the virtuous hero into kissing her and then proceeded to seduce him. Marilyn's solo version captured the gossamer precision of Genée's dancing, if not the sexuality.

Audiences' enthusiastic response to the Genée impersonation encouraged Marilyn to add others to her repertoire. She came to master impressions of the top female personalities of the day, including Lillian Russell, Elsie Janis, Eva Tanguay, Nora Bayes, Bessie McCoy, Marie Dressler, and Gaby Deslys. Among the males, Marilyn picked two of the most eccentric. Her impression of Julian Eltinge was more complex than any in her catalog: a young girl imitating a middle-aged man who impersonated women. The Five Columbians had once done a twenty-week tour with Eltinge as the headliner, so Marilyn knew all his tricks and mannerisms. Her double-edged impression of Eltinge impersonating English ballerina Maude Allen in her famous "Salome" dance was a show-stopper. For her tribute to Bert Williams, the foremost black entertainer of the day, Marilyn did not darken her face. Outfitted in satin, a silk top hat, and the oversize white gloves that were a Williams trademark, Marilyn sang and did flashy dance steps to his "When You're All Dressed Up and No Place to Go."

Between working, rehearsing, and learning new routines, neither Marilyn nor her sisters ever went to school. But very early on, Ada Miller taught them reading, writing, and simple arithmetic. When they were on the move, whether it was on trains, ships, or the occasional stagecoach (there still were some in remote parts of the United States), there was always a satchel full of books and study materials, which were compulsorily dipped into during what would have been the girls' normal school hours. Since many vaudevillians traveled with their families in tow, some theaters had backstage classrooms for the children, with parents and local teachers sharing the instruction.

If anyone so much as insinuated that her daughters' educations were being neglected, Ada Miller would produce a letter signed by Mayor Harrison of Chicago that said, "If these children are the products of the stage, let us have a theater in every home and school in America." The document looked and sounded so official that its authenticity went unchallenged. Ada Miller never said how she obtained it, but it may very well have been a fake. Such a piece of paper often meant the difference between the Five Columbians working or not working in places where the Gerry Society or an equivalent was active.

Vaudeville families such as Marilyn's tended to be very close and self-sufficient. Young Marilyn never had the chance to make lasting friendships, but her two older sisters were more than suitable companions. The three girls were inseparable, on and off the stage. They had to be, to protect themselves from all sorts of types, college boys and pimps alike, who lingered outside the stage door.

Seasoned troupers and well in the spotlight by the time that Marilyn joined the Columbians, neither Ruth nor Claire resented Marilyn taking a bigger and bigger role. In fact, they welcomed it because it meant they wouldn't have to work as hard and would be spared some of their stepfather's tantrums. Everyone was aware, however, of the pressures that could build up among five people who worked closely together under constant pressure. There was a rule in the Miller family that once the curtain came down, no one was to speak a word until the makeup was off and street clothes were on. By that time, any quarrels that might have been caused by someone's error or awkwardness in the performance would be avoided.

The Millers usually traveled by train. To economize, Caro Miller would book a sleeping berth for Ada and himself and then at bedtime search for a vacant one for the girls, tipping the porter half the regular rate. Marilyn and her sisters always shared one upper berth. Squashed tightly in the cramped quarters, they sweltered in summer and froze in winter. Not surprisingly, they were constantly getting trainsick. There were times when the family had to change trains in the middle of the night, getting off at three in the morning and sitting and suffering in the station until their connection came along hours later.

Many of the trains lacked dining facilities, so the Millers packed sandwiches and cold meals and ate in their seats. They'd arrive at their destination early in the morning, check into their boarding-house or hotel, and report to the theater at nine o'clock for re-hearsals. If they were delayed for some reason, they had to change into their costumes on the train and rush directly to the theater. Between performances they'd be so exhausted that they'd just stretch out on the floor in the dressing room and rest; there wasn't enough time between shows to really sleep.

Some of the small-time circuits that the Millers played were in such isolated areas that they were known as "the Death Trail" and "the Aching Heart." Once, in a tiny theater in North Dakota, a bat swooped down through the spotlight at Marilyn while she was in the middle of a dance. Most of these theaters had no dressing rooms; everybody changed in the basement, with a sheet down the middle to divide the sexes. Sanitary facilities were shared by all. It wasn't uncommon to see a sign backstage that said "PLEASE DON'T FLUSH THE TOILET WHILE THE ACT IS ON."

Marilyn's youth onstage and backstage was subject to the constant torment of Caro Miller's "guidance." The experience left her indelibly scarred. She had been so disciplined that she never learned to play; too early her career became her life. It was during this time that Marilyn began to acquire the quietly smiling, detached air that remained with her into adulthood. It was a characteristic that often puzzled her friends, that mysterious impression that Marilyn gave of being somewhere else, simply not part of whatever was happening around her.

$\mathbf{S}$HUBERT DISCOVERY

"BEING AN INFANT PRODIGY and living it down is no easy matter," said the teenage Marilyn Miller. "For twelve years I was under the spell; but my emancipation—my escape, as it were—came in 1914 when I appeared at the Winter Garden in New York. Up to that night I was a prodigy, with no hopes of escape till my final day of rest came. But after that night—after that ordeal—I was just myself, Marilyn Miller, dancer and mimic. The slate was wiped clean, the stigma was removed. I was free!"

Marilyn's journey to the stage of Broadway's leading showplace began in 1911, the year that she entered her teens and sprouted to what would be her full adult height—slightly over five feet. Convinced that Marilyn could pass for sixteen, the minimum working age in big cities, Caro Miller put her to the test by obtaining a booking for the Five Columbians in Chicago. At the end of the first show, a child labor inspector who'd been in the audience served Miller with a subpoena. Not only couldn't the Columbians finish the engagement, but they also were barred from working in Chicago for three years and fined $250, a considerable sum at that time.

After that experience, Caro Miller decided that until Marilyn turned the legal age, the Five Columbians would work abroad, where they were seldom hassled and were much in demand. The Old World was going crazy for the uniquely American popular music that was developing out of ragtime, minstrel songs, the blues, and jazz. Preferring to book talent wholesale and far in advance, British and European entrepreneurs were offering tours of two and three years duration to such acts as the Five Columbians, whose repertoire of songs and dances was as American as their name.

During their extensive foreign travels of 1911–14, Marilyn and her family were seldom aware of the political turmoil that was escalating toward a world conflict. The event that touched them most deeply was the sinking of the ocean liner *Titanic* on its maiden voyage to the United States in April 1912. Several of the Millers' show business friends, returning from tours similar to their own, were among the fifteen hundred people killed.

In the three years between 1911 and 1914, the Five Columbians introduced English and continental audiences to many new American songs that became all-time standards, including "Alexander's Ragtime Band," "Everybody's Doing It," "I Want a Girl Just Like the Girl That Married Dear Old Dad," "Memphis Blues," "Oh, You Beautiful Doll," "My Melancholy Baby," "Waiting for the Robert E. Lee," "Moonlight Bay," "Peg O' My Heart," "You Made Me Love You," "That Old Gal of Mine," "Row, Row, Row," and "Let Me Call You Sweetheart." The Columbians also featured the latest American dance crazes—the turkey trot, the grizzly bear, the ball and jack, the shimmy, and the Brazilian-originated maxixe.

By February 1914, the Five Columbians were in London, winding up a tour of the Stoll Circuit. Impressed with their work, Oswald Stoll signed them to appear in a revue called "Oh, Joy" that he was assembling for the Coliseum Theatre. But during rehearsals, Caro Miller decided that he liked neither the material nor the Columbians' slot in the program, which amounted to warming up the audience for the bigger acts to follow. Miller requested a withdrawal and was handed another tour of the British provinces instead.

Meanwhile, romance was threatening to break up the Five Columbians. Now in their early twenties, Ruth and Claire Miller had fallen in love with two young American tourists, Dr. John Sweeney and his friend, James B. McKowen, a theatrical agent. The two couples were married when the Columbians returned to London. Caro Miller, who might have been expected to oppose the double wedding, actually was quite pleased. Ruth and Claire were starting to lose the youthful appeal that was so essential to a family act; their marriages spared Miller from being saddled with their support later on.

At fifteen, Marilyn was experiencing heart flutters as well. Ironically, the object of her interest was the man who would be the great love of her life, although no one could have known it then. He was a twenty-one-year-old American named Frank Carter. A singer and dancer himself, Carter was working at the London Hippodrome in *Hello, Tango*, a musical starring Ethel Levey, the "queen of ragtime" and the former wife and performing partner of George M. Cohan. Marilyn and her family were staying in the same building of furnished apartments as Carter, but she never actually met him. "I used to watch him going to his theater," Marilyn Miller said later. "I was too young for him to pay any attention to me, but I thought him wonderful. Frank was so handsome. I think he was the first fellow who ever really appealed to me. At that age girls are so romantic."

Just before Marilyn's sisters and their new husbands were to depart for the United States, Caro Miller booked the Columbians into the Lotus Club, one of the smartest dance spots in London. Near all the West End theaters and adjacent to Covent Garden, it featured afternoon and evening *dansants*, plus a supper cabaret with American entertainers and musicians, many of them black. The club made its reputation with ragtime, but now was veering more toward the tango, which had taken London by storm, and the controversial bunny hug (condemned from church pulpits because of the close body contact between partners).

The Lotus management decided that the name of the Five Columbians was more suited to vaudeville than to a sophisticated nightclub, and the family became known merely as the Millers. So that no one should mistake the ripening Marilyn for an adult or a midget, she was introduced as "Baby" Miller. Between her newly mastered tango *sur les pointes* (danced on the tips of her toes) and her charming impersonations and renditions of "Has Anyone Here Seen Rover?" and "Where Did You Get That Girl?" Marilyn never failed to win an ovation. A critic for the influential *Dancing Times* magazine wrote, "She is a born dancer, a wonderful little mimic, and absolutely unspoiled with success."

Although Marilyn Miller never developed into the toast of London, she quickly became a favorite of the wealthy, titled set that frequented the Lotus Club. Sir Philip Sassoon, scion of a banking family that rivaled the Rothschilds, became one of Marilyn's most devoted fans, turning up almost every night of the engagement. After the show, when it was club policy for the performers to mingle among members of the audience and chat with them, Sir Philip invariably invited Marilyn to do the tango with him. Since he towered over her, she had to dance on her toes to bring herself up to within reach of his arms.

One evening at the Lotus Club, Sassoon showed up with the second most important person in all the British Empire, his friend Edward, Prince of Wales. King George V's heir apparent was then nearly twenty, four years older than Marilyn. Although it would have been a breach of royal etiquette for the prince to dance with her in a public place, Sassoon did introduce them, and Marilyn told him the story of dancing for his grandfather, Edward VII, when she was a child. The meeting sparked a casual friendship that would last for years.

Gossip soon had it that the Prince of Wales had fallen in love with Marilyn Miller. More than likely, the rumors originated in the imagination of Caro Miller, who saw the publicity value of such a connection. Edward, of course, later demonstrated a preference for women older than himself.

Another important person visiting the Lotus Club during the Millers' engagement was Lee Shubert, the American producer and theater owner, who was making one of his semiannual trips to London to recruit talent for upcoming shows. When Shubert strolled in that evening, Marilyn was in the midst of her Bert Williams routine, dressed in a white satin suit and with her long, Pollyanna curls topped by a silk hat. As she continued with impressions of Sophie Tucker, Fritzi Scheff, and Adeline Genée, Shubert recognized Marilyn's appeal immediately. She wasn't the most beautiful girl he'd ever seen, but she had great rapport with the audience and seemed to be enjoying herself immensely while entertaining them. She reminded Shubert of a young Elsie Janis, one of the biggest stars on the American stage at that time, who also started her career in vaudeville doing imitations similar to Marilyn's.

Lee Shubert was even more captivated when he saw Marilyn come out into the audience after the show and dance with Sir Philip Sassoon. She had a pixie quality that was irresistible. Despite her youth (or perhaps because of it), every man in the room seemed to be focusing on her. But what was most attractive to Lee Shubert was the knowledge that he could hire Marilyn, an unknown, for a pittance. The shrewd and stingy practices of Shubert and his brother, Jake, had been a primary impetus for the formation of the first theatrical labor union, Actors Equity, in 1913.

Lee Shubert invited Caro Miller to his table and told him that he wanted to engage Marilyn for the next edition of *The Passing Show*, which was to open on Broadway in the late spring. With the Five Columbians about to break up, plus the opportunity to really launch Marilyn, Caro Miller couldn't afford to haggle. He shook hands on a deal that guaranteed Marilyn $75 a week to start. If she was a success, her salary would be doubled and she'd also receive a contract with the Shubert production company.

Since Lee Shubert never bothered to ask about Marilyn's age, Caro Miller didn't tell him that she wouldn't be sixteen years old until some months after *The Passing Show* opened. He was afraid that the prospect of problems with the Gerry Society might kill the deal.

The full details of the arrangement were kept from Marilyn. Caro Miller didn't want to involve her in wheeling and dealing that had nothing to do with her talent as a performer. Why distract her from concentrating on her art? All the teenager knew was that she was going back to America to appear at the Winter Garden, a theater that her stepfather said was the most wonderful on Broadway and perhaps in all the world. She was, of course, overjoyed.

As soon as the Lotus Club booking ended, the Miller family sailed for New York from Southampton on the S.S. *Brittanic*, the sister ship of the tragic *Titanic*. The voyage, a belated honeymoon for Claire, Ruth, and their new husbands, was hardly a pleasure cruise for Marilyn. She spent most of the seven days in the ship's gymnasium with Caro Miller, exercising, practicing, and learning new dance routines. She also took some rudimentary lessons in fencing, which proved so beneficial to her balance and coordination that a morning workout with the foils became a part of her regular routine.

Upon her arrival in New York, Marilyn was taken directly to the Winter Garden to start rehearsal. The Winter Garden was the most elegant theater she had ever seen. The auditorium was decorated in the style of an English garden. It had a trellised ceiling, and latticework graced the walls. But what was most exciting to Marilyn was the opulence of the costumes and stage settings. Although they were gaudy in comparison to the trimmings of the Shuberts' main competitor, Florenz Ziegfeld, Marilyn didn't know any better. As far as she was concerned, she'd been dropped into fairyland.

Marilyn wasn't quite sure what she'd gotten herself involved with, except that it was called *The Passing Show of 1914*. Harold Atteridge, who wrote what little there was of an actual script, tried to explain it to her. Since 1912, the Shuberts had been producing one of the revues at the Winter Garden every spring or summer.

Poking fun at that year's Broadway plays and musicals, they were intended to run only for a limited time and then go on tour, hence the handle "passing show." Although there was a slight thread of story and Marilyn would portray a character named Miss Jerry, her main job was to offer impersonations of some of the stars and personalities who were being spoofed.

Although she grew up backstage and thought she'd seen just about everything, Marilyn was shocked by another aspect of *The Passing Show*. For all its humor and music, it was really a glorified "girlie" show, with sixty young chorines parading straight into the audience on a ramp provocatively referred to as "the bridge of thighs." The runway was touted as a Shubert invention. Actually, they stole the idea from one of Max Reinhardt's experimental theaters in Berlin.

Marilyn's eyes were opened even further as she watched the "half-naked" women performing onstage. She had always seen them wear full body tights under their costumes, sometimes flesh-colored, but more often pink or white so that no one out front should mistake them for real skin and be offended. But in *The Passing Show of 1914*, legs, arms, shoulders, and even midriffs were bare. A typical chorus outfit was a blouse or halter, short trunks, and anklet socks. Even the public beaches couldn't provide such a wealth of uncovered feminine pulchritude.

During the initial rehearsals, Marilyn's performance was disappointing; she seemed to have lost much of her usual sparkle. Although she'd been performing now for almost seven years, she had never worked outside the family act. She obviously missed their support and encouragement, especially that of her sisters, who were her best friends. Realizing that, Caro Miller persuaded the Shuberts to send Marilyn for outside coaching. Thrown in among girls her own age, the camaraderie and competitiveness soon revived her spirits.

Marilyn studied classical ballet with Theodore and Alexis Kosloff, the Russian brothers who were among the first great dancers from the Imperial Theatre of Moscow to perform in the United States.

At the Ned Wayburn School, she was drilled in tap and so-called "acrobatic" dancing, which included such flashy specialties as the split and the backbend.

At both the Kosloff and Wayburn studios, Marilyn kept running into a saucy girl with long blond curls like her own, who spoke with a delicious stammer and was named Marion Davies. A year older than Marilyn and several inches taller, she became a lifelong friend, although they weren't classmates very long. Mainly interested in going on the stage to attract a rich husband, Marion lacked the dedication of the dancer. She abhorred the rigorous daily practice sessions. She used to tell Marilyn: "It's b-b-bad for the s-s-system. It'll k-k-kill you." Marilyn would only giggle and work all the harder.

Noticing Marilyn's rapid improvement, Jake Shubert started taking a fatherly interest. During rehearsals one morning, he introduced her to the show's music composer, Sigmund Romberg. "I predict a great career for this girl," Shubert said, as Marilyn stood beside him, smiling shyly. "Let's see what you can do to get her established, Romy."

As Marilyn scampered away, Romberg followed her with his eyes. There was something fresh and different about the girl. She had a winsome manner. If he could only project this quality undiluted across the footlights, he thought, Marilyn would enchant everyone who saw her. He began dreaming up a song, something very special and unusual, for her to perform.

It was the third Shubert show for Sigmund Romberg, a twenty-seven-year-old Hungarian immigrant who had conducted dance bands in New York's beer gardens before establishing himself as a composer of theater music. Although he was well paid and highly regarded by the Shuberts, he'd not yet written the kind of smash hit that would send audiences home humming and whistling. In Marilyn Miller's fresh face and talent, he saw an opportunity. Wouldn't it be wonderful, he thought, if she and a Romberg song could simultaneously capture the public's heart?

Several days later, Romberg handed her a sheet of music. "Look this over, Marilyn. You will sing it in the second act. It's called 'Omar Khayam.' You must know the poem. 'A loaf of bread, a jug of wine...' See how you like it."

Marilyn thanked him and went to find a pianist to play for her. Soon, from a back corner of the stage, Romberg could hear her singing. Her voice was pure and sweet, and as she began to learn the melody and lyrics, he grew more and more certain of success. At the end of the afternoon, Marilyn went fluttering back to Romberg and hugged him: "Oh, Romy, I like it. I like it so much. Thank you." Needless to say, Romberg's predictions came true.

When *The Passing Show of 1914* opened on the night of June 10, Marilyn Miller was still unknown to most of the public, so her name was hardly mentioned on the bill. The leading members of the cast were prima donna José Collins and comedian George Monroe, but the main attraction was really the production itself. "A twelve hour show squeezed into three...an uproarious upheaval of lingerie and laughter—the mastodon of musical extravaganza...a wiggling wave of winsome witches. It washes out care and irons out wrinkles...a reeling riot of resplendent revelry," the advertisements described it.

It was the most spectacular *Passing Show* to date. The finale recreated the San Francisco earthquake of 1906, showing an even more beautiful Golden Gate city rising from the ruins. Costumed in ways that a program note boasted would "make Mother Eve envious," the chorus girls played football on the runway and pranced up and down four slanting tiers that swept from stage floor to roof. They "floated" off in a Zeppelin on a fantasy flight to Paris and pounded out the new eagle rock dance craze.

Maude Adams, John Barrymore, Vernon and Irene Castle, Ruth Chatterton, Salvation Nell, and Prunella were among the personalities and characters included in the travesties of current shows. No longer a competitive entertainment form that could be ignored, the "flickers" were also spoofed, with portly George Monroe in drag as "Little Buttercup, queen of the movies," modeled after Mary Pickford.

In the first act, Marilyn Miller appeared only once, dancing about in an impression of Adeline Genée. On stage a mere two minutes, she'd spent the previous hour limbering up, but it was worth the effort; she received an ear-shattering ovation. In the second act, she sang Romberg's "Omar Khayam," with an extended appearance featuring more of her impersonations, including Bert Williams, Ethel Levey, and Julian Eltinge. Two new characterizations were inspired by recent movies, swim champion Annette Kellerman as "Neptune's Daughter" and Russian tragedienne Olga Petrova as "the Vampire."

During the final curtain calls, Marilyn received the majority of the applause. When she finally left the stage, her face was flushed and her eyes moist with tears. Bumping into Sigmund Romberg in the wings, she threw her arms around him and kissed him. Romberg pried himself loose of her embrace, turned her around, and propelled her back out to the stage. "Get out there and take another bow," he said. "This is the very greatest moment in your life."

Newspaper reviews hailed a new star. "Marilyn Miller is a sort of calcium sunshine; she is to 'The Passing Show' what Roosevelt is to the Bull Moose," said the *Sun*. "A hitherto unknown young woman named Marilyn Miller—an exceedingly clever person who will be much better known before long—made one of the hits of the piece. She looked well, danced well and did some capital imitations," wrote the *Herald*'s reviewer. "The real hit of the entire performance was little Miss Marilyn Miller, who is youthful and pretty, who dances as if she enjoyed it, and who as an imitator approaches very closely to Miss Elsie Janis," according to the *Telegram*. "With their usual uncanny eye for talent, the brothers Shubert introduced a dancing sprite—mercurial, lovely Marilyn Miller," raved the *Morning Telegraph*.

Cosmopolitan magazine noted that Marilyn's "illusive, lilylike figure, at 5'1", makes her look tall enough for a front line show girl. Her voice is phenomenal, in high soprano notes as well as in the almost baritone range brought into play by her uncanny bits of masculine impersonation. Here is an original sort of ingenue who lives still in the blissful age of innocence."

By the time of the opening, the Shuberts had discovered Marilyn's true age. Their press agents made certain that it was never mentioned until after she turned sixteen on the first of September. Apparently, the Gerry Society had younger fish to fry; there never was any trouble in the nearly three months that Marilyn appeared at the Winter Garden in violation of the child labor law.

For a birthday present, the Shuberts gave Marilyn a five-year contract that immediately raised her salary to $150 a week and promised regular raises after that. Now in a much better bargaining position, Caro Miller included himself in the deal. He was to be employed as a stage manager on Shubert shows, Marilyn's primarily, but others when she was inactive. Miller's argument was that Marilyn's solo career ruled out reviving the family act, and that he and Ada Miller had no other way of earning a living. He felt the Shuberts owed them something for all the years they had put into Marilyn's development.

Even if Marilyn had been consulted in the matter, she wouldn't have dared object. Caro Miller ruled her life, disciplining her as if she were still a child. When she came home late from dance classes or didn't practice as hard as he thought she could, Miller punished her, occasionally caning her across the backside when he was really angry. Since his maltreatment of Marilyn seemed to get worse as she reached her full physical development, it is conceivable there was a psycho-sexual component to it. Driven by impulses that his conscience told him were wrong, Miller exorcised them through physical violence.

Becoming an overnight celebrity further complicated Marilyn's relationship with "Papa Gig." As befitted the ingenue of one of the most popular shows on Broadway, she was besieged by stage-door Johnnies. The Winter Garden, of course, had more than its share of them. The choice seats bordering the stage runway were highly prized by Ivy League college boys and a whole range of wealthy, more mature men who could have been their fathers and grandfathers, brothers and uncles. Caro Miller didn't want Marilyn mixing with that crowd. Although he may have been jealous, he'd also been in show business long enough to have seen too many innocent girls get into trouble. They became pregnant and had to settle for being mistresses instead of wives. Many ended up as prostitutes. With such a promising future ahead of her, Marilyn wasn't going to meet that fate if he could help it.

At her stepfather's insistence, Marilyn was to be chaperoned at all times. When Miller was unavailable, her mother took over. Ada Miller accompanied Marilyn to and from the theater and stayed in her dressing room during performances. No one could enter without her permission. In time, Ada Miller became noted for her condescending attitude toward visitors. "I wouldn't let some of them into my house," she once said. "We meet all sorts of rich and titled people, but what do they amount to? The only one I really liked was Prince Paul of Serbia. He was a very nice man. But I don't want Marilyn marrying any title."

Although she'd done it in the past, Ada Miller no longer assisted Marilyn with her makeup and costume changes. Ada made it clear that she was above that now and insisted that the Shuberts provide Marilyn with a "colored" maid—Violet Ordley, who'd worked on and off for the Millers since the days of the Columbians. On the rare occasions when Ada Miller was absent from the dressing room, Violet took over as Marilyn's chaperone.

All that sheltering made Marilyn seem very innocent in comparison to girls like Marion Davies, who, with more suitors than she could handle, was out partying every night. For lack of any real social life, Marilyn's career in the theater became everything to her. It was magical and exhilarating. Although the work was exhausting and often excruciating, the applause and the adulation of the public made it all worthwhile.

The Passing Show of 1914 ran on Broadway for 133 performances, all that was intended; its main purpose was to keep the Winter Garden filled during the summer doldrums that affected most other theaters in that era of no air conditioning. In the autumn, the revue started a road tour that extended to the West Coast and back, playing one- or two-week engagements in Shubert-owned theaters. By that time, *The Passing Show* had more than recouped its investment, so everything that the tour earned above operating costs was profit for the Shuberts. That was standard business procedure then, an added benefit being that the Broadway run provided sufficient advance publicity and word-of-mouth to penetrate the hinterlands. News traveled slowly then; radio and television were, respectively, years and decades away.

Although Marilyn was only featured during the Broadway run, she was raised to star billing when *The Passing Show of 1914* went on the road. Now that war had broken out in Europe, the original leading lady, José Collins, felt it her patriotic duty to return to her native England to help entertain the troops. Caro Miller was quite pleased with Collins's departure, and not only because of what it meant to Marilyn's career. Along with the majority of Americans, he was unsympathetic to the Allied cause and didn't want his country to become involved.

The *Passing Show* tour was twice as long as the Broadway run; it did not end until March 1915. After a short vacation with her parents at Lake Muskegon, a Minnesota resort very popular with show people, Marilyn was whisked back to New York to begin rehearsals for the next edition of *The Passing Show*. Although she was now the only performer in the family, the pattern of their lives hadn't changed much from the days of the Five Columbians.

Having passed her novitiate as a Broadway celebrity, Marilyn was promoted to leading lady and *premiere danseuse* of *The Passing Show of 1915*, which opened at the Winter Garden on May 29.

Featuring more dancing than any of the previous editions, it included elaborate production numbers built around the two big crazes of that year, the Hawaiian hula and the pan Pacific drag, which had originated at an international exposition held in San Francisco.

For the first time on Broadway, Marilyn danced as herself, rather than impersonating Adeline Genée or some other idol of the time. The Shuberts spared no expense, closing the first act with a "spring ballet" featuring Theodore Kosloff, his wife, Maria Baldina, and a large corps. In the dance finale, Marilyn pranced out from the wings and joined hands with the Kosloffs for a *pas de trois*.

The vague and scattered plot coupled Marilyn with the handsome baritone John Charles Thomas. As his "first love," Marilyn follows Thomas to the big city, where he takes a course in "the spacious halls of experience" and narrowly escapes being seduced by several parasitical damsels before the inevitable happy ending. Along the way, Marilyn sang "Every Small Town Girlie Has a Big Town Way," "My Trombone Man," and a duet with Thomas called "Any Old Time with You."

Filled with travesties of the previous stage and movie season, the targets of *The Passing Show of 1915* included Ethel Barrymore, *Androcles and the Lion*, Charlie Chaplin, Theda Bara, Trilby and Svengali, Will Rogers, and *Raffles*. Marilyn wore a man's three-piece suit and derby hat to impersonate Clifton Crawford, a middle-aged matinee idol from Scotland who was famous for being the first actor to perform readings of Kipling's "Gunga Din."

For her second *Passing Show*, Marilyn's reviews were more enthusiastic than ever. "A year has seemingly intensified her youth and charm, her airy lightness, the nimbleness of her toes and the sparkle in her eyes. Artistic? Perhaps, but enchanting, certainly. There is only one Marilyn Miller," said the *New York Globe*. Colgate Baker of the *New York Review* called her "one of the daintiest, prettiest and cleverest girls on the American stage. She is a vision of delight at all times." The *New York Dramatic Mirror* said "Miss Miller made the hit of the evening with her adorable smile and blithesome dancing. Her reception at her every appearance was deservedly uproarious. The gain she has made the past year in poise and assurance has made her personality even more awesome."

Heartened by such praise for his prodigy, Caro Miller urged the Shuberts to star Marilyn in a vehicle of her own, but the producers were not agreeable. Although the United States was still neutral in the European war, public nervousness over eventual participation was starting to affect theater attendance. Fewer productions were being mounted, and 1915 generally was not a time for risk taking. Marilyn had to be content with another long road tour with *The Passing Show* after it ended its run of 145 performances at the Winter Garden in September.

By the summer of 1916, Jake Shubert had relented slightly and decided to release Marilyn from that year's *Passing Show* and use her elsewhere. Charles Dillingham, a sometime partner of Florenz Ziegfeld and another arch rival of the Shuberts, had struck gold with a colossal spectacle at the Hippodrome that was modestly entitled *The Big Show*. The spectacular included everything from vaudeville and circus acts to swimming and ice-skating, plus the incomparable ballerina Anna Pavlova dancing a condensed version of *The Sleeping Beauty*. Jealous of Dillingham's success, and at the same time longing to deflate his ego through derisive satire, the Shuberts assembled *The Show of Wonders* to inaugurate the Winter Garden's autumn season. Featured along with Marilyn would be Willie and Eugene Howard, considered by their peers to be the funniest of all comedy teams, and George Monroe, the Winter Garden's perennial drag impressionist.

Employing some of the same creative talent as did *The Passing Shows*, including Sigmund Romberg and writer-lyricist Harold Atteridge, *The Show of Wonders* finally convinced the Shuberts that Marilyn Miller had the makings of a major star. On opening night, she received a standing ovation, led from the first row by none other than Lillian Russell and Diamond Jim Brady. In outfits that ranged from a scanty, revealing deer skin to dazzling rhinestone knickerbockers, she was "so completely adorable" that the critic for the *Tribune* wanted to "hang her on a Christmas tree and light pretty candles all about her. To look at Marilyn Miller is to remember what a beautiful thing is youth at its youngest and prettiest."

The *Sun* concurred: "She may not be Pavlova, but with her youth, which is very real and alive, her beauty and a demure grace not found too often in Winter Garden stars, her performance last night was delightful. Miss Miller is so refreshing that it is a pleasure merely to look at her."

As the show progressed, Marilyn found herself more and more ensconced in and drawn toward the relentless and haphazard life of the stage. One day during rehearsals, the ballet master Theodore Kosloff, usually the most sure-footed of men, slipped accidentally and struck Marilyn in the nose. Although she suffered only slight pain, the blow was severe enough to splinter a tiny bone. The incident seemed trivial, and she laughed it off—she was only eighteen years old. The Winter Garden's house doctor said it would quickly heal of its own accord. But he was wrong. Marilyn developed a chronic sinus condition that became progressively worse.

The Show of Wonders also set forces in motion that later affected Marilyn's professional as well as personal life. Among the celebrities present at opening night was the exquisite red-haired star of light comedies Billie Burke, conspicuously without her husband, Florenz Ziegfeld, who once said the only thing that would get him into a Shubert theater was the funeral of any of the brothers. But Billie Burke felt no such animosity toward the Shuberts, nor could she afford to. Since her producer-manager Charles Frohman's death in the sinking of the *Lusitania* the previous year, she'd become dependent on people like the Shuberts for employment.

Marilyn's act impressed Billie Burke, who guessed that her husband would have a similar reaction. "Marilyn was the vision of perfection, representing in beautiful flesh all the things that all his life Flo Ziegfeld had sought to dramatize," Billie Burke said later. "Marilyn summed up and symbolized the grace and joy which were what Flo reached for in everything he staged. She was, as every male with reasonable eyesight knew, extraordinarily enticing and special."

The Ziegfelds lived on upper Broadway in a sumptuous thirteen-room suite in the Hotel Ansonia, a monument to the Beaux Arts style. When Billie Burke returned from her visit to *The Show of Wonders*, she was ready to sign Marilyn Miller herself, if her husband wouldn't, for his next edition of the *Follies*. Ziegfeld pretended not to be interested, but he was inwardly pleased. He'd been following Marilyn Miller's progress for some time, but he didn't want his wife or the Shuberts to know about it.

CHAPTER FOUR

ZIEGFELD STAR

NED WAYBURN, THE ROLY-POLY, three-hundred-pound dalai lama of the Broadway musical scene, was the first person to alert Florenz Ziegfeld to Marilyn Miller's potential. She'd been studying at Wayburn's dance academy since her arrival in New York in 1914. When Wayburn went to work for Ziegfeld the following year as director of the *Midnight Frolic*, an offshoot of the *Follies*, he'd mentioned Marilyn as a potential star, but thought she'd need a few more years of training and practical experience before she'd be ready.

This was fine with Ziegfeld. Although his productions were famed for their glittering "name" casts—the 1916 *Follies* boasted Fannie Brice, Will Rogers, Bert Williams, W. C. Fields, and Ina Claire— Ziegfeld wasn't really a builder of stars. He preferred to buy them ready-made; if he had to pay them exorbitant salaries, he didn't care. It was an essential component of the extravagant Ziegfeld image, more than worth it in terms of publicity and prestige. In the case of Marilyn Miller, Ziegfeld knew that her development couldn't have been in any more capable hands than the Shuberts'. And when Marilyn was ripe for picking, he looked forward to the satisfaction he'd get from stealing one of their prize jewels.

Meanwhile, Marilyn's association with the Shuberts continued along the lines set with her first *Passing Show*. After 209 performances at the Winter Garden, *The Show of Wonders* began a cross-country tour in April 1917. It was the year of President Wilson's declaration of war against Germany, hardly the most propitious of times. Box-office receipts plummeted as the public spent potential ticket money on Liberty Bonds. Nearly a million men volunteered for military service; conscription took away another million men. *The Show of Wonders* was one of the first musicals to eliminate male chorus lines, more out of necessity than patriotism. Backstage technicians also soon became irreplaceable.

The Shuberts decided to let *The Show of Wonders* struggle on, confident that the public would seek relief in entertainment once the initial shock and hysteria over the war started to wear off. Once again their instincts paid off, particularly in areas with military camps and war-related businesses. In those boom markets, the Shuberts found no resistance to a top price of $2 a seat for *The Show of Wonders*, a new high for a touring production.

As Marilyn traveled from city to city, she found herself becoming included in the war effort. An entertainer in the true sense of the word, she was constantly being invited to perform at bond rallies and recruitment drives. How could she refuse? She not only enjoyed it, but Caro Miller was quick to point out how beneficial such active patriotism could be to her career. Playing before a crowd of 150,000 on Boston Common got her more exposure in five minutes than *The Show of Wonders* would in a hundred nights. Marilyn's war work over the next two years endeared her to the public and established her as a national celebrity.

Marilyn's tour with *The Show of Wonders* resulted in a series of scattered circumstances that would eventually introduce her to Florenz Ziegfeld. Another eighteen-year-old named Olive Thomas, whose delicate, heart-shaped face had earned her a reputation as the most beautiful of all the *Follies* girls, ended a turbulent and much-publicized romance with Ziegfeld by marrying Jack Pickford, the actor brother of "little Mary." Pickford then persuaded Thomas to quit the stage for a career in the movies, where she was soon earning an astronomical $2,500 a week.

Those developments left Ziegfeld with two vacancies to fill— one in the *Follies* and the other in his personal life. He was known to take a "personal interest" in one or more of his young female employees (stars and chorus girls alike), something that Billie Burke had learned to tolerate, if not sanction. The affairs never lasted long and rarely intruded on Ziegfeld's role as husband and as father to their baby daughter, Patricia.

Olive Thomas quit Ziegfeld's employ during the Atlantic City tryout of the 1917 *Follies*. Since it was too late to replace her, Thomas's scenes were revamped and divided up among other women in the cast. That gave Ziegfeld more than enough time to find a new star for the next edition, which wouldn't start rehearsals until the spring of 1918.

Ziegfeld started taking an active interest in Marilyn Miller when she returned to New York at the end of *The Show of Wonders* tour. While awaiting her next Shubert assignment, she caught up with all the shows that had opened while she was away and attended a few parties and banquets chaperoned by her parents. It was at one of these celebrated fetes that Ziegfeld spied Marilyn—not as beautiful as Olive Thomas, but shapelier and, from what Ziegfeld could see of her ankles, possessed of terrific legs. Flo Ziegfeld always judged girls by their ankles; they were the first thing the audience saw when the curtain went up. Marilyn's halo of blond hair was another big attraction; most of the past Ziegfeld glamor girls, including Olive Thomas, were sultry brunettes.

Wary of tipping his hand, Ziegfeld began checking into Marilyn's status with the Shubert organization. Much to his disappointment, he discovered that her contract didn't expire until 1919. Of course, he could try to buy it out, but that would have meant placing himself at the mercy of his worst enemies. Instead, he instructed his attorneys to look for a possible legal solution. Shubert contracts were notorious for fine-print "joker" clauses that voided or changed the original intended purpose of the document.

Unaware of what was going on in the Ziegfeld camp, the Shuberts didn't let Marilyn sit idle very long. After much badgering from Caro Miller, they decided to give her a chance to act as well as sing and dance in a conventional "book" musical that was being readied for the Astor Theatre, an elegant Broadway house the Shuberts leased from George M. Cohan and Sam Harris.

Fancy Free was designed to feature Clifton Crawford, the multitalented Scotsman whom Marilyn had impersonated in her second *Passing Show*. Marilyn was cast as the ingenue, Betty Pestlewhite, sharing costar billing with the stylish comedienne Marjorie Gateson.

Fancy Free's uninspired plot doesn't stand retelling; it was set in Palm Beach and dealt with love and mistaken identities among the millionaire set. Augustus Barratt wrote the music and lyrics, Dorothy Donnelly the book; they were two of the most prolific composers and authors on Broadway, though far from the best.

In March 1918, *Fancy Free* launched its tryout tour quite successfully in easily pleased Providence, Rhode Island, and then headed on to Chicago for its first confrontation with major critics. The reviews were less than encouraging. *Variety*'s Chicago critic claimed: "Marilyn Miller was superb in dancing, but misses much when singing or talking.....As for the play itself, the producers have a nerve to charge $2.50 and $3.00 on Saturday nights!"

By the time *Fancy Free* opened in New York in April, critics were still carping about Marilyn's vocal abilities. The *Globe* said that "her chief charms are her well-shaped legs, her vivacity and spontaneity. If she learns to sing she will have an immense advantage over other young women in musical comedy." But Heywood Broun of the *Tribune* didn't seem to mind: "Miss Miller presents an eloquent argument for immortality. How can anybody believe in the end of things, death and such like, if he will only observe how much bounce there is in the best of us."

Marilyn's mixed notices didn't seem to diminish Florenz Ziegfeld's interest in her. On the second night of *Fancy Free*, Ada Miller shooed everyone from Marilyn's dressing room to relate some thrilling news. That afternoon, she had received a call from Ziegfeld's business manager with an offer for Marilyn to appear in the next *Follies*, which was soon to start rehearsals. Marilyn thought that someone was playing a joke on them; she was positive that the Shuberts would never release her.

But Marilyn knew it was true when Ada explained to her that Ziegfeld's lawyers had discovered that the Shubert contract was in fact invalid. When the original deal had been made, Marilyn was still a minor, so Caro Miller signed the contract on her behalf. But Miller had never bothered to obtain power of attorney over Marilyn; he assumed, quite wrongly, that his marriage to her mother automatically made him Marilyn's legal guardian. Without a judicial sanction, only the signatures of Ada Miller or Marilyn's real father, Edwin Reynolds, would have made the Shubert contract binding.

Marilyn Miller signed with Florenz Ziegfeld. The Shuberts were furious but helpless. All they could do was fire Caro Miller, who'd been working for them as a stage manager. Miller was devastated, not only by the loss of his job, but also by the damage to his professional reputation for dealing so unwisely. Marilyn couldn't have been more delighted; it was a first step toward ending Caro Miller's domination over her life.

After giving two weeks formal notice, Marilyn left *Fancy Free* on May 4, 1918. By that time, she'd been working for the Shuberts for four years and was being paid $450 a week. Her contract with Ziegfeld was for one year only at $600 a week, with an option for a second year at $750 a week. In addition to the *Follies*, Marilyn also would make occasional appearances in the *Midnight Frolic*, which played in the roof cabaret atop the New Amsterdam Theatre on Forty-second Street near Times Square.

According to a widely circulated rumor of the time, Marilyn Miller slept her way into Flo Ziegfeld's employ (the same was said of practically every woman who ever worked for him). To clinch the deal, Marilyn allegedly spent a few nights with Ziegfeld in an apartment that he kept for trysting purposes at the Hotel Ansonia, three floors above the one he shared with Billie Burke and their daughter.

People who knew Marilyn well doubted the truth of such rumors. After four years with the Shuberts, Marilyn was well established and much sought after by producers; there was no need for her to resort to sex as a bargaining tactic. In fact, at that point, Ziegfeld needed Marilyn Miller much more than she needed him. In addition to a replacement for Olive Thomas, he found himself with another vacancy in the 1918 *Follies* when Bert Williams, a fixture since 1910, had to drop out due to illness.

Marilyn was then nearly twenty years old. Ziegfeld, at forty-nine, was more than twice her age. Unlike her friend Marion Davies, who'd recently started an affair with the fifty-five-year-old press baron William Randolph Hearst, Marilyn wasn't attracted to older men. She considered Ziegfeld no more appealing than most such men. A few inches taller than Marilyn, he was stocky and round-shouldered, with receding hair, a beak-shaped nose, and a sardonic gleam to his eyes. He spoke in high-pitched tones and dressed too ostentatiously for her taste. His silk shirts and ties, running to purples and pinks, reminded her of the pimps who lingered in the shadows of theater alleys trying to recruit chorus girls.

Ziegfeld's history as a womanizer was well known to the public, as well as to Marilyn. The son of the founder of the Chicago Musical College, Florenz Ziegfeld, Jr., entered show business as a sharp-shooter in Buffalo Bill's Wild West Show. During the Chicago World's Fair of 1893, he launched his career as a flamboyant show-man with Sandow the Strong Man, who appeared on stage as naked as the law permitted, performing such superhuman feats as lifting grand pianos and wrestling lions. After a couple of record-breaking cross-country tours with Sandow, Ziegfeld started to acquire a rep-utation as the logical successor to P. T. Barnum.

But the real breakthrough for Flo Ziegfeld came on a trip to London in 1896, when he saw the scintillating Polish-French sou-brette Anna Held on a variety bill and brought her back to New

York to star in such shows as *Papa's Wife*, *The French Maid*, and *The Parisian Model*. Anna Held drove men wild with her saucy renditions of naughty songs such as "Won't You Come and Play with Me" and "I Just Can't Make My Eyes Behave." Through clever promotion that focused on her gorgeous hourglass figure and her beauty regimen of bathing daily in a tub filled with forty quarts of fresh milk, Ziegfeld created the reigning sex symbol of the time and then married her, which gave him absolute control over her career as well as her earnings.

It was Anna Held rather than Ziegfeld himself who came up with the idea for the first *Follies* in 1907. She suggested that he produce an American version of the Parisian *Folies*, which were collections of comedy sketches, vaudeville turns, dances, and songs—all presented in a rapid succession of varied costumes and sets. Ziegfeld converted the roof garden of the New York Theatre into the *Jardin de Paris* and astonished the opening-night audience with an elaborate show that rivaled any across the Atlantic. The hit of the evening was, of course, the glamorous line of fifty exquisite "Anna Held girls," who were, in effect, the first "Ziegfeld girls."

Although Ziegfeld turned the *Follies* into an annual tradition, he continued to produce other shows as well, including *Miss Innocence* with Anna Held and *The Soul Kiss* with Adeline Genée (the ballerina who had made such an impression on the young Marilyn Miller). During the rehearsals for *Miss Innocence*, Anna Held discovered that she was pregnant, but rather than postpone production or find a replacement for her, Ziegfeld wanted his wife to have an abortion. When she refused, Ziegfeld and a doctor brutally overpowered her and knocked her out with chloroform. The operation was performed. Incredibly, Anna Held went on to do the show, but she never forgave Ziegfeld. She eventually divorced him after he started an affair with the voluptuous Lillian Lorraine, who was a featured player in *Miss Innocence*.

Dubbing her "the most beautiful woman in the world," Ziegfeld starred Lillian Lorraine in the 1909 *Follies*; the professional and personal relationship continued until 1913, when he discarded her

for Billie Burke. A great fashion trend setter of the time, the bub-
bling, romantic comedy actress was one of the era's most popular
and highest paid stage stars. When Ziegfeld started courting Billie
Burke, he was as much interested in her bank accounts, real estate
holdings, and social position as he was in the woman herself. They
were married in 1914 and had a daughter, Patricia, two years later.

Twelfth in the series of annual productions, *The Ziegfeld Follies of
1918* was scheduled to open at the New Amsterdam Theatre on
June 18. In addition to Marilyn Miller, the featured performers
(no one in the *Follies* was billed above the title or in type larger
than Ziegfeld's name) included lariat-twirling Will Rogers, the
homespun humorist-philosopher; banjo-eyed Eddie Cantor, whose
frenetic, risqué fun making was usually performed in blackface;
and bulbous-nosed W. C. Fields, whose rather eccentric juggling
act and raspy wisecracks placated the audience between lengthy
scene changes. Among the other women were Ann Pennington, a
peppy little "hooch" dancer famous for her long blond tresses and
dimpled knees; Lillian Lorraine, the singer who was once Ziegfeld's
number-one box-office attraction as well as his mistress; and Dolores,
the silent mannequin whose haughty grandeur and extravagant
costumes earned her the title "empress of fashion."

Marilyn Miller wasn't the only important newcomer to the *Follies*. Appearing opposite her as the male juvenile was Frank Carter,
the darkly handsome American whom she'd secretly admired when
their paths had crossed in London in 1914. In the intervening four
years, Carter had developed into one of the most promising entertainers on Broadway, mainly in shows with Al Jolson and Eddie
Cantor, the latter responsible for his joining the *Follies*.

Since rehearsals began on an individual basis, Marilyn didn't
meet Frank Carter until the entire company was assembled for the
dress run-throughs. "I had just completed a very difficult dance
and sat on a chair in the wings to rest," Marilyn said later. "A young
man came over and cautioned me about the draught. Imagine my
surprise, and I must confess, my delight, to behold Frank Carter.

I told him I thought it was too warm to catch cold, but he advised me to be careful and covered my shoulders with his coat. I thought that very considerate and nice. That little incident quickly developed into a love affair.

"Frank was forever doing unexpected, thoughtful things. From the day he covered my shoulders, I felt there was someone who had real interest in me, and to think it was Frank made it all the pleasanter. He had a country place on Long Island and kept an old-fashioned flower garden. He used to bring me huge bouquets that he had picked himself."

Born in Fairbury, Nebraska, in 1892, Frank Carter also was a former child performer, billed as "the boy grand opera artist." After his voice changed, he worked for a short time selling programs in theaters and then became a circus high diver, quickly ending up in the hospital for eight months when he misjudged a ninety-foot descent into an artificial pond. Once recovered, Carter started a song-and-dance career with the help of his uncle, Wellington Cross, who was a headliner in that field. Following a stretch in vaudeville, Carter switched to Broadway revues and musical comedies, where he became the protégé of George M. Cohan and his wife, Ethel Levey. Carter was rumored to be one of the reasons why the Cohans were divorced. In any case, Ethel Levey made Carter her leading man in *Hello, Tango*, which took him to London at the time Marilyn first fell under his spell.

Frank Carter had black hair, large and luminous eyes, and a slender, boyish figure. Often described in advertising as "the man with the 100 horsepower personality," he was extremely popular with women. Prior to Marilyn, his most serious involvement had been with Lucy Weston, the luscious British music hall star whom Ziegfeld had introduced to America in the 1908 *Follies*. Carter and Weston may have been married briefly. Newspapers said that they were, but the couple denied it when they broke up. More than likely, they had just been living together.

Marilyn Miller's relationship with Frank Carter really didn't heat up until after the *Follies* opened and the pressures of rehearsals were over. Although Caro Miller now was in a somewhat precarious position where Marilyn's career was concerned, she still relied on him for coaching, and that meant working from twelve to eighteen hours a day to perfect her *Follies* routines. She went to sleep easily at night, exhausted and mentally drained, but she would wake up an hour or two later, haunted by a recurring nightmare in which she was paralyzed and unable to dance.

During rehearsals for the *Follies*, Marilyn often worked with an enthusiastic and genial young piano accompanist who called himself George Gershwin. He was just beginning to acquire a reputation as a composer of popular songs, but was not yet able to make a full-time living from it. Discovering that they were born only three weeks apart, they became great friends. During rest breaks, Gershwin loved to demonstrate his latest tunes for Marilyn while she improvised dances to them. Ziegfeld stumbled upon such a scene one day, disliked Gershwin's music, and told him to stick to songs written for the show, which were by Irving Berlin and several other leading composers of the time.

If Ziegfeld was taking any special interest in Marilyn, she wasn't aware of it. But she had no way of knowing when he might be watching her from his concealed spying places in the New Amsterdam's first and second balconies. When his sharpshooter's eyes spotted something that displeased him, Ziegfeld had his own way of communicating with Marilyn—he sent her a telegram. When the very first one was delivered to her dressing room, criticizing her for crooked seams in her stockings, she thought it was a joke. But she learned that Ziegfeld continually "wired" everyone who worked for him. He had an arrangement with Western Union whereby he could send as many as a million words a year for a flat fee of $25,000 annually.

Marilyn's chores in the *Follies* were similar to those that she had had in the Shubert revues, except that Ziegfeld operated on a grander and more expensive scale. The 1918 *Follies* cost $140,000, a new record both for Ziegfeld and Broadway. Half the budget went for the opulent sets designed by Joseph Urban and Ben Ali Haggin, who were as much "stars" of the *Follies* as Ziegfeld or any of the performers. Urban's *pièce de résistance* this time was a living tableau entitled "The Warring World," which included, in one stunning panorama, doughboys charging over a trench amid deafening gunfire, Red Cross nurses attending the wounded, little French waifs in rags begging for food, and bare-breasted Kay Laurell on top of a revolving globe of the world as the "Spirit of the *Follies*," leading the Allied forces to victory.

And that was just the opening scene of the 1918 *Follies*; there were twenty-five more to follow. The patriotic theme pervaded it, but there were also comedy sketches and production numbers unrelated to the war. Eddie Cantor in blackface pranced out to sing "But After the Ball Was Over" and appeared in other scenes, for the first time in his career minus the burnt cork. Will Rogers and W. C. Fields teamed up in "The Lower Regions," a spoof of Gorky's then highly controversial *The Lower Depths*. The big hit song of the show, "Garden of My Dreams," brought to life the scene on an ornamented Japanese bowl, with Frank Carter and Lillian Lorraine performing on a bridge over a real running stream, surrounded by row upon row of flowering cherry trees.

Marilyn appeared throughout the revue. In the first act, she did two solo dances, including one called "Yankee Doodle," which was preceded by Frank Carter singing Irving Berlin's "I'm Gonna Pin a Medal on the Girl I Left Behind." During the second act, Marilyn appeared in a ballet fantasy, "A Dream," with Frank Carter as the dreamer and sixteen of Ziegfeld's most nimble coryphees dancing with her. In one of Ziegfeld's most extravagant gestures, he ordered Marilyn a fresh costume for every performance at $175 a throw. He believed it was more than worth it in terms of the publicity it received.

But Marilyn's real moment of triumph came in the solo number "Mine Was a Marriage of Convenience," in which she impersonated Ziegfeld's wife, Billie Burke. Marilyn created pandemonium in the audience, not only with the audacity of the spoof, but also with her exquisite silk and satin gown of baby blue, which was Billie Burke's trademark color.

Marilyn Miller put it all together with this show. On opening night, eight taxicabs were needed to carry all her flowers home. The audience loved her and so did the critics. Louis Sherwin of the *Globe* probably summed it up best: "Marilyn Miller, radiant with smiles and grace of exuberant adolescence, seems to dance for the sheer joy of dancing. What makes her still more delightful is the fact that she is the only dancer who has a voice of any real quality."

Harper's Bazaar said: "Other girls can dance. Other girls can smile. But Marilyn Miller's the only girl who can do both at once— with her tongue in her cheek, so to speak, and her hands tied behind her, as it were. There is a clear-eyed, open air virility about her work that is indescribably refreshing."

Several days after the opening, Marilyn was summoned to a private audience with Anna Held, who'd heard nothing but praise about her ex-husband's newest star and wanted to meet her. It was a moment that Marilyn never forgot. At age forty-five, Anna Held was dying from a rare bone disease; probably the greatest beauty of the turn-of-the-century era, she had wasted away to seventy pounds. As she spoke to Marilyn from her bed in the royal suite of the Hotel Savoy, she could barely raise her head from the pillow.

It turned out that Anna Held had really invited Marilyn there to counsel her. Held said that Ziegfeld had broken her heart and ruined her life; if Marilyn wasn't careful, he'd do the same to her. He'd done it to every woman that he'd been involved with and Billie Burke would prove to be no exception.

Marilyn grasped Anna Held's clammy hand and told her not to worry. Flo Ziegfeld was definitely not her type. The only man that she was interested in was Frank Carter. Maybe someday she would even marry him.

She never saw Anna Held again. The first Mrs. Ziegfeld died two months later.

Chapter Five

Young Mrs. Carter

Marilyn Miller's love affair with Frank Carter developed against a background of two wars, the one still raging in Europe and, closer to home, her own battle with Flo Ziegfeld and her stepfather. Whatever separate personal jealousies they might have had, Ziegfeld and Caro Miller were united in the belief that Marilyn was throwing away a brilliant future by getting involved with Frank Carter or, for that matter, any man. Total commitment to career and training was imperative; no romantic distractions were to be tolerated. Look what had happened to poor Olive Thomas, who since quitting Ziegfeld to marry Jack Pickford had become hopelessly addicted to drugs and alcohol.

Although Marilyn was now twenty years old and earning $600 a week, she still lived with her mother and stepfather, which was the "proper" thing for a young single woman of that era. Home was in the Idaho Apartments, on Seventh Avenue between Fifty-fourth and Fifty-fifth streets. Within the family quarters, Marilyn had her own bedroom and practice space, but if she wanted to entertain friends it had to be in the parlor with either or both of her parents present. Frank Carter was not welcome there. Ada Miller disliked him as much as her husband did; she thought that

Carter was a scheming opportunist whose main interest in Marilyn was to form a husband-wife team similar to Vernon and Irene Castle, once the highest paid attraction in all of show business. (After heroic service as a volunteer pilot for the British Royal Flying Corps in the first years of the war, Vernon Castle had returned to America to train new recruits, only to be killed in a plane accident.)

Ironically, it was the war that gave Marilyn and Frank Carter the initial opportunity to be together. Both were very active in the war effort, Marilyn most of all because beautiful blondes were reputed to be the best fund raisers and morale boosters. In one evening, she sold $1,250,000 worth of Liberty Bonds at a booth in the middle of Times Square. Magazines loved to use her as a model for all the young women waiting for their lovers to return from the front. In a typical pictorial layout in *Vanity Fair*, Marilyn posed as "the wartime bride," wearing a gown of white pussy willow satin and lace and carrying a bouquet of lilacs and white pansies.

Since they were working together in the *Follies*, it seemed only natural that Marilyn Miller and Frank Carter should do volunteer service as a team. There was nothing that Ziegfeld or her parents could do to stop them without seeming horribly unpatriotic.

New York was swarming with thousands of military men who were on leave or waiting to be shipped overseas. Marilyn and Frank did what they could to entertain them, usually at the Soldiers, Sailors and Airmen's Club on Madison Avenue. Afterward, the couple would dash off to Carter's apartment for some hasty love-making. According to a rule strictly enforced by her stepfather, Marilyn had to be home no later than one o'clock sharp.

Marilyn and Frank had the help of their friend and *Follies* co-worker Eddie Cantor in circumventing her parents' no dating rule. Ada and Caro had no objections to Marilyn going out to dinner after the show with Cantor, who was a happily married man with children and considered very respectable. After the curtain came down, Cantor would put on his dinner jacket and take Marilyn to Frank Carter's apartment. Then he'd go to one of his favorite delicatessens and kibitz with friends until it was time to pick her up and take her home.

The lovers were looking forward to going on the road with the *Follies* because it would give them more unchaperoned time together. But business was so good in New York that Ziegfeld did the unprecedented and moved the show to the Globe Theatre for an extended run (the New Amsterdam had a prior booking). The transfer couldn't have taken place at a worse time. An epidemic of Spanish influenza, apparently brought over by returning servicemen, was spreading all over the United States. By the time it subsided, half a million Americans had died. The toll worldwide was over 21 million—more than twice the number killed in the war.

With the public warned to avoid crowded conditions, theaters throughout the country were shut down, but the ones on Broadway remained open as a symbolic gesture to the time-honored tradition that "the show must go on." Although business was terrible at first, it began to pick up for the *Follies*, once word got around that choice seats usually impossible to obtain were now readily available.

The flu pandemic and the world war terminated almost simultaneously. Mourning quickly changed to rejoicing when the armistice was declared on November 11, 1918. With its patriotic theme, that night's performance of the *Ziegfeld Follies* stirred the audience to a ten-minute standing ovation at the conclusion. Along with everyone else on both sides of the footlights, Marilyn Miller was teary-eyed as the cast and audience joined in singing "The Star Spangled Banner."

One of the first postwar engagements for the *Follies* was in Washington, D.C., where President and Mrs. Wilson attended the opening performance. Afterward, when the entire cast was lined up for an introduction, President Wilson complimented Marilyn on her war work and told her to expect a surprise in the mail. A few weeks later, both she and Frank Carter received bronze medals from the War Department. President Wilson's portrait was embossed on one side, his signature and the message "Well done!" on the other.

Life on the road proved unbelievably romantic for Marilyn and Frank. Ziegfeld was stuck in New York, where he was preparing the next edition of the *Follies* and several other projects. Caro Miller, who couldn't get a job in New York after the embarrassing incident over Marilyn's Shubert contract, had gone to the West Coast to be a road manager for Klaw and Erlanger. Ada Miller had chosen to stay behind to travel with Marilyn, but she no longer opposed the affair. Frank Carter had charmed his way into her heart with his gentleness and courtly good manners.

By the spring of 1919, Marilyn and Frank were engaged. In May, they returned to New York for an event that became a Broadway legend, Ziegfeld's *Follies-Frolic Ball of 1919*. The 1918 *Follies* had been such a smash that to celebrate, the producer brought the cast back to New York and merged it with that of the *Midnight Frolic* for a single performance in the New Amsterdam roof cabaret.

Held on a Sunday night so that the stars of all the other Broadway shows could attend, the super revue was the zenith of Ziegfeld extravagance. Joseph Urban's shimmering set was all gold leaf, real diamonds, emeralds, and amethysts; the souvenir program was printed on lustrous, perfumed pink satin. In addition to Marilyn and Frank, the performers included Will Rogers, Fannie Brice, Bert Williams, W. C. Fields, Van and Schenck, Eddie Cantor, Lillian Lorraine, Ann Pennington, and many others, plus the combined roster of two hundred Ziegfeld girls.

As their next assignment, Marilyn and Frank were to appear in the 1919 *Follies*, which was to open on June 23. To take advantage of the lull before rehearsals started, they dashed off to Maryland, got married before a justice of the peace, and returned the same day without telling anyone what they'd done. But Ziegfeld had spies everywhere and he was livid when he found out. He fired Frank Carter from the *Follies* and swore that he'd never work in any Ziegfeld production again.

Marilyn threatened to quit as well, but Ziegfeld retaliated by promising to sue her for breach of contract and to make sure that she never appeared on Broadway again for *anyone*. After a long and noisy battle in which the usually dainty and feminine Marilyn surprised Ziegfeld with the number of obscenities in her vocabulary, she decided to stay.

But the newlyweds had the last laugh. The Shuberts quickly signed Frank Carter for a new show called *See Saw*. Hoping to annoy Ziegfeld even further, they went through another marriage ceremony in New York at the Church of the Ascension, followed by a two-day "honeymoon" in the royal suite of the Astor Hotel. Marilyn sent the bill to Ziegfeld, who knew when he was beaten and paid it without protest.

The couple happily set up housekeeping in her parents' former apartment in the Idaho. "Frank was a husband to be proud of," Marilyn Miller said later. "I was terribly in love with him. He filled my life. Have you ever had a load lifted from your mind? Well, that's how I felt when I married Frank. It made the whole world brighter. We were just two chums. We talked over our plans and how we would develop our careers. We built castles in the air in our spare hours.

"Our domestic life was ideal. I was free from the annoyance and distractions of the so-called stage Johnnies. It was a constructive love. Frank was so encouraging. He wanted me to succeed; he believed in me. He told me, 'This will be your banner year—this year you'll become a big star. You're ready for it!' I didn't think I was. I was afraid of it. But Frank kept urging me on, giving me belief in myself, confidence in my own powers. And my desire to justify his belief in me, my longing to make good for him, did for me what nothing else has ever done."

Although he disapproved of her marriage, Ziegfeld continued to feature Marilyn as the principal female in the 1919 *Follies*. He told a reporter at the time that "if all the girls in the company were simply lined up in a row, you might perhaps pick out several whom you thought prettier than Miss Miller. Then why does she deserve to be a headliner? Because Marilyn Miller is like a burst of sunshine. She is very pretty in face and has a beautiful figure; she dances exquisitely; and she has a wonderful personality. She is the incarnation of freshness, of youth, of vitality."

Every *Follies* was intended to be bigger than the year before, but this one was so gargantuan that Ziegfeld discovered he'd commissioned his designers, Madame Frances and Lucille, Lady Duff Gordon, to make more costumes than were really needed. Since it was too late to cancel them, he added a fashion parade number and asked Irving Berlin to write a song especially for the act. The result was "A Pretty Girl Is Like a Melody," sung in the show by John Steel. The tune would live on as the Ziegfeld national anthem. Marilyn didn't appear in the number, but, because she was the star of that *Follies*, the song became her trademark as well. While it was running, she couldn't stroll into a nightclub without the band striking up "A Pretty Girl."

Marilyn's big solo number in the 1919 *Follies* was "Sweet Sixteen," in which she and sixteen handmaidens toe-danced through one of Joseph Urban's most magical settings, all delicate flowers and lush greenery. Marilyn also joined Eddie Cantor and Bert Williams in a ten-minute minstrel segment that cost $35,000 and featured over a hundred of the usual Ziegfeld lovelies plus a chorus of forty-five "pickaninnies" dancing the shimmy. With Bert Williams making his farewell appearance in the *Follies*, it was the only time except for that one night at the *Follies-Frolic Ball* that Marilyn worked opposite the man she'd idolized and impersonated since childhood.

Irving Berlin revived "Mandy"—the minstrel song that had been so popular in *Yip, Yip, Yaphank*—expressly for Marilyn. Marilyn danced to the tune, accompanied by the close harmony team of Gus Van and Joe Schenck. Dressed in a form-fitting trouser suit and top hat of pink satin, she made her entrance from the top of a magnificent Urban staircase, strutting down to stage level in an impression of the early minstrel star George Primrose.

Later, in a scene spoofing Prohibition, she danced "A Syncopated Cocktail," in which bartenders were turned into soda jerks. In a circus ballet composed by Victor Herbert, Marilyn entered on a white horse and proceeded to bring the house down as she twirled and leaped nimbly through space. Billie Burke, watching enviously from the audience, said later that "Marilyn's legs have never been matched for slim, provocative beauty."

Marilyn Miller cemented her position as the toast of Broadway with the 1919 *Follies*. "No audience is immune from the infection of her joyous and enthusiastic youth," said *Vanity Fair*. New parents started naming their babies after her. Young girls became her most ardent fans, probably because she still looked like one herself. Her hair styles were widely copied as she switched back and forth from long curls to short ringlets. The sale of corn cob pipes soared when Marilyn happened to mention to a reporter that a man wasn't really a man unless he smoked one.

Marilyn received the royal seal of approval when her old friend, Edward, Prince of Wales, attended the *Follies* while on a tour of the United States and visited her dressing room afterward. She was dressed in an old pongee kimono and her face was smeared with cold cream when the prince arrived, but she showed a charming lack of vanity and chatted with him comfortably.

Edward loved the show's exquisitely designed production of "Tulip Time in Holland" and regretted that he could not see it again because he was leaving New York the next day. After he left Marilyn's dressing room for the nightclub on the New Amsterdam roof, she coaxed Ziegfeld to move the "Tulip Time" scenery, costumes, and working windmill upstairs by elevator for a repeat performance. The prince got a delightful surprise when the number turned up unannounced in the middle of the *Midnight Frolic*.

Meanwhile, Frank Carter received much acclaim for his new musical, *See Saw*; the critics praised not only his acting and dancing, but his merry, ingratiating personality as well. With both their careers booming, neither Marilyn nor Frank had reason to be jealous of the other's success. The marriage flourished because of their mutual support. In their spare time, they dreamed about their future together. "We wanted to make a lot of money so that we could be independent in our old age," Marilyn Miller said. "We studied voice and technique and practiced new dance steps. We just burned up with ambition and serious determination to go higher. Of course, we always found time to have fun. We both loved swimming, golf, tennis, all sorts of active things."

At the end of November, Marilyn and Frank held a Thanksgiving supper at the Astor Hotel for friends from both of their shows. Ziegfeld was not invited. The gathering was something of a farewell party, since the couple was about to be separated for the first time since their marriage. Carter was going on the road with *See Saw* that weekend, and Marilyn soon would with the *Follies*. They wanted to meet whenever and wherever they could, not only when they happened to be working the same cities; they would get together on their Sundays off, as time and distance allowed. They also swapped lists of all their hotels and theaters, together with telephone numbers and telegraph addresses. Eddie Cantor, who traveled with Marilyn in the *Follies*, said that she and Frank were so much in love at the time that they spent most of their salaries on long-distance calls.

In the spring of 1920, they managed a second honeymoon of sorts when their tours converged in Chicago; in between performances they had two full weeks to enjoy themselves before they would have to part again. One afternoon, they attended the annual automobile show, where Marilyn fell in love with a customized Packard touring car. She wanted to buy it, but Frank said it was far too expensive. The price was $10,000, an enormous sum even for a luxury auto maker such as Packard; the standard version of the same car cost $3,500.

But Frank's disapproval was all pretense. Their first wedding anniversary was coming up soon and he could think of no better way of expressing his adoration of Marilyn than by presenting her with that exquisitely crafted machine. The next morning, while Marilyn was still asleep, he returned to the auto show and made a down payment. The car was to be royal blue, with the monogram

"MM & FC" on all the doors, and would be ready by the time Carter finished his tour. Marilyn would be in Philadelphia then with the *Follies*, and he intended to deliver the car personally. She loved surprises; he couldn't wait to see her reaction to this one.

See Saw gave its last performance in Wheeling, West Virginia, on Saturday night, May 8. As he was checking out of his hotel, Frank telephoned Marilyn to confirm that he was leaving immediately for Philadelphia, not mentioning the new car but just that he was sharing a ride with three friends from the show who also were heading in that direction.

Marilyn tried to persuade Frank to wait until daylight. Like many people in that era, she was terrified of driving in the dark. Roads and highways, especially in rural areas, were treacherously constructed, usually without any illumination except for the vehicle's own headlights.

But Frank couldn't be discouraged. "Don't worry, Lumpy. We'll be very careful. Sleep tight and dream only of me."

Keeping to his promise, Frank drove cautiously, notching only 106 miles from midnight to dawn. Around Grantsville, Maryland, he saw the first good stretch of open road ahead and stepped on the accelerator to make up time. While traveling at 65 miles per hour, he misjudged a sharp curve and slammed on the brakes. The Packard spun around and crashed into an embankment beside the road, flipping over like a turtle on its back.

◆ CHAPTER SIX

A WAIF NAMED SALLY

"AT SIX O'CLOCK ON a Sunday morning, I received a telephone call that my husband had met with an accident," Marilyn Miller said later. "The voice at the other end said that Frank's car was wrecked near a small town in Maryland and that I should come immediately.

"My sister Claire was staying with me at the time. We got dressed, rushed to the Philadelphia terminal and then had to wait two hours for the next train to Cumberland, a journey that took another five hours. When we got there, two young men were waiting for us. Their clothing was torn and mud-stained, and their faces were sunburned from sitting outside all day watching every train that came in.

"They had been in the car with Frank. They both looked solemn and asked me to sit down. A fear grew in my heart. 'Frank is dead,' one of them announced, sadly casting his eyes downward.

"'But the message said he was unconscious and in the hospital,' I protested.

"'We thought it would make your trip easier if you didn't know the whole truth,' the other man said. 'But Frank was killed instantly. He was crushed between his seat and the steering wheel.'

"I was devastated," Marilyn Miller said. "I couldn't believe it.

Frank and I had so many wonderful things planned. We had even talked of old age together, and there he was, just a few months after his twenty-eighth birthday, laid out in that horrid morgue in Cumberland.

"When I saw that stunning new Packard that he meant to surprise me with, I felt even worse. Frank was dead, but the car was little damaged except for a dented roof and cracked windshield. The fourth passenger broke his collarbone and four ribs and was hospitalized for six months. I couldn't get over the feeling that it all might not have happened if I'd never raved about that car to Frank in the first place. I should have realized that he'd rush out and buy it for me. He was always so impulsive and generous that way."

Two days after the accident, funeral services were held for Frank Carter in New York at Campbell's Chapel on upper Broadway. Conducting them was the same clergyman who officiated at Marilyn and Frank's wedding only eleven months before. In the throng of celebrity mourners, Flo Ziegfeld's absence was conspicuous, although he sent a spray of flowers more elaborate and beautiful than any on the bier.

The young widow, her face covered by a long black veil, watched her husband's casket being lowered into a temporary grave at Woodlawn, the vast parklike cemetery in the Bronx that was a favored last resting place for the rich and famous. For all her grief, Marilyn had already made up her mind to build Frank a magnificent memorial. A few weeks later, she sold the unlucky Packard and, adding some of her own money, commissioned a $35,000 white marble mausoleum. Although the memorial resembled a Greek temple, it was supposed to symbolize the little white cottage in the country that Marilyn and Frank had dreamed of retiring to one day. Like that cottage, it was intended only for two. Marilyn left instructions in her will that when she died, she was to be interred next to Frank Carter and the crypt was to be sealed forever.

Immediately after the funeral, Marilyn returned to Philadelphia to resume working in the *Follies*. Since Carter died on a Sunday, she had missed only one performance. She didn't really want to go back: "I thought that I had been killed, too. I didn't want to live. I didn't want to do anything but be left alone."

But everyone urged her to keep on working, that it was the only thing that would help her to forget. Eddie Cantor said, "Lumpy, you're a terrific performer. You sing, you dance, you have youth. No matter whatever happens, you'd be the kind of trouper who'd go on."

Marilyn came round. "The things you've seen on the stage and read in books about the clowns whose hearts are breaking—the Pagliaccis and the shows that carry on—are true," she said later. "It was the hardest thing I ever had to do, but through it I learned that I could always perform. It seems that the more unhappy I am, the faster I dance, more lightly, more easily than at any other time. I did then. I was told I had never danced so well. But it was the singing that nearly did me in. As a dancer, your muscles are disciplined and respond automatically. But the voice is something else; your throat closes, you can't open your lips, you're choked."

Her opening number in the *Follies*, in which she was supposed to be a deliriously happy "sweet sixteen" experiencing first love, was a terrible ordeal for the youthful widow. "I thought I would never get through that song," Marilyn Miller said. "I had to give orders that no one should speak to me before I went on. I'd crouch like a runner in my dressing room until I heard the opening bars, then dash to the stage. If anyone had spoken to me, I would have been lost."

When she was onstage, Marilyn's performances seemed as magically doll-like and technically flawless as ever, but offstage she was falling apart. Eddie Cantor later described taking Marilyn back to her hotel suite one night: "Frank's pictures were all over the place, three or four of them. She went around the room, looking into Frank's face and crying hysterically. I had to get a doctor to give her a shot and put her to bed."

Night after night, Marilyn sat or stood passively in her dressing room, tears rolling down her cheeks while her maid, Violet Ordley, changed her costumes and led her out to the wings. "It was a dreadful time for us all," Ordley said. "For weeks, Miss Miller didn't seem conscious of what she was doing or where she was at."

For the balance of the tour, Eddie Cantor, Gus Van, and Joe Schenck appointed themselves Marilyn's court jesters. They put on impromptu shows in her dressing rooms and in her hotel suites afterward; they would have followed her to the bathroom if it would have helped. "We couldn't make her laugh, but we could keep her from sobbing herself sick," Eddie Cantor said.

Late one night, at about 2:00 A.M., Cantor donned a pair of knickerbockers and a tam-o'-shanter, took his golf clubs, and sent Van and Schenck to fetch Marilyn and bring her out into a corridor of the hotel where they all were staying.

"Eddie, what are you doing?" Marilyn asked when she arrived.

"Well, Lumpy, I want to get out on the golf course before it gets too crowded," Eddie Cantor said.

"Marilyn laughed and laughed until she was tired enough to sleep," Cantor remembered later. "This went on day after day until the season closed, and somehow that gallant girl managed to get through every performance."

Under the circumstances, Ziegfeld decided to drop Marilyn from the 1920 edition of the *Follies*, replacing her with another blonde named Mary Eaton, who was probably a better dancer but couldn't match Marilyn's charisma. For publicity purposes, Ziegfeld tried to create a rivalry between the two stars, but they had been good friends since childhood; Mary, too, had grown up in a family of entertainers. Marilyn later served as matron of honor at Mary's wedding to film director Millard Webb.

What Ziegfeld had planned for Marilyn Miller instead of the *Follies* was unclear. But when she finished touring, he invited her to spend a fortnight's vacation at Burkeley Crest, the estate in Hastings-on-Hudson that Ziegfeld had been calling his own ever since marrying Billie Burke, to whom the house really belonged. Because Burke was on the road with a play at the time, Marilyn was afraid of being left alone with Ziegfeld and declined his invitation.

Not easily rebuffed, the producer suggested that Marilyn go abroad for the summer at his expense, provided that she spend part of the time improving her voice and acting talent. He felt that she was ready to branch into other fields of performance, and talked vaguely of starring her in a show of her own at the end of the year.

Marilyn was quick to accept the offer. She welcomed a chance to escape New York and its many memories of Frank Carter. She also needed a vacation from her mother, who was turning to her with complaints about Caro Miller and their deteriorating marriage. Marilyn kept telling her to stop moaning and divorce him, advice Ada Miller finally followed while her daughter was abroad.

No longer able to rely on her mother for understanding and comfort, Marilyn had grown very close to her mother-in-law, Carrie Carter. Mrs. Carter was not a performer herself, but she understood their problems; she was the proprietor of a rooming house for young women who were just starting out in the theatrical profession. Still deeply in mourning and not about to play the merry widow, Marilyn asked Mrs. Carter to accompany her on the trip to help ward off the wolves of London and Paris.

"I worked like a Trojan during that trip," Marilyn Miller said later. "I studied dramatic art, elocution, Delsarte, and French. I took a voice lesson every morning. Anything to get Frank's death out of my mind. For weeks and months I was frightfully unhappy. Then time began to heal. But you never get over love, properly speaking. I shall love Frank as long as I live."

While Marilyn was staying at the Ritz Hotel in Paris, she received a condolence note from her Ziegfeld predecessor, Olive Thomas, who'd known Frank Carter in her theater days. Thomas was in Paris for a second honeymoon with Jack Pickford and invited Marilyn to join them for dinner one evening. Not yet feeling up to that kind of socializing, Marilyn delayed answering and eventually forgot all about it.

Soon after she returned to New York in September, Marilyn learned that Olive Thomas had died in Paris five days after swallowing a solution of bichloride of mercury that was sufficient to kill twenty-five people. The Paris police first declared it an accident, but subsequent investigation suggested otherwise. At age twenty-four, Olive Thomas probably committed suicide. But why? According to one theory, she was being menaced by a gang of Montmartre drug peddlers to whom she owed an enormous sum of money. Another explanation was that Thomas and Jack Pickford were out carousing all that night and returned to their hotel suite sky high on cocaine. They quarreled, Thomas threatened suicide, and Pickford dared her to try it, never believing that she would.

The tragedy, the first major Hollywood scandal, made headlines all over the world. In those highly puritanical times, the public was outraged by the mere mention of drug addiction and sexual profligacy in connection with the case. The mercury solution that Olive Thomas swallowed was the most widely used medication for treating the sores and lesions of syphilis, which was then incurable. That Thomas and Pickford had the substance in their possession implied that at least one of them was afflicted with the disease. Not surprisingly, Jack Pickford's image as the "ideal American boy" was irrevocably tarnished. He was accused of being a dope fiend and a degenerate. While he was taking his wife's body back to the United States on the *Mauretania*, Pickford made a dramatic attempt to jump overboard, but was restrained by another passenger who was standing at the rail nearby.

Marilyn did not attend Olive Thomas's funeral when it was held in New York on September 29, 1920. It had only been four months since Marilyn had buried Frank, and she wanted no more reminders of that ordeal.

Flo Ziegfeld, again absent from the funeral, blamed Jack Pickford for Thomas's death and swore he'd kill Jack if he ever set eyes on him again. But Ziegfeld did arrange the services for Olive Thomas and contributed the burial plot as well. It, too, was located in Woodlawn Cemetery, not far from the one that Marilyn had bought for Frank Carter.

*   *   *

While Marilyn had been in Europe, Ziegfeld had started hunting around for the perfect script for her first starring role. One day he ran into the writers Guy Bolton and P. G. Wodehouse and told them of his search. "You ought to have a huge success with Marilyn," Bolton said. "She's got the same sort of quality Maude Adams had. A wistful charm that goes right to the heart."

Ziegfeld asked Bolton and Wodehouse if they'd be interested in working with Jerome Kern, their friend and frequent collaborator, on a musical version of Clare Kummer's *Be Calm, Camilla*, a successful Broadway comedy of 1918 that had starred Lola Fisher and Walter Hampden.

"Isn't that the play in which the heroine breaks her ankle in the first act?" Wodehouse said innocently.

"That's it," Ziegfeld replied.

"I shouldn't have thought it would be an ideal vehicle for a dancer," Wodehouse replied.

Ziegfeld asked if they had a story of their own that might be more suitable. They suggested *The Little Thing*, a play that Bolton had written years before. Jerome Kern had composed a few songs for it, but they hadn't been able to find a producer.

As they explained it to Ziegfeld, *The Little Thing* concerned a waif who washes dishes in a theatrical boardinghouse. Found abandoned in a New York telephone booth, she's been named Sally Rhinelander, after the telephone exchange. Sally dreams of being a great dancer, encouraged by two comical and elderly boarders, a former star ballerina and her faithful but now decrepit lover.

When Ziegfeld seemed interested, Wodehouse and Bolton described the songs that Jerome Kern had composed so far. Two of the numbers contained some of Wodehouse's own favorite lyrics; one was in celebration of the Little Church Around the Corner, where he'd been married, and the second was "Bill," discarded from one of the trio's legendary collaborations of the World War I era at the tiny, jewellike Princess Theatre.

Ziegfeld liked the basic idea, but immediately started making suggestions of his own. Loathing older female comedians of the

Marie Dressler type, he wanted the ex-ballerina to be rewritten for a younger woman or even a man. And the little dishwasher must aspire to be not just a famous dancer, but a great star of the *Ziegfeld Follies!*

But now that he'd committed himself, Ziegfeld wondered if Marilyn Miller was equal to the demands of the assignment. Could she act and sing well enough to carry a work by one of the top creative teams in the musical comedy theater? Marilyn assured Ziegfeld that she could and promised to work harder than she ever had before. Work was what she needed, more than time alone, to forget Frank Carter.

While the new play was in preparation, Marilyn spent from twelve to eighteen hours a day getting in shape. Her schedule began with an hour's dancing lesson and two hours with vocal coach Robert Hosea. In the afternoon, she attended drama classes, and in the evening she practiced and exercised, often until midnight or later.

When Marilyn started working out with Ziegfeld's music director, Gus Salzer, he told her, "Don't try to *sing* your songs. Just *talk* them."

Marilyn hesitated a moment, then said, "But I think I could *sing* them, if you'll let me."

"Oh, very well, try it if you want to," Salzer said, well aware of her vocal shortcomings in the past.

But when Marilyn began to sing this time, Salzer was astonished. She had a new voice, pure and sweet, with an affecting quality to it that had never been there before.

"But how?" Salzer stammered when Marilyn finished. "Why, we have a Patti here," he said, referring to a famous bel canto virtuoso of the time. He was exaggerating, of course. But Marilyn's hard work, plus the emotional experience she had been through over Frank Carter's death, had given her a voice which, although hardly the best in the musical comedy field, was more than adequate for the job.

Ziegfeld had several other composers and librettists developing projects for Marilyn, including one based on *Captain Jinks of the Horse Marines*, the 1901 play that was Ethel Barrymore's first starring vehicle on Broadway. The producer needed to protect himself against the chance that the Kern-Bolton-Wodehouse collaboration would not be ready in time. The script was almost delayed when Wodehouse was called away to England. But Guy Bolton took over full responsibility for the book, with Clifford Grey writing additional lyrics.

Ziegfeld was so delighted with the results that he gave designer Joseph Urban carte blanche to make it the most lavish musical that Broadway had ever seen, a tribute to life and beauty. Canceling two other plays that he was preparing for the comedians Leon Errol and Walter Catlett, Ziegfeld made them Marilyn's costars and shot his entire bankroll on what amounted to three shows in one.

In its final form, Guy Bolton's rags-to-riches plot resembled two other musicals that were current hits on Broadway, *Irene* and *Mary*. Not surprisingly, this one would be called *Sally*, and it was cleverly worked out as a display case for Marilyn Miller and Ziegfeld showmanship. The story opens with a socialite settlement worker, wealthy Mrs. Ten Broek (played by the mannequin Dolores, in her first speaking role) taking a group of orphaned young women to the fashionable Alley Inn in Greenwich Village to interview for the job of dishwasher. Sally is hired and soon strikes up a friendship with the usually soused and insouciant waiter Connie (Leon Errol), who has fallen on hard times but whose true identity is the exiled Duke Constantine of Czechogovinia.

When Blair Farquar, scion of a rich Long Island family, stops by the Alley Inn to make a reservation, he literally bumps into Sally and is fleetingly captivated. She falls in love with Blair at first sight, but has little hope of ever meeting him again. An opportunity presents itself, however, when Connie, the duke in disguise, is invited to a ball at the Farquar estate. It just so happens that Otis Hooper (Walter Catlett), the theatrical agent supplying the entertainment for the evening, is a guest at the Alley Inn and looking for a Russian ballerina to replace one who has suddenly become indisposed. Hooper notices Sally dancing for some of the staff and is so impressed that he persuades her to impersonate his client.

At the gala, Sally's hopes are destroyed when Blair Farquar fails to recognize her. Obviously he has forgotten their previous brief encounter. She berates him, they argue, and the hoity-toity guests are scandalized when Sally is exposed as nothing more than a common scullery maid. Connie takes the humiliated girl back to the Alley Inn, where she appears destined to spend the rest of her life in servitude.

But of course she doesn't, because Otis Hooper is stricken by a guilty conscience and arranges for Sally to appear in nothing less than the *Ziegfeld Follies*. In a show within the show, she astounds the audience in her sumptuous "Butterfly Ballet," with music by special guest composer Victor Herbert (who conducted the orchestra for that one number on the opening night of *Sally*).

Sally realizes the dreams of every American girl of her generation by becoming a Ziegfeld star and marrying a millionaire. In the spectacular finale, Sally and Blair Farquar, Connie and Mrs. Ten Broek, and Otis Hooper and his fiancé have a triple wedding and parade down the steps of Joseph Urban's stunning recreation of one of New York's most romantic landmarks, the Little Church Around the Corner.

Because of the many departures from Bolton and Wodehouse's original concept for *Sally*, the Jerome Kern song "Bill" was dropped and eventually turned up seven years later in Ziegfeld's *Show Boat*, where it became a show-stopper for Helen Morgan (who, ironically, was a dancer in the last row of the chorus in *Sally*). From a flop that never reached Broadway called *Zip Goes a Million*, Kern salvaged two songs with lyrics by Buddy De Sylva—"Look for the Silver Lining" and "Whip-poor-will." Together with the newly written "Wild Rose," they became the biggest hits of the *Sally* score.

Since Ziegfeld and Kern both wanted a star entrance for Marilyn in the first act, they detested Guy Bolton's idea of bringing her on as one of six orphan girls dressed in drab cotton dresses, laced-up ankle boots, and poke bonnets that obscured their faces. But Bolton found an unexpected ally in Marilyn herself, who thought the situation was just right for her to break into an eccentric dance. Ziegfeld begrudgingly allowed it for the Baltimore tryout, but said it would have to be rewritten for New York if it didn't go over.

On the first night in Baltimore, a delighted gasp went through the Academy of Music when the last of the orphans was yanked out of the line by the owner of the Alley Inn and revealed herself as Marilyn Miller. The opening was not changed.

Sally opened at the New Amsterdam Theatre in New York on December 21, 1920. Marilyn's surprise entrance received the expected reaction. "When I heard the deafening applause, I thought I would faint with fright," she said later. "All I could see was the face of my mother, smiling encouragement to me from a seat in the boxes. And then I began to dance. I always lose myself when I dance. I seem to be another, projected personality. After that I wasn't a bit nervous. It was all so wonderful—and I'll never regret the hard work I had to do to achieve such a result."

But Marilyn's most triumphant moment in *Sally* came later in the first act, when still dressed in orphan drab she sang "Look for the Silver Lining." She would seem to be lost in daydreams and unaware of the audience's existence and then suddenly look them straight in the eye and smile irresistibly as she came to the last four lines of the refrain:

> A heart full of joy and gladness
> Will always banish sadness and strife.
> So always look for the silver lining
> And try to find the sunny side of life.

There was a hush for a moment as the last note died away, followed by a storm of applause. Again and again, Marilyn had to repeat the chorus, and each time she sang it there was that awed silence before the ovation. The plea for practical optimism was obviously the kind of sermon audiences wanted to hear in that time of postwar economic depression. Performance after performance, the response was always the same.

On one evening in particular, the final curtain ovation was so overwhelming Marilyn couldn't leave the stage. She had to run down a ramp into the aisle and straight out of the theater into Forty-second Street. Some of the audience followed her, formed a circle around her, and brought her back inside for several more rounds of cheering.

As befitted a Ziegfeld star, Marilyn's wardrobe consisted of more than the drudge's colorless outfits. Amidst Urban's exquisite sets of the estate ball and the simulated *Follies* number, she had a sumptuous ballet dress of white ermine, as well as another one of rainbow silk with simulated butterfly wings. In the finale, she paraded in a $10,000 lace wedding gown with a long train that required the attentions of fifty beautiful bridesmaids. So that the audience could have a peek at Marilyn's twinkling feet, Ziegfeld installed a mechanical platform that rolled out over the orchestra pit during her dance numbers.

According to an eyewitness account by the critic for the *New York Sun*, Marilyn had undergone a miraculous change in the year since her last *Follies* appearance: "She used to be a gangling minx with alacritous legs twinkling beneath a rigid torso and fixed smile, who twittered now and then in a squeaking voice. In the interval, she has come to dance with more than her former swiftness and with a new suppleness and abandon. Somewhere she has acquired a singing voice of resonance and body, together with a knack of twirling off comedy lines with a tricksy spirit of mischief. Somewhere too, she has picked up a personality. Her chryselephantine beauty has a charm, a grace, a fragrance of springtime, which are poignantly delightful."

The reviewer for the *New York Clipper* noted: "Miss Miller is a delight throughout. Not only does she strike the keynote of loveliness in her terpsichorean bits, but she sings in a manner just as delightful. She strikes her zenith in the butterfly ballet. She was greeted with as much applause as the well-known 'Babe' Ruth receives when he dispatches the globule on a hurried flight over the Polo Grounds grandstand."

Because of the lengthy ovations from the audience, the opening night of *Sally* started at 8:15 and didn't end until long after midnight. *Variety* said "Ziegfeld has turned the clock back fifteen years and produced a pictorial extravaganza reminiscent of 'The Wizard of Oz' and 'Babes in Toyland.' There's enough material to make two or three comic operas, a couple of revues and a perfectly good farce." The *Graphic* commented: "Ziegfeld has eclipsed all his former productions, even the most famous of the 'Follies'!"

Although *Sally* turned Marilyn Miller into the undisputed queen of American musical comedy, the triumph of opening night was diminished for her by the unshakable awareness that Frank Carter hadn't lived to see it. When Eddie Cantor came to her dressing room to offer congratulations, Marilyn broke down in his arms and sobbed.

Trying his best to console her, Cantor paraphrased some advice that Will Rogers had once given him under similar circumstances. "Lumpy, this should be the happiest night of your life," Cantor said. "I have a feeling that Frank did see it, and from a very good seat."

CHAPTER SEVEN

FAIRY PRINCESS

SALLY, STARRING MARILYN MILLER, became the biggest Broadway musical hit of its time. Both the play's title and star had to be mentioned in the same breath, because Ziegfeld decreed that the public would get no other *Sally* but Marilyn Miller. He would permit no road companies; the only way the rest of the United States was going to see *Sally* was when the Broadway run ended and Marilyn took it on tour.

Overnight, she became Ziegfeld's fairy princess. Tearing up her contract, he gave her a new one that made Marilyn Miller the first female star of musicals to receive a percentage—10 percent of the weekly gross against a guarantee of $2,500. Throughout most of the run, grosses were at or close to capacity, between $36,000 and $40,000 a week. (Those figures seem paltry by modern standards because Broadway ticket prices were only one twelfth of what they are today. Marilyn's takings now would be equivalent to about $45,000 a week.)

Ziegfeld ordered her dressing room at the New Amsterdam to be completely renovated by Elsie Sloan Farley, the leading society decorator of the time. He wanted everything in pink satin and velvet. To take Marilyn around town as well as back and forth to the theater every day, the producer provided her with a chauffeur-driven, pearl-gray Minerva, a Belgian-made limousine with silver replicas of the Roman goddess of wisdom on the front radiator and hubcaps.

If Ziegfeld's generosity seemed absurd, his sense of good business was not. He knew that whatever salary or gifts he gave Marilyn were nominal compared to what Hollywood could pay her. Olive Thomas, for example, had been earning $8,000 a week at the time of her death. Bigger stars such as Mary Pickford and Charlie Chaplin were getting million-dollar deals and sharing in the profits of their films.

Although Marilyn had received movie offers while she was in the *Follies*, they poured in once *Sally* opened, and she made sure that Ziegfeld knew about every one. While she took her time considering the offer, Ziegfeld would get anxious and buy her an emerald brooch, a chinchilla coat, or some other ultraexpensive present to persuade her not to accept.

But Marilyn was simply squeezing Ziegfeld for all he was worth. Different from most young women of her generation, she had no dreams of becoming a movie star, something that she would never have admitted to Ziegfeld. She was exceedingly happy working in the theater, which was far more prestigious, if not as lucrative. If moving pictures weren't a silent medium, she would have been more interested. But as she often asked herself, what moviegoer in his right mind would plunk down 35¢ to watch a nonsinging, nondancing Marilyn Miller? Although she was a wonderful mimic and probably could have succeeded in movies as a comedienne, she considered that a waste of her other talents.

The relationship between Marilyn and Ziegfeld had everyone puzzled. For all the superextravagance of his productions, Ziegfeld was known in the business as a tightwad when it came to anything not visible on stage. His openhandedness with Marilyn didn't jibe. People observing them got the idea that Ziegfeld was in love with Marilyn. Some even thought that Marilyn was in love with Ziegfeld.

But if love was involved, it wasn't the romantic, hearts-and-flowers variety. Marilyn's motives were simple; she had a love for the kind of beautiful, expensive things that only a man like Ziegfeld could provide. If he was foolish enough to give them to her, she would accept them. She felt no obligation to grant any favors in return.

Ziegfeld's feelings for Marilyn were more complex. Marilyn Miller was his prize jewel, his dream of the glorified American girl come true. His obeisant and possessive treatment of Marilyn was similar to a collector's passion, which explained why he was so hostile to Frank Carter or any other man who threatened to remove her from her glass case.

There was a perverse paternal impulse involved as well, not unlike the one between Marilyn and Caro Miller. Marilyn's child-like qualities were naturally endearing to the much older Ziegfeld, but they also excited him sexually. Since Marilyn made it quite plain that they could never be lovers, he got his pleasure through indulging her, at times all but groveling at her tiny, size-one feet.

"Ziegfeld spoiled the hell out of her," an associate said later. "If Marilyn wanted the moon, he'd give it to her, plus Mars." As time went on, such pampering was to make Marilyn extremely demanding and difficult to deal with, or at least where Ziegfeld and similar authority figures were concerned. Among her fellow workers, she was always known as a "good scout" whose success never turned her into an "upstage" snob.

But sweet, childlike Marilyn could turn into a tough, foul-mouthed bitch when she wanted to, and no one was exposed to that unpleasant side of her more than Ziegfeld. It was undoubtedly his own fault. Unintentionally, he gave her such a feeling of self-importance that whatever he did for her was never enough. She always demanded more.

Meanwhile, Billie Burke was watching the Marilyn-Ziegfeld association with increasing alarm. Thirteen years older than Marilyn, Burke saw her as a serious threat to her marriage, and she became almost paranoid in her hatred for the younger woman. Burke and Ziegfeld's only child, Patricia, later vividly described the bitterness and insecurity that existed on all three sides of the developing triangle.

For a treat on her fifth birthday, Patricia Ziegfeld wanted to be taken to see *Sally*, but Billie Burke said it was unsuitable. "Unsuitable?" Flo Ziegfeld retorted. "Beautiful music, marvelous scenery—what's unsuitable about it, for God's sake? Anyway, the child will adore seeing Marilyn dance."

"Oh, of course, I almost forgot," Billie Burke said. "Marilyn is in the show, isn't she? Well, you know, it might be a good idea for Patty to see her at that. Before it's too late, I mean. . . . Poor Marilyn, she used to be such a lovely thing. That's one of the heartbreaks of show business, dear," she told Patricia. "I want you to remember when you see Miss Miller that she was once a graceful, pretty dancer."

"Why do you keep calling her poor Miss Miller?" Patricia asked. "Is she sick?"

"Not *sick* exactly," Burke said. "Try to be kind when you see her, dear. Someday you'll begin to grow old, too, and then you'll want people to be kind to you."

Patricia Ziegfeld was left spellbound by the theatrical magic of *Sally*. Her favorite moment was the "Look for the Silver Lining" number: "When Marilyn Miller came dancing out on her toes to that haunting melody she seemed to be floating above the stage like a thistledown angel." After the final curtain came down, Patricia wanted to remain in her seat forever for an endless procession of *Sally*s. Ziegfeld finally got her unstuck by offering to take her backstage to meet Marilyn.

When father and daughter arrived, Marilyn was at her dressing table applying cold cream to her face. She still wore the wedding gown from the finale. "Hello, you lousy son of a bitch," Marilyn said to Ziegfeld. "Hello, you no-good bastard."

"Now, Marilyn," Ziegfeld said. "Now, dear, I've brought my little daughter especially to meet you. You've heard me talk about Patricia, haven't you?"

"To the point of nausea," Marilyn said, finally acknowledging Patricia with an unenthusiastic hello.

"What seems to be the trouble, Marilyn dear?" Ziegfeld said. "Is something bothering you?"

"You know goddam well what's bothering me," Marilyn shouted. "It's this piece of crap you call a costume. I've told you a thousand times that it weighs a ton, and as far as I'm concerned you can just take it and shove it!"

Ziegfeld hastily said, "This is the first Broadway show Patty has ever seen in her life. The very first!"

"What the hell are you being so goddam quaint about?" Marilyn asked. "You sound like Daddy Long Legs."

When Marilyn started calling him "Buster" with a violent glare in her eyes, Ziegfeld hustled Patricia away. As the dressing room door slammed behind them, they could hear glass shattering against it, apparently the cold cream jar that Marilyn had brandished in her hand as they left.

After that confrontation, dealings between Marilyn and Ziegfeld went into a deep freeze, much to Billie Burke's delight. But it didn't last very long.

By May 1921, Frank Carter had been dead a year. To recognize the anniversary, Marilyn and Frank's uncle, Wellington Cross, arranged the first of what was to be an annual Frank Carter Memorial Benefit for the Service Club for Soldiers, Sailors and Airmen, which Carter had helped to establish during World War I. At a banquet that raised $15,000 for the club's peacetime continuance, Carter was awarded a posthumous medal made from scrap salvaged from the U.S. battleship *Maine*, which Marilyn turned over to Actors' Equity for safekeeping.

That night seemed to mark the end of Marilyn's official period of mourning. No one would ever see her cry again. What they would witness was the twenty-three-year-old widow's emergence as a playgirl. For three hours every night, she could lose herself

in the role of Sally. After the curtain came down, she wanted to
go out and have fun, to keep dancing and smiling brightly—or she
might remember Frank Carter.

Jane Franklin, a reporter who knew Marilyn well during that
time, said, "I'll never forget her habitual entrances, whether into
a nightclub or a private party. You saw three or four or five very
handsome young men, and then you saw Marilyn. One escort was
never enough for her. The band had to shorten its interludes, or
the Victrola had to play constantly, so that Marilyn could dance.

"It was as if she'd rededicated her life to having fun. I don't think
Marilyn ever had a serious thought in her head. Someone would
start talking about the League of Nations and she'd say, 'Oh, come
on, let's have a pillow fight.' One afternoon, between a matinee
and evening performance of Sally, she went up to the Plaza Hotel
and danced with forty Harvard boys who'd invited her for tea."

As the star of the biggest hit on Broadway, Marilyn never had
a shortage of suitors to choose from. But she wouldn't go out with
anyone considerably older than she, no matter how rich and attentive he might be. She might accept bouquets and trinkets as
her rightful due, but she kept the donors themselves dangling until
they gave up. Young socialites and college men had a better chance,
but she felt most at ease with her own kind—entertainers and
especially dancers. It didn't matter if they were no more than
chorus boys. Usually the most handsome men in the show, they
were also the most anxious to please and the supply was never
ending.

Marilyn briefly was involved with Irving Fisher, who played Blair
Farquar in Sally. He had a fine light baritone voice, a magnetic
personality, and was reminiscent of Frank Carter. But Fisher was
also involved with Nora Bayes, the great vaudeville star who had
introduced "Shine On, Harvest Moon" and many other hit songs.
The fortyish Bayes had a fierce temper and threatened to break
Marilyn's legs if she didn't stop keeping company with Fisher.
Marilyn quickly complied.

Marilyn then took up with actor George Stewart, the younger brother of Anita Stewart, who had been one of the first major movie stars. George Stewart was a boyish Richard Barthelmess type, and Marilyn fell for him instantly when they met at a party. Sadly, their love affair didn't last. Stewart had his skull broken in a roadhouse brawl with actor-director Ralph Ince and spent the rest of his life as a helpless invalid, nursed by his sister after she retired from acting.

It was starting to look as if Marilyn was jinxed in her selection of men, but she carried on anyway. For the summer of 1921, she rented the Edmund E. Frisch estate in Great Neck, Long Island, and plunged into the hectic social life of that North Shore community.

There was a saying popular then: "To live in Great Neck is synonymous to being a national success." Nowhere else in America was there such a large cross-section of celebrities from the worlds of industry and finance, publishing and the arts. Marilyn's neighbors included show business friends Eddie Cantor, W. C. Fields, Ed Wynn, George M. Cohan, Leslie Howard, Fannie Brice, Jane Cowl, Lillian Russell, Laurette Taylor, and Groucho Marx; the writers F. Scott Fitzgerald, Ring Lardner, Robert Benchley, and Alice Duer Miller; and tycoons such as Solomon Guggenheim, Vincent Astor, Walter Chrysler, and Joseph Pulitzer.

On the Fourth of July, Marilyn attended a fireworks party at Ed Wynn's place. Before it got dark, all the guests joined in a treasure hunt for items that Wynn had hidden in the shrubbery. Marilyn came up with a pair of sapphire cuff links, which she was only too happy to exchange with Harpo Marx for the gold-plated compact that he had found.

After Ed Wynn detonated $5,000 worth of fireworks, everybody got pie-eyed on illegal mint juleps and gin rickeys. (It was still the era of Prohibition.) The party lasted all through the night and into the next afternoon, when the fun moved to movie actor Thomas Meighan's estate. All the Great Neck notables started putting on a show, but none could top Marilyn and Fannie Brice doing impressions of each other. Marilyn croaked her way through "My Man" and Fannie absolutely murdered "Look for the Silver Lining."

Marilyn had a small woolly dog named Bolivar Brown that she took with her everywhere. At a party at the Great Neck home of film director Allan Dwan, Bolivar wandered out on the grounds and didn't return. Since it was pitch black outside, Marilyn became very concerned and called for a volunteer to help her look for the dog.

Nearly every man in the room stepped forward for the chance to be alone in the dark with Marilyn Miller, but Jack Pickford got there first. Oddly enough, they'd never actually met, although they seemed to have been on a collision course for years because of their mutual Olive Thomas–Flo Ziegfeld connection.

Host Allan Dwan said later, "It took a helluva long time for Marilyn and Jack to find that little pooch. I didn't know that my grounds extended that far." When they finally did return to the party with Bolivar Brown yapping at their heels, Marilyn and Pickford were holding hands. Couples were dancing, so they joined in when the pianist started playing the current hit, "There'll Be Some Changes Made." Marilyn and Pickford were clutching each other so tightly that it seemed likely the song's title would turn out to be prophetic.

Marilyn Miller never kept it a secret that her initial attraction to Jack Pickford stemmed from his resemblance to Frank Carter. "Jack is the only man I've met since my husband's death who reminds me of him," she said shortly after the romance became public knowledge. "Jack is the same type physically, dark-haired and slender, but his eyes are dark gray while Frank's were black. Jack is like Frank reincarnated—the same point of view and everything.

"I suppose it's a horrible thing to say, but I couldn't really love a man if he wasn't wonderful looking. And Jack Pickford just fills the bill. No one ever had a more winning smile nor a sweeter way. Jack's never grown up. He'll always have the heart of a youngster.

Though he's twenty-five, he looks and acts and thinks like twenty. Just a blessed boy he is—and that's another reason why I love him."

Born in Toronto, Canada, on August 18, 1896, he was the youngest of the three Smith children who adopted the professional name of Pickford. Gladys, the oldest and Jack's senior by three years, changed her first name as well and became Mary Pickford. The middle child was Lottie Pickford, who later couldn't cope with Mary's much greater fame and developed into an incurable alcoholic. And then there was the awesome Charlotte ("Ma") Pickford, who was known as the patron saint of stage mothers and also as "the Hetty Green of Hollywood" because of her shrewd and enormously successful management of Mary's career.

Although he didn't have Marilyn Miller's song-and-dance background, Jack Pickford also started his career as a child, acting in stage plays at the age of eight and in movies at nine. He also appeared in small parts in some of Mary's early films for Biograph and D. W. Griffith.

When Mary was barely in her teens, her sudden popularity was especially beneficial to Jack, who found himself being swept up along with her. It was one of Mother Pickford's iron-clad rules that any studio interested in hiring Mary also had to take Jack for his own series of pictures. While Mary was affiliated with Adolph Zukor's Famous Players, Jack, under contract as well, starred in such films as *Tom Sawyer*, *Seventeen*, *Great Expectations*, *The Little Shepherd of Kingdom Come*, and *His Majesty, Bunker Bean*. In 1918, when Mary went to First National in the highest-paying film contract up until that time—$750,000 for three pictures, plus a bonus of $100,000 just for signing—Jack was also taken on for three, though only at $50,000 each.

Jack's films were reasonably successful and he was known internationally, but he deeply resented being dominated by Mary and their mother. He reacted like a combination of Peck's Bad Boy and Dorian Gray, endlessly embarrassing his family by evading the draft, sleeping around, and by his addiction to drugs and alcohol.

At the time he met Marilyn, he was just emerging from what for Jack Pickford was an unprecedented ten months of hermitic life, forced upon him by the scandal over Olive Thomas's death.

Marilyn Miller didn't seem to be bothered by his notorious reputation. She was dazzled, as most women were, not only by Pickford's handsomeness and gallantry, but also by his effervescent sense of humor. Writer Adela Rogers St. John, who knew practically everybody in Hollywood from the early silent days onward, said that Jack Pickford had a sharper wit than any person she had ever met.

Within a short time, they had fallen in love. Both carefree, fun-loving, and tough show business veterans, they were well matched. Spoiled and irresponsible, they lived only to enjoy themselves and didn't worry much about the consequences.

Another of Jack Pickford's attractions for Marilyn was his family connection. Mary Pickford and her husband, Douglas Fairbanks, known as "the royal couple of Hollywood," were treated adoringly all over the world because of the fantastic popularity of silent films, which eliminated language barriers like no other medium before or since.

Doug and Mary's "Pickfair" estate in Beverly Hills was second only to the White House in the range and number of dignitaries and celebrities who were entertained there. Although Marilyn Miller was famous enough in her own right, her acceptance into this exalted society, perhaps even an in-law-to-be of the "king" and "queen," was a very exciting prospect.

But what really clinched the romance between Marilyn Miller and Jack Pickford was Flo Ziegfeld's fierce opposition. They were like two rebellious teenage sweethearts; the harder Ziegfeld tried to drive them apart, the closer and more attached they became.

CHAPTER EIGHT

A TURBULENT COURTSHIP

"MILLIONAIRE OR BILLIONAIRE, I could have had them all, but I'm particular and I chose Jack Pickford. Ten thousand men have loved me, but I love only one, and that's Jack," Marilyn Miller supposedly told a reporter when the tabloids first caught on to the affair in December 1921.

Although it was the heyday of sensationalist "yellow" journalism, a more bizarre article never appeared than the two-page spread in Hearst's Sunday supplement *American Weekly*, which was illustrated with a pen-and-ink drawing of Marilyn being courted by Jack Pickford in the middle of Woodlawn Cemetery! They were pictured cuddling on a bench surrounded by tombstones, Marilyn dressed in a stylish black mourning outfit and furs. A caption claimed that the couple had been meeting there regularly while visiting the graves of their late spouses. The story went:

> Finally, on a day when the cold winter weather was setting in, Jack pressed Marilyn's hand and felt an answering squeeze as they bent over the grave of Olive Thomas. Both gave expression to the thoughts that had formed the silver lining to their cloud of grief.

"I am sure they would want it this way," said Jack. He looked tenderly at the tomb of Marilyn's husband and then at the tomb of his wife.

"I'm sure they would," said Marilyn.

For all its absurdity and sentimental tastelessness, the article did contain a speck of truth. Soon after they met, Marilyn learned that Pickford had not yet selected a monument for Olive Thomas's grave. When she motored up to Woodlawn with him for a look at Frank Carter's white marble mausoleum, Pickford was impressed enough to order a similar though smaller one for Olive Thomas. But that was the extent of their graveyard rendezvous. It's doubtful that either of them gave much consideration to whether or not Frank or Olive would have approved of the match.

Distance proved no impediment to the relationship. Marilyn was committed to *Sally* and Jack was working in Hollywood, but he came to New York whenever he could. Within six months, they were engaged. "We are not going to be married *for ages*," Marilyn said. "Jack will stay in pictures and I'll stay on the stage, so we probably won't see much of each other. I think people are happier if they don't see too much of each other."

Marilyn's dressing room abounded with pictures of her fiancé: Jack Pickford serious, Jack smiling; Jack in a polo suit, Jack in a two-piece bathing suit; Jack behind the wheel of his Alfa-Romeo two-seater. Some were studio glossies, others Marilyn had taken herself with a Kodak Brownie. Almost all were autographed in Jack's boyish slant, with inscriptions such as "To my own darling little girl" or "To Pink Foots," his pet name for Marilyn.

A large portrait of Frank Carter still remained on prominent display. "My perfect first husband and my wonderful next husband," Marilyn said, pointing them out to a backstage visitor. "Sometimes I think I've had more sorrow than most girls, but then I look at those pictures and know I've been blessed above all women, for never did a girl have the love of two such men.

"Why do I love Jack?" Marilyn asked. "Why does any girl love a man? Because he's 'different,' because there's not another man on earth so good, so tender, and so thoughtful. As every woman knows, it's the little things that count, and Jack has a happy faculty for remembering little things. For instance, he knows I just adore old-fashioned chocolates, so he buys them for me in an old-fashioned paper bag. He knows I love white roses, so he gives me a single bud, the kind I like to wear pinned to my dress.

"He never forgets the things I like to eat, and the things I hate to eat. He's the most wonderful man to go out to dinner with— just orders everything himself and never makes a mistake. He remembers that my favorite color is purple and my favorite perfume essence of violets. That I love chiffon stockings and puppy dogs and funny dolls, and that I'd rather have a bag of peanuts than a quart of champagne."

Meanwhile, Flo Ziegfeld was irate. His anger was directed mainly at Jack Pickford, whom he'd never forgiven for stealing Olive Thomas away from him and who now seemed on the verge of a repeat performance with Marilyn. But this time Ziegfeld had much more to lose; Marilyn Miller had become his biggest drawing card, and he had even more ambitious plans for her after *Sally* finished its phenomenal run.

Those plans seemed to include sexual intentions, or so Marilyn presumed when the producer started lavishing his attentions on her. "Ziegfeld haunted my dressing room. He flooded it nightly with flowers and candy. He sent similar tokens to my apartment," Marilyn said later. "The nearest he ever came to making love to me was to pat me on the cheek and to slip his arm around my waist before I could free myself. After that, I never permitted him to set foot across the threshold of my dressing room unless my sister Claire or my maid was there. And I never went to his office on business without my mother or sister as chaperone."

Not the least of the reasons why Marilyn became engaged to Jack Pickford was to provoke Ziegfeld. She succeeded, and in this continuing game both played, he retaliated by threatening to sue her for $5 million for breach of contract. There was a clause in her

Sally contract that stipulated she couldn't marry while the show was running, which could be for up to five years from the 1920 signing. Marilyn's attorney retaliated by pointing out another clause that said Ziegfeld couldn't put on *Sally* without Marilyn Miller as star. If he wanted the biggest money-making show of his career to continue, he would have to stop meddling in Marilyn's private life.

While the opponents figured out their next moves, *Sally* continued to prosper. It was such a tremendous hit that Ziegfeld was forced to break an eight-year tradition and move the opening of the 1921 *Follies* from the New Amsterdam to the Globe. Van and Schenck paid tribute to Marilyn's absence from that edition of the *Follies* by dedicating a song to her entitled "Sally, Won't You Come Back?"

By the time *Sally* closed in April 1922, it had become the most successful Broadway musical up to that time, grossing $3,286,000 in 570 performances. It was far ahead of the previous record holder, *Irene*, which had played a hundred more performances but in a theater less than half the size of the New Amsterdam.

But Marilyn's connection with *Sally* was far from over. She would tour with it through the end of 1923, including six months in Chicago, sixteen weeks in Boston, and nine weeks in Philadelphia. In the full three years that she was with the show, Marilyn gave more than one-thousand-five-hundred performances. With her percentage of the gross, she earned about half a million dollars and became a rich woman in those times of low income taxes.

To celebrate the closing of the Broadway run and the start of the tour, the cast of *Sally* held a farewell dinner in the New Amsterdam roof cabaret. Walter Catlett, the fidgety, stone-faced comedian whose trademark was huge horn-rimmed glasses without lenses, wrote a burlesque of *Sally* with rubber-legged Leon Errol in drag in the title role. For the first and only time in her career, Marilyn Miller was relegated to the chorus line.

Marilyn hoped that the road tour and distance would put an end to Ziegfeld's meddling, but she was wrong. *Sally* no sooner opened in Boston than he started sending her telegrams and letters that viciously attacked Jack Pickford's character and past. Marilyn tore them to shreds and flushed them down the toilet. "If Flo Ziegfeld ranted until doomsday, he couldn't do anything but increase my admiration and infatuation for Jack," she said later. "The more Flo tried to hurt Jack, the more he hurt me and the more I despised him for it."

The conflict worsened when Marilyn was caught up in a scandal that had nothing to do with Jack Pickford but, in Ziegfeld's opinion, blackened both her good name and that of *Sally*. After the show one night in Boston, Marilyn and others from the cast attended a party at the home of millionaire art dealer Benjamin Kabatznick. The proceedings got a bit wild and the police were finally summoned when one of the showgirls stripped naked and auctioned herself off to the highest bidder.

Marilyn escaped arrest through the back entrance, but someone told reporters that she'd been there and it was her name that dominated the next morning's headlines. One story even said that Marilyn was having an affair with Kabatznick, the evidence being an autographed picture of her that graced the top of his grand piano! When she read that, Marilyn lost her temper and phoned the newspaper for a retraction. It wasn't the mention of an affair that she minded so much as the man she was supposed to be having it with. She said that Kabatznick was too old and fat, that the very thought of Marilyn Miller being interested in a man like that was ridiculous.

When Kabatznick read Marilyn's comments he threatened a libel suit, but changed his mind when Marilyn apologized for what she readily admitted was inexcusable behavior. She'd known Kabatznick for many years, ever since her first *Passing Show* had played in Boston, and was actually mildly fond of him and his "sugar daddy" ways.

The Kabatznick incident triggered a barrage of vitriolic cables from Flo Ziegfeld, who was in London for what turned out to be unsuccessful negotiations for a British-European version of the *Follies*. His onslaught finally convinced Marilyn and Jack to retaliate with news that was guaranteed to devastate him. They announced plans to be married as soon as *Sally* took its hot-weather recess in August.

It was as if another world war had suddenly been declared, such was the press's reaction to the exchange of bombshells that took place in June and July of 1922. Ziegfeld's first "shot" was to make public the charges against Jack Pickford that he'd already expressed privately to Marilyn. The crux of Ziegfeld's complaint was that Jack Pickford had been dishonorably discharged from the U.S. Navy and that he also was directly responsible for Olive Thomas's death.

With the help of a private investigator, Ziegfeld unearthed secret Navy Department files that showed Pickford, while serving as a coxswain, had paid a bribe of $500 to a Navy physician to get a deferment from combat duty during World War I. Furthermore, Pickford had acted as go-between for the doctor and other wealthy "slackers." For arranging the introductions, the doctor gave Pickford prescriptions for morphine and other drugs. Pickford escaped a prison term by agreeing to testify for the prosecution in the doctor's trial by court-martial.

According to Ziegfeld, Jack Pickford destroyed Olive Thomas by getting her hooked on drugs and—the ultimate degradation— infecting her with syphilis. Horrified by the discovery that she was diseased, Ziegfeld claimed she had deliberately swallowed poison.

Ziegfeld was too shrewd a promoter and too fearful of a libel suit to state his case against Jack Pickford directly to the press. He relied on publicity agents to do that for him through personal, rather than written, contact with reporters and editors. After going through so many hands, the version the general public heard had been cleaned up and expurgated, but the smear effect was still very potent.

Jack Pickford never uttered a word in his own defense. But Marilyn, quoted in newspaper accounts, had plenty to say: "Ziegfeld is nursing an old grudge against Jack Pickford. He has done everything in his power to discredit Jack in my eyes. His attack on Jack is a perfect parallel of his attack on Frank Carter, which was less conspicuous because Frank wasn't as widely known as Jack Pickford. But in both cases, Ziegfeld wasted his spleen. He failed with Frank Carter as he has failed with Jack Pickford. I shall marry Jack in spite of the ravings and rantings of a regiment of Ziegfelds and am only too eager, too proud, and too happy to do so."

Marilyn said that Ziegfeld's "big aim in life appears to be to discredit Jack Pickford. He's a wretch to say what he has about Jack. On what authority has he set himself up as a paragon of virtue? His position is ludicrous. He is guilty of an absolute falsehood when he says Jack was dishonorably discharged from the Navy in connection with fraud revealed in draft slacker cases. Jack was honorably discharged and can reenlist tomorrow if he cares to. The judge advocate wrote Jack a letter to that effect. Jack has the letter, and I saw it." What Marilyn didn't say—and probably didn't know—was that the letter was part of Pickford's deal with the Navy Department for testifying against the doctor.

"Flo Ziegfeld holds a contract signed by me," Marilyn said. "But that contract relates solely to business. He has not the slightest control over my private or social affairs. Who is he that he should try to dictate to me or to tell me whom I should or should not marry? Mind you, I hate to tell these things. It is against my grain and impulse, but Ziegfeld struck at Jack and me and I shall strike back at him. I do this not in a spirit of vengeance or ingratitude, nor to hurt anybody. He gave me no choice. He injected himself and his wrath and must take the consequences."

Ziegfeld's countermove was to start rumors circulating that Marilyn and Pickford didn't really love each other, that they were only getting married for the sake of publicity and to further their careers. At Ziegfeld's instigation, his Boston coproducer, Edward Royce, told reporters that he thought it was a pity for Marilyn Miller to marry while she was enjoying such phenomenal success. It was the old show business theory that a star's romantic appeal to the public was greatly enhanced if she or he was single and—if only in fantasy—attainable.

Marilyn thumbed her nose at those suggestions. "Our marriage will be the result of a real love match," she said. "It will not be a show marriage, or a press agent's dream, or a snare for oodles of publicity. All our friends know it, and so does Flo Ziegfeld, and that's what makes him all the more furious."

She believed that marriage would help her career rather than hurt it. "Marriage is the very finest state for a person on the stage. I certainly found it to be so as Frank Carter's wife. It made a new being out of me. I made more rapid progress. My confidence grew. My ambition soared. I expect that the same thing will happen with Jack Pickford. As my employer, Ziegfeld should appreciate that."

Marilyn saved her best fusillade for last. She suspected that what really motivated all of Ziegfeld's invectives and innuendos was his disappointment over her rejection of his romantic advances. "I am paying the price for being good," Marilyn said. "Flo Ziegfeld is a persevering, subtle type. He will say that his attentions were that of a manager who wished to please or flatter the star, but don't believe it. I was obliged to hold him at arm's length. He resented such treatment. It was not easy for a man of his many conquests. But he was too callous to take the hint. He was annoyingly persistent. I never saw his like, and I've been on the stage for most of my life!"

Marilyn said there were nights when she had to barricade herself in her dressing room to fend Ziegfeld off. She also accused him of having indiscreet affairs with chorus girls and conducting all-night orgies with four or five of them at a time in his private office at the New Amsterdam Theatre.

Ziegfeld had gone so far as to propose marriage to her, Marilyn claimed. But she laughed in his face, she said, knowing full well that Flo Ziegfeld would never divorce Billie Burke for any woman. If he did, she would make sure that he never saw their daughter, Patricia, again.

"Billie waves that child at him like George M. Cohan waves the flag!" Marilyn said.

* * *

While Ziegfeld was abroad tending to business, Billie Burke was spending the summer at Norwood Farms, an estate that she owned in York Harbor, Maine. When she read a newspaper account of Marilyn's statements, she flew into a rage, immediately cabling Ziegfeld for an explanation. But before he could reply, a carload of reporters from New York descended on her, and Burke found herself pouring more venom into the already boiling scandal pot.

"Bah!" said Billie Burke in her inimitable addlepated way. "Likewise pish-tush! Flo jealous of that Pickford—which isn't his name at all, I'm told. The very idea! And as for this Miller person thinking she has a place in any but the professional and business thoughts of Mr. Ziegfeld! Well, the poor child's brain can't be functioning properly, that's all. She certainly flatters herself immensely if she thinks for one moment Flo Ziegfeld wants to keep her from marrying that Pickford boy because *he* is in love with her. She must have those delusions of grandeur that poor Harry Thaw suffers from.*

"It only shows," Billie Burke continued, "how foolish and nonsensical a woman can be when she falls under the hypnotic influence of such a man as Pickford, an influence that—well, just wait and see."

Billie Burke spoke lovingly of Ziegfeld for a moment and then issued a warning: "Let Marilyn be careful. I have some questions I'd like her to answer before she utters any more lies about my husband! Come on, young Miss Miller. Tell the truth about yourself. Tell the world what Flo Ziegfeld, my husband, has done for you! Tell the truth, the naked truth—if you dare!"

Marilyn was angry, Burke said, because Ziegfeld had interfered in her private life on numerous occasions. "It isn't only this Pickford business. Flo has had lots of trouble with Miss Miller. Last year she threw a tantrum because he called a halt on some parties she held at Great Neck, Long Island, when the good name of *Sally*

*Harry Thaw, murderer of architect Stanford White, was acquitted on a plea of insanity after enormous publicity.

was being endangered by her conduct. So Flo set his foot down. Set it down hard. And then Marilyn got mad and threatened all sorts of things. That's what's behind all this fuss and fury.

"Why doesn't Miss Miller tell the world the names of the very nice people, oh, so very nice, who attended those parties at Great Neck? Let her answer that. Let her tell the truth about Marilyn Miller, not lies about Flo Ziegfeld!"

No answer was forthcoming, at least not from Marilyn herself. But rumor had it that the persons Billie Burke referred to were a group of high-society good-for-nothings. But Burke also could have meant any number of bootleggers, drug peddlers, and other underworld types who were usually much in evidence at any large gathering of celebrities during the Prohibition era.

Billie Burke received a reply to the cable she had sent Ziegfeld asking for an explanation of Marilyn's accusations:

> BILLIE DARLING. I AM NOT AFRAID OF THE TRUTH AND I SWEAR TO GOD THERE IS NOTHING TO WHICH YOU CAN TAKE EXCEPTION. WAIT UNTIL I AM PROVEN GUILTY. YOU AND PATRICIA ARE ALL THAT MEAN ANYTHING TO ME. BE FAIR DEAREST. WILL SAIL ON NEXT BOAT.

Before he left Paris for Cherbourg, Ziegfeld issued a rebuttal to the International News Service. "Everyone knows that Jack Pickford was discharged from the Navy because of his connection with draft fraud cases," he said. "Marilyn should have picked a real man. Her brilliant prospects will not be improved by marrying Pickford. I wish her every happiness, but she is taking awful chances, especially in view of the tragic end of Olive Thomas."

Ziegfeld confessed that "Billie Burke's husband is too lucky to be jealous of anybody's attentions to Marilyn Miller. Billie Burke fascinates me more than ever. She is the most charming woman in the world, and Patricia is a wonder baby."

* * *

The mudslinging might have continued indefinitely were it not for the intervention of Ma Pickford, who could no longer tolerate the blackening of her family's reputation. Every time some new attack was made on Jack Pickford, it reflected back on sister Mary, who was "America's sweetheart" and the most popular female movie star in the world. Her career, as well as Jack's, could be ruined.

Mrs. Pickford decided that the only solution was to have a heart-to-heart talk with Marilyn. Traveling to Boston unannounced, she surprised Marilyn by turning up in a front-row seat at a performance of *Sally*. When Marilyn finished her butterfly ballet in the last act, an usher rushed down the aisle to the stage with a huge bouquet of roses in varying degrees of red and pink. The clean-up campaign had begun.

Ma pursued her children's interests with single-minded determination and an astute business and public relations sense. Over a midnight supper in Marilyn's suite at the Copley Plaza Hotel, Mrs. Pickford told Marilyn that if she really loved Jack, she should stop feuding with Ziegfeld immediately. No further bombasts were to be fired. Marilyn needed little persuading. All the tensions of recent weeks had left her on the verge of nervous collapse.

Ma thought that Marilyn and Jack should be married as soon as possible. The engagement period had gone on long enough. It was obvious that they were having a sexual relationship and the puritanical American public did not approve of such conduct.

Marilyn favored an elopement, but Mrs. Pickford decided that would be a missed opportunity for some much needed image enhancement. She envisioned a big public event, a lavish formal wedding that would wipe away memories of the dirty linen recently on display. And what better place to hold it at than Pickfair? It was only proper that the "queen of Broadway" should be married at the home of the "king and queen of Hollywood."

Without bothering to consult Mary and Doug, let alone the prospective bridegroom, Marilyn and Mrs. Pickford fixed a tentative date of August 1. When Ada Miller expressed resentment

over being left out of the planning, a royal battle developed between the two archetypal stage mothers, but the victor was never
in doubt. A sore loser, Ada Miller vowed to boycott the wedding
and kept to her promise.

When news of the forthcoming nuptials reached Ziegfeld, he
sent Marilyn (with copies to the press, of course) what soon was
labeled "the cablegram with the sting." It said:

> I PRAY THAT ALL YOUR EXPECTATIONS WILL BE REALIZED
> AND THAT GOD HAS HAPPINESS AND PROSPERITY IN STORE
> FOR YOU IN TAKING THE STEP YOUR HONEST FRIENDS
> CONSIDER THE MISTAKE OF YOUR LIFE. GOOD LUCK MY
> DEAR MARILYN. FLO.

◆ CHAPTER NINE

Mary Pickford

ON HER WEDDING DAY, Marilyn Miller became not only Mrs. Jack Pickford, but also, for obvious reasons, "America's other sweetheart." Bide Dudley, poet laureate for Pulitzer's *New York World*, celebrated the occasion by writing:

> Oh, Marilyn, oh, Marilyn,
> You now are Mrs. Jack,
> And hearts are glad and hearts are sad,
> From Newfoundland to Yak.
> Oh, Marilyn, sweet Marilyn,
> It's joy we wish you, dear.
> We're all worked up; we lift the cup
> And drink to you near beer!

The ceremony was held at Pickfair on July 30, 1922. Two weeks before that, *Sally* gave its final performance of the summer in Boston and Marilyn took the midnight train to New York to select her honeymoon trousseau. Apparently, the newlyweds weren't planning to stray far from the bedroom. Although Marilyn spent nearly $3,000, most of it went for lingerie, including fifty ultrasheer

105

nightgowns and dozens of "teddies," "step-ins," slips, and petticoats, all newly imported from Paris.

Traveling from coast to coast with Marilyn was her soon-to-be
ex-mother-in-law, Carrie Carter, who somehow had managed to
pass muster with Ma Pickford and was to give the bride away in
the absence of Ada Miller. Marilyn had severed all contact with
Caro Miller since his divorce from her mother.

Marilyn expected the wedding to be held on August 1, but when
she arrived at Pickfair, she discovered that the date had been
advanced to Sunday afternoon, July 30. Mother Pickford had made
the change so that there'd be no interruption of film production
schedules; otherwise, Hollywood would have been forced to shut
down for the day. Jack Pickford was working in *Garrison's Finish*,
Mary in *Tess of the Storm Country*, and Douglas Fairbanks in
Robin Hood, and the invited guests were involved with at least a
dozen other films.

The wedding was to be the first major family function held at
Pickfair since Douglas Fairbanks had made a present of it to Mary
Pickford on *their* wedding day in 1920. Formerly a hunting lodge,
the estate was situated high on a mountain crest between Benedict
and Coldwater canyons, with an unobstructed view of the Pacific
Ocean. Covering nearly three acres, the grounds contained a Tu-
dor-style mansion, riding stable, tennis court, miniature golf course,
and Beverly Hills' first swimming pool, which was a hundred feet
long, with its own sand beach.

Mary Pickford was then twenty-nine, five years older than
Marilyn, and Douglas Fairbanks was thirty-nine. Their regal life-
style was not Marilyn's. Although she found the couple cordial,
she never really felt comfortable in their lofty company. Mary in
particular was a problem because she seemed to resent Marilyn,
both as a potential husband stealer and as a threat to her extremely
close relationship with Jack, the spoiled rotten apple of her eye.

Since her hosts left for the studio at five in the morning and
usually didn't return until late in the evening, Marilyn saw little
of them until the night before the wedding, when everyone—Jack

and Ma Pickford included—dined *en famille* on a solid gold dinner service while attended by eight footmen in full-dress uniform. When the pomp and ceremony got too much for Jack Pickford, he registered his displeasure with a stentorian fart. Only he could get away with such impudence. Even Ma Pickford laughed.

By Hollywood standards, the wedding was an intimate affair, with about forty guests and an equal number of reporters and photographers. Mary Pickford's red, yellow, and blue Mexican parrot squawked hello to everyone as they arrived. Hanging over the orchid-laden, improvised altar in the Pickfair living room was a huge wedding bell made of white chrysanthemums.

The string quartet that provided background music at the Pickford-Fairbanks studio played the processional as Mary, the matron of honor, descended a staircase, followed by Marilyn, exquisite in a gown of white georgette crepe and princess lace. Looking spruce in black cutaway and gray pin-striped trousers, Jack Pickford was accompanied by his best man, film director Victor Heerman.

The scene was reminiscent of the wedding finale in *Sally*. The Reverend Neil Dodd, rector of the Little Church Around the Corner, which figured so prominently in the show, came from New York to conduct the Episcopal service. As soon as it was over, everybody rushed to kiss the bride, but Charlie Chaplin, almost unrecognizable dressed as a toff instead of a tramp, got there first.

A champagne reception was held on the lawn in front of the house. Topping the six-tier wedding cake were a kewpie doll bride and groom standing under a candy trellis of roses and lilies of the valley. Just as Marilyn and Jack were ready to cut the first slice, a small single-engine plane suddenly appeared in the sky above, swooped down, and dropped a hundred "bombs" of fresh flowers on the assemblage.

Outside Pickfair, a great mob had collected. Extra police had to be called, sight-seeing buses clogged the narrow mountain road, and gatecrashers were apprehended as they tried to scale the garden walls.

When the wedding couple finally drove off, escorted by six patrolmen on motorcycles, there were three old shoes hanging from the rear bumper of their Rolls Royce. One was a dainty, toeless slipper once worn by Mary Pickford. The second was a scuffed Oxford that belonged to Douglas Fairbanks. The third was a dried out leather bootee of Charlie Chaplin's.

There was no honeymoon in the regular sense. As her son's manager and producer, Mrs. Pickford refused to give him more than two days off from filming *Garrison's Finish*. Not wanting to waste any time traveling, the newlyweds checked in at the Ambassador Hotel for what the press presumed would be a forty-eight-hour orgy. Surprisingly, they spent every night in the hotel's Coconut Grove, dancing and socializing with friends.

For the remainder of August, they rented a small furnished house that reporters naturally called their "love bungalow." Posing for photographers as she picked flowers in the front garden, Marilyn said, "I dread the day when I must start east again. I'd like to stay here always. It's as nearly perfect as any earthly place could be."

While her husband was working, Marilyn loafed and swam the afternoons away at Pickfair. She also found time for dance lessons with Theodore Kosloff, her coach from Shubert times, who now had his own ballet studio in Hollywood and was closely allied with Cecil B. De Mille in movie work.

The Hollywood of 1922 offered little in the way of public nightlife, so Marilyn and Jack spent most of their evenings at parties and dances at the homes of friends. Charlie Chaplin, whose estate bordered Pickfair, was the first to fete them, and that set off a chain of similar gatherings hosted by Harold Lloyd, Alla Nazimova, Rudolph Valentino, Tom Mix, and Mabel Normand.

Another party giver was Samuel Goldwyn, who was getting ready to sell his Goldwyn Pictures Corporation to Marcus Loew's Metro Pictures and become an independent producer. When Goldwyn saw Marilyn delighting his other guests with a sensuous demonstration of the shimmy, he got so fired up with excitement that he later took her aside and tried to sign her to a movie contract.

Marilyn couldn't have cared less—she'd turned down many such offers in the past—but when Goldwyn persisted, she agreed to make a screen test.

When Ma Pickford learned of Goldwyn's interest, she insisted on taking on the role of Marilyn's business manager. Ma wasn't going to permit the former glove salesman to take advantage of her daughter-in-law's lack of experience with double-dealing Hollywood executives. Mrs. Pickford's interest, of course, wasn't purely protective; as Marilyn's manager, she would be entitled to a percentage of her movie earnings.

Marilyn's screen test soon became a family project. Jack Pickford volunteered to direct it, and Mary was coerced into serving as technical adviser. The idea wasn't as crazy as it might have seemed. Jack already had directed portions of his sister's films, including the highly successful *Little Lord Fauntleroy*. And who knew more about makeup, lighting, and camera angles than Mary, who at twenty-nine was still portraying youngsters and getting away with it?

Filmed at the Pickford-Fairbanks studio, the test pleased everyone but Marilyn. She chose to do some comic and dramatic bits from *Sally*, plus a couple of minutes of ballet twirling and tap dancing. But without the benefit of music, sound, and color, she saw on the projection room screen only a pale shadow of what she imagined Marilyn Miller to be on the stage. Even worse, she detected an eerie resemblance to Mary Pickford, which wasn't surprising given the latter's behind-the-scenes participation. Her sister-in-law even dressed Marilyn's hair in the long Pollyanna curls that were a Mary Pickford trademark.

Ma Pickford never forgave Marilyn for rejecting Samuel Goldwyn's offer, thinking the decision very selfish. Apart from adding to the family treasury, Mrs. Pickford saw Marilyn's working in films as a steadying influence on her son. Jack had never been very dedicated to his career and was likely to become even less interested if he was going to be chasing around the country after Marilyn while she was appearing in plays. If it had been up to Ma, Marilyn and Jack would have become a steady movie team, a rarity for two stars actually married to each other.

At the end of August, Marilyn headed back to the East Coast for the Labor Day reopening of *Sally* in Boston. Jack Pickford wasn't going to let his new bride travel all that distance alone, so he left his *Garrison's Finish* literally without one. Due to that and subsequent delays caused by Jack, the film took six months, rather than six weeks, to complete.

The six-day journey was transformed into a bonus honeymoon, since the couple never strayed from their compartment except to change trains. When they reached Boston, Jack continued on to New York to look into the possibilities of settling there permanently, which would make for fewer separations. Although he wasn't keen on working in movies, he could do it just as easily in New York, where nearly all the Hollywood studios had branches grinding out well over a hundred features a year.

Marilyn's return to *Sally* was being eagerly awaited by the scandal press, which anticipated a resumption of the hostilities with Flo Ziegfeld that had dominated headlines and front pages at the beginning of the summer. But hopes were dashed when the two adversaries decided to declare a truce. Marilyn had promised Ma Pickford to stay out of trouble. Ziegfeld, on the other hand, needed to keep Marilyn happy; he didn't want her walking out on him before *Sally* finished its tour.

Marilyn made her position plain when she told a reporter, "Flo Ziegfeld is the best in his line. There's no reason why we shouldn't continue working together as long as we don't let our personal feelings interfere."

Much to everyone's surprise (but in the best interests of *Sally*'s tour), Ziegfeld issued a statement in which he refuted previous remarks about Marilyn and Jack Pickford: "I have no grudge or personal feelings against Mr. Pickford. Whatever interest I showed was prompted solely by commercial and artistic reasons. I simply wished to advise Marilyn as her manager. I felt that a girl of her age and wonderful opportunities should defer marriage for a few years. Her choice of husband was never the issue. That attitude on my part has been misjudged, misunderstood by Marilyn and everybody else."

But the calm proved brief. Jack Pickford was named as corespondent in director James Young's divorce action against film star Clara Kimball Young. Since the alleged intimacies between Pickford and Mrs. Young were supposed to have taken place long before Marilyn became involved with him, she had no reason to be jealous. But it was an embarrassing business, blown up by the press, which relished any opportunity to create a scandal and raise doubts about the durability of the Miller-Pickford marriage.

In November, Marilyn was reportedly stricken with appendicitis during the Philadelphia engagement of *Sally*. Mary Eaton, then appearing in the 1922 *Follies* in New York, was rushed down to substitute. (Months before, Ziegfeld had insisted that Eaton learn the part of Sally in case of just such an emergency. Ziegfeld preferred not to use unknown understudies, although it sometimes couldn't be avoided for a performance or two. If people were willing to pay up to $3.50 a ticket for *Sally*, they were entitled to a star.)

Marilyn recovered in a week. It turned out that her indisposition wasn't caused by a ruptured appendix at all, but by nervous exhaustion. Surprisingly, Ziegfeld had little or nothing to do with her breakdown, nor did her enforced separation from Jack Pickford. The trouble this time was mainly with her family.

The pressure had been building for some time. When Marilyn became famous, her immediate relatives in a sense became famous too. As Marilyn Miller's mother, or Marilyn Miller's sister, they were regarded as celebrities even if it was just by friends and neighbors. They had to be seen to dine well, dress well, and live well, and they made constant demands on Marilyn for money and attention. They were so convincing that Marilyn always felt she owed them something, that whatever she did for them was never enough.

Marilyn's mother was starting to regret divorcing Caro Miller, driving Marilyn to distraction with her weeping and wailing. But a more serious problem was with Marilyn's twenty-seven-year-old brother, Edwin Reynolds, Jr., who had been drummed out of the Columbians at an early age and raised by their uncle and aunt in Memphis. Marilyn had very little contact with Edwin until she became a Ziegfeld star and he started writing to her for financial assistance. By that time he was married and an expectant father, so Marilyn responded by giving him the down payment for a house that he wanted to buy in Minneapolis. The baby turned out to be a girl and was named Marilyn. Over a period of four years, Aunt Marilyn gave Edwin about $25,000, which she thought was being used for his family's welfare. It wasn't. Edwin was a compulsive gambler. He lost all the money and more; Marilyn didn't find out until his creditors tried to collect and he disappeared, abandoning his wife and daughter in the process.

If he'd just been Edwin Reynolds, Jr., the incident might have passed unnoticed, but since he also was Marilyn Miller's brother, the press had another field day. Her worst upset came when Edwin was apprehended in Chicago and hauled back to Minneapolis in handcuffs to face charges of deserting his family.

Meanwhile, Marilyn's sister Claire, who was carried on the *Sally* payroll as a substitute chorus girl but was really a traveling companion for the star, picked that same week to announce that she was divorcing talent agent James B. McKowen, her husband of eight years. That in itself was no bombshell, but Claire also announced that she intended to marry a certain W. Robert Montgomery of Boston. The name registered with at least one reporter with a long memory. It quickly was headline news that Marilyn Miller's sister was engaged to a man who had served two years in Sing-Sing for grand larceny. Needless to say, Marilyn Miller was not available for comment.

Life turned considerably brighter for Marilyn when *Sally* moved on to Pittsburgh and Jack Pickford arrived from California to celebrate Thanksgiving with her. When they sat down to dinner in their hotel suite, Marilyn squealed with delight when Jack lifted the lid off the turkey tray and she spotted a glimmering diamond-and-emerald earring dangling from each of the drumsticks. At Christmas in Detroit, Pickford completed the surprise with a matching bracelet concealed in plum pudding.

By that time, Marilyn and Jack had been married five months, although it seemed to them more like five weeks because their careers had kept them apart so much. Since they still were behaving like honeymooners, it was a bit early to tell whether they could avoid the all too obvious pitfalls of their unconventional living arrangements. It wouldn't be easy and might even be outside their control. They were darlings of the public, much fancied and pursued. There were too many temptations, too many opportunities for infidelities to take place.

Although it was apparent that they were very active sexually, Marilyn and Jack kept the details of their intimate moments private. But because of Jack Pickford's history, there were all sorts of rumors about drug and alcohol binges. Gossipers also claimed that Marilyn had become infected with syphilis on her very first night with Pickford. If true, that would have made her a sort of Typhoid Mary of the American musical theater, given the number of men she was involved with *after* Jack Pickford.

As for Jack Pickford giving her VD, Marilyn was both sexually sophisticated and fanatical about personal hygiene—and certainly aware of Jack's history—so the gossip would seem to be unfounded.

Although it was true that Jack Pickford used drugs and drank heavily, there is no evidence that Marilyn did much of either. Since Jack Pickford was a very charming and persuasive man, she may very well have experimented with cocaine and marijuana and got drunk occasionally. But had she been a heavy user, there was no way that she would have been able to appear in a strenuous, three-hour musical such as *Sally*, which she did six days and eight times a week virtually nonstop for three solid years.

Also, Marilyn's serious sinus condition resulted in blinding migraine headaches, which she overcame much of the time through sheer force of will. She could not tolerate hard liquor or tobacco, so it was unlikely that she would have snorted cocaine or smoked marijuana with any regularity. When she did drink, it was champagne or wine, but more than a glass or two made her ill.

Unlike hers and Frank Carter's synchronized itineraries, Marilyn and Jack had no fixed schedule for spending time together. Since she was restricted to whatever city *Sally* happened to be playing in at the time, Jack did most of the traveling. They had no real home, just the series of luxury hotel suites that Marilyn rented while touring. The frequency and duration of the meetings seemed to depend on how randy they were feeling and whether Jack could be spared from his moviemaking activities.

After celebrating Christmas and New Year's in Detroit with Marilyn, Jack returned to Los Angeles to start a new film, *Valley of the Wolf*. No sooner did he get there than he turned right around and went back, this time chartering a private plane because he couldn't tolerate another four days on the train. Ma Pickford, who was producing the movie, finally had to go to Detroit herself to bring her son back.

Jack was concerned about Marilyn receiving too much attention from some of the Detroit automobile magnates and other big-spending types. After a performance, they were lined up in the corridor outside her dressing room, waiting for an audience. The couple's first quarrels were over whether or not she should accept gifts from admirers that went beyond the usual flowers and boxes of candy. A pearl necklace or diamond wristwatch wasn't the sort of thing Jack wanted his wife taking from other men. When she did, he suspected she was granting intimate favors in return.

Marilyn denied it, probably with her fingers crossed behind her back. She was seen gallivanting about town with many of those admirers, especially the younger and most handsome ones. When they went back to Marilyn's hotel suite after the joints started to close down, it's doubtful that it was to play Parcheesi. Marilyn would dismiss her maid for the night and her beau would discreetly press a ten- or twenty-dollar bill into the girl's hand as she left.

By the spring of 1923, rumors were circulating that Marilyn and Jack were considering a divorce. She was in Chicago with *Sally*. He reportedly could no longer tolerate his wife being anywhere but by his side. The press, always looking for an angle to exploit in the absence of any hard news, saw no reason for them to stay married if they were going to be living apart so much.

Marilyn denied that she and Jack were having problems. She said it was all malicious gossip stirred up by her old and devoted friend Benjamin Kabatznick, the millionaire art dealer from Boston, who was obsessed with the idea of marrying her himself. She claimed that he'd offered her "yachts and automobiles and plates of diamonds" if she would divorce Jack Pickford. This was indeed true, but Kabatznick had about as much chance of marching down the aisle with Marilyn as Ziegfeld did. They simply weren't her type; money and/or power in themselves couldn't buy her affections.

Kabatznick did succeed in inflaming Jack's jealous streak, causing Marilyn to spend $50 a day (an enormous sum then) on long-distance phone calls to placate her husband. Peace finally was restored when Marilyn sent Jack a costly gold-and-platinum cigarette case that was inlaid with a mother-of-pearl heart engraved with their two sets of initials.

All seemed serene by summer, when Marilyn took her August vacation from *Sally* and joined Jack in Los Angeles for the celebration of their first wedding anniversary. Buster Keaton, who'd known Marilyn since they were children in vaudeville and also was one of Jack's best friends, threw a party in their honor. When they arrived at the Keaton mansion, it looked as if a funeral were underway. There was a big black hearse parked in the driveway. It turned out, however, that it was only being used to deliver twenty cases of bootleg liquor.

While Marilyn and Jack were enjoying an infrequent month together, it seemed a natural time to discuss their future. Her contract with Ziegfeld expired at the end of the year, and she would be free to do as she pleased. She could renew with Ziegfeld or accept another of the offers that always were coming her way, the most recent being from the Keith-Orpheum Circuit for a vaudeville tour at $5,000 a week. Ma Pickford kept badgering her about a movie career, but Marilyn still wasn't interested, although she realized it was probably the most logical solution to finding more time to spend with her husband while his work kept him in California.

Jack favored Marilyn remaining on the stage. He hated movie work himself and the dominating ways of Ma and Mary even more. He recently had purchased a racehorse named Doctor Winifred and was thinking of giving up films to start a stable of his own. He and Marilyn talked of buying an estate on the North Shore of Long Island, where Jack could breed and train horses while Marilyn continued her theater career.

Interestingly, Marilyn and Jack never, at any time, said they planned to raise a family of their own, obviously because he was syphilitic. But in her autobiography, Mary Pickford later blamed the eventual breakup of the marriage on Marilyn's refusal to have children. "She had the attractiveness and sparkle of youth, but I always thought he looked upon her as his child, rather than his wife. Perhaps if they had had a baby themselves, it might have been different," Mary Pickford said. "Jack always wanted children, but for Marilyn a career came first. She was probably the most ambitious human being I have ever met. A baby, needless to say, had no place in a life of such unsparing professional drive."

A bizarre statement, written in Mary Pickford's declining years. She had either forgotten or didn't want to admit that her brother had venereal disease. Also, Mary herself never had any children for the same reason she speculated Marilyn hadn't. During her first marriage, to actor Owen Moore, Mary once deliberately aborted herself by going horseback riding so that she could avoid disrupting her career.

When Marilyn returned to the tour of *Sally* in September, both Jack and Doctor Winifred went east with her for the opening of the fall racing season. For a change, the couple would be near each other; Marilyn's tour was starting in New York and going on to Buffalo and New England.

Ziegfeld had booked *Sally* back into the New Amsterdam Theatre for two weeks, advertising it as "New York's last chance" to see it with the original star. That was Ziegfeld's way of determining the leverage that he would have when it came to bargaining with Marilyn over a new contract. If the engagement sold out he knew that she would give him a difficult time. It did.

Marilyn had no agent. She always knew in broad terms exactly what she wanted, leaving it up to her lawyer, Moses Masalansky, to negotiate the details of the final contract. She wasn't sure whether she wanted to stay under Ziegfeld's management or not. The only certainty was that if she did, it would have to be in a new show. Nearing the end of three years with *Sally*, the novelty long gone, she couldn't wait for the moment when she could hang up that wretched orphan's uniform for good.

She rejected Ziegfeld's first idea, which was to team her with Eddie Cantor in *Kid Boots*, a zany musical about a caddy master at a Palm Beach country club who bootlegs "loaded" golf balls. Although Marilyn adored Eddie Cantor and would always be grateful to him for helping her get through Frank Carter's tragic death, she also had very strong opinions about her status as a star. After establishing herself in *Sally*, she didn't want to appear in a show named for a character other than the one she herself would be playing. Furthermore, the part of the romantic ingenue that Ziegfeld described to her wasn't nearly as important as Cantor's. She told Ziegfeld to give it to her perennial backstop, Mary Eaton, which was exactly what he did.

Ziegfeld's next suggestion was more to Marilyn's liking. It was a musicalization of *Peg O' My Heart*, the 1912 comedy by J. Hartley Manners that ran a record 603 performances on Broadway and helped establish the playwright's wife, Laurette Taylor, as the most revered actress of her time. The sentimental story of a poor Irish colleen who inherits an enormous fortune but must go live in

England in order to collect it, *Peg* seemed a natural choice for Marilyn after *Sally*. But it was a big undertaking and Ziegfeld would need time to clear the rights and commission the book and music, possibly with Jerome Kern or Victor Herbert as composer.

In the meantime, Marilyn had no choice but to fulfill the remaining months of her contract for *Sally* and await further developments. In the following weeks, Ziegfeld became increasingly attentive and solicitous, sending her a diamond-and-ruby pendant, bottles of Chanel No. 5 by the case, and other expensive gifts. She wasn't sure if they were contract bribes or a renewal of Ziegfeld's old romantic interest; probably they were a mixture of both.

Whatever Ziegfeld's motives were, Jack Pickford resented his approach, and the two men soon were at loggerheads again, with Marilyn caught in the middle. Jack believed that the only way peace could ever be restored was for her to leave Ziegfeld rather than sign a new contract with him. Perhaps she should even stop working altogether. She had lots of money and so did he. They could purchase that estate on Long Island, travel, or do whatever they pleased. His argument was extremely appealing to Marilyn, who had been toiling continuously for the last twenty of her twenty-five years.

When Marilyn told Ziegfeld that she'd decided not to renew her contract after all, bitter words were exchanged and her last weeks in *Sally* were disastrous. To spite Ziegfeld, she started making cuts in some of her dance numbers and even missed a few performances, claiming to have injured a knee. After Ziegfeld discovered that Marilyn and Jack were seen attending various Broadway plays when she should have been resting, he sent her a special-delivery letter blasting her for unprofessionalism and blaming it on Jack Pickford's bad influence.

On December 18, 1923, Marilyn sent a telegram to all fifteen of New York's morning and evening newspapers stating that she was ending her contract with Ziegfeld and that she would never work for him again because of his meddling in her private life. The next day, Ziegfeld wired the same papers: "If that statement is any satisfaction to her, I am satisfied. I simply refer to my letter to her dated last Friday and ask you to ask her to publish it."

Marilyn and Jack Pickford had been staying at the Ambassador Hotel on Park Avenue. When reporters went there to question her about Ziegfeld's cryptic message, the couple already had checked out, leaving no forwarding address. Marilyn knew when she was licked. There was no way she could defend her recent shameful conduct. If she even tried, Ziegfeld would unleash further bombast and they would be right back making nasty headlines again. It was time to fold her tent until the air cleared.

CHAPTER TEN

SPRITE AND CIRCUS QUEEN

SINCE IT WAS THE dead of winter in New York, Marilyn and Jack had decided to head west for Beverly Hills to spend the Christmas holidays at Pickfair. On Christmas Eve, Charlie Chaplin, who had a reputation for thriftiness, dropped by in a moth-eaten Santa Claus costume and proceeded to dole out gifts purchased at a five-and-ten-cent store. Marilyn, Mary, and Ma Pickford all received pink rayon bloomers. Jack Pickford got a bottle of Glover's Imperial Mange Medicine and Douglas Fairbanks a kiddie bow-and-arrow set.

After a New Year's Eve party at John Barrymore's house that lasted well into the second day of January 1924, Marilyn woke up with a terrible migraine headache, turned over, and remained in bed another two days to recuperate. But in the weeks that followed, she quickly became bored with having nothing to do except run around town with Jack every night. Having worked since childhood, she had never had a chance to develop any interests outside her career. Her reading consisted mainly of newspapers, and that was just to get the latest show business news and gossip. Without the purpose in life that her work provided, she felt lost.

The cure for Marilyn's problem was obvious. The hitch was that if she did sign up for a new show, what about her marriage? Although there hadn't been that many problems so far, they were bound to develop if she and Jack continued to be separated so much of the time. In just a few weeks in Hollywood, she'd seen it would be very difficult for her husband to remain faithful, even if he tried. There were as many femmes fatales waiting to pounce on him as there were oranges on the trees.

Among dozens, Marilyn considered her greatest threat raven-haired Bebe Daniels, who was then on a par with Gloria Swanson and Pola Negri as a screen sex siren. A close friend of Mary and Lottie Pickford, Daniels was a regular at Pickfair. High-spirited and mischievous, she had been one of Jack's first serious romances. In fact, Marilyn might never have become Mrs. Jack Pickford if Daniels had not earlier rejected his numerous proposals of marriage. Marilyn feared the love affair would flame anew while she and Jack were living apart.

Marilyn thought it might be wise to accept one of those Hollywood contract offers after all. It wasn't what she really wanted, but it would enable her to keep an eye on Jack and also make her less of an outsider where her in-laws were concerned.

As luck would have it, she discovered that First National Pictures had just acquired the movie rights to *Sally*, probably as a vehicle for their current box-office darling, bob-haired Colleen Moore. Marilyn was tempted to make a bid for the role herself, but decided not to bother when she thought it out. To suit the requirements of the silent medium, *Sally* would have to be revamped as a comedy without music or dancing. What could Marilyn Miller bring to the project that Colleen Moore, with her extensive filmmaking experience, couldn't do just as well or better?

Seeing a lesson in that, Marilyn realized that she had no choice. Kissing Jack a temporary good-bye, she went back to New York to find out what Broadway producers had to offer that might make fuller use of her talents. Since Ziegfeld was still very much the enemy and she wasn't keen about rejoining the moneygrubbing Shuberts, she set her sights on Charles Dillingham. He'd produced everything from *When Knighthood Was in Flower* to Victor Herbert's *The Red Mill* and George Bernard Shaw's *Man and Superman,* as well as eight years of superextravaganzas that had earned the New York Hippodrome its reputation as the temple of illusion and wonderment.

The balding, white mustachioed Dillingham was then fifty-five years old and a beloved theatrical character, regarded as the unofficial mayor of Broadway because he resided square in its center in the Astor Hotel and owned the beautiful Globe Theatre, which was famous for a sliding roof that was left open to the sky on fair warm-weather nights. To work for C. B. Dillingham carried as much prestige as working for Ziegfeld, which was Marilyn's reason for putting him at the top of her list of prospective employers.

She also knew that Dillingham would give her none of the personal problems that she'd had with Ziegfeld. Although the two men once were partners in a number of shows, including *The Century Girl* and one of Broadway's most colossal flops, *Miss 1917,* Dillingham was always honest and aboveboard in his dealings with people. If he tended to take a fatherly interest in performers he liked, the interest was at least genuine; his advice and counsel were much sought after by stars and newcomers alike.

Although they now were business rivals, Dillingham still was friendly with Ziegfeld and well aware of the difficulties that he and Marilyn had experienced. Dillingham thought it was a tragedy of sorts, because Marilyn Miller and Flo Ziegfeld were two of a kind in the way that they could create theatrical magic; if they could have worked amicably together, there was no limit to the successes they might have achieved.

When Marilyn visited Dillingham in his office at the Globe Theatre one February afternoon, he told her that she should really try to make it up with Ziegfeld, but if she couldn't, he would be only too delighted to take her under his management. Marilyn needed no time to consider, provided, of course, that Dillingham would pay her what Ziegfeld had been paying her—a guarantee of $2,500 a week against 10 percent of the gross. Dillingham would. They shook hands on it and started to discuss their first collaboration.

Both agreed that another big musical on the order of *Sally* was what they wanted. Marilyn was enthusiastic about a story suggestion made to her by comedian Walter Catlett while they were working together in *Sally*. It was about life in the circus, with a clown adopting an orphan waif and helping her to become the star attraction, possibly as an aerialist or bareback rider. Dillingham saw many possibilities for spectacle in the circus background and promised to discuss the idea with some of his associates.

But a new show could take up to a year of preparation, and Dillingham thought it would be wasteful to keep such a valuable box-office property as Marilyn Miller sidelined that length of time. Something else would have to be found for her to do in the interim.

Dillingham suggested *Peter Pan*. He'd once intended to stage it at the Hippodrome, but had been unable to get permission from James M. Barrie, who considered his play the exclusive property of its original star, the inimitable American actress Maude Adams.

Marilyn thought Dillingham was joking, but his arguments did intrigue her. Although acting was the least developed of her skills, she realized that her spritelike qualies and dancer's agility were well suited to the physical demands of the role. Furthermore, *Peter Pan* was not so much a play as a magical theatrical experience. And although not a musical either, there were opportunities in her role for her to sing and dance. Under the circumstances, Dillingham thought it was the best project for her unless she wanted to do a revival of *Little Miss Fix-It* or some other early musical that was probably better off left forgotten. She did not.

Nothing further could be done until Dillingham cleared everything with James M. Barrie in England. The part of Peter Pan had never been played in America by anyone but Maude Adams—first in 1905 for several years and again in 1915—and Barrie still had hopes of her doing one more revival. But Maude Adams now was fifty-two, twice Marilyn's age, and all too happy to let go of a role that she was sick to death of.

When Dillingham finally made a public announcement of his

plans for *Peter Pan*, he said that James M. Barrie had selected Marilyn Miller from a list of ten American actresses. The names of the other nine women never were revealed, not to spare them embarrassment but because they didn't exist. Barrie actually made his decision after discussing Dillingham's proposal with a close friend, the director Basil Dean, who'd seen Marilyn in *Sally* and had been enchanted. At Barrie's insistence, Basil Dean was to direct Marilyn in *Peter Pan*, and the distinguished British actor Leslie Banks was to portray Captain Hook.

Much to Dillingham's dismay, the publicity about *Peter Pan* brought some unexpected competition from Hollywood. There had never been a movie version of *Peter Pan*, again because of Barrie's loyalty to Maude Adams, who considered film work beneath her dignity. But now that Barrie had given permission for Marilyn Miller to do the play on the stage, it seemed only fair to consider movie bids as well. Dillingham was powerless to prevent it because he'd neglected to ask for an exclusivity clause in his contract with Barrie.

The Hollywood bidding was intense, becoming a touch ludicrous when William Randolph Hearst's Cosmopolitan Pictures entered the competition in behalf of its principal star, Marion Davies, the boss's mistress and America's most criticized courtesan. But James Barrie finally made a deal with Famous Players-Paramount, which assigned a seventeen-year-old unknown named Betty Bronson to play Peter.

Conspicuously absent from the negotiations was Mary Pickford, who was rabid over these developments because she'd been badgering Barrie for years to let her do *Peter Pan* on the screen. But now that Marilyn had beaten her to it, if only for the stage, Mary wasn't going to be dragged into a comparison contest with her sister-in-law and possibly come out the loser. Mary's dealings with Marilyn, which had never been overly friendly, frosted over even further.

In the end, Dillingham decided to go full speed ahead with his production of *Peter Pan*, figuring that the film version might help promote the play rather than detract from it. They weren't really competing for the same audience, and the combined publicity could only help both projects. Dillingham also doubted that any silent movie (black and white or hand tinted), no matter how much it depended on special effects and trick photography, could duplicate the experience of seeing the much-beloved fantasy in a richly colorful live performance.

Marilyn and Dillingham were agreed that their *Peter Pan* should use the magnificent set and costume designs from the original Maude Adams version, which were impossible to improve upon. While Dillingham attended to the details of mounting the production, Marilyn returned to California for what might be her last chance for some time to be with her husband.

Jack Pickford had been an actor since childhood, and Marilyn was hoping that he would be able to help her prepare for what promised to be the most difficult assignment of her life. Not only was drama her weak point, but she also would have to contend with critics comparing her to Maude Adams, whose portrayal of Peter Pan was considered one of the greatest stage performances of the previous hundred years.

But Marilyn got no help at all from her husband, who thought he had as much competence to be an acting coach as Rin Tin Tin. Instead, he passed her along to sister Mary, who, of course, was in no mood to teach Marilyn anything about playing a role that she'd long coveted for herself.

The only member of the family to offer Marilyn assistance was brother-in-law Douglas Fairbanks. He gave her the use of the fully equipped gymnasium and swimming pool at the Pickford-Fairbanks Studio as a training camp. Whenever his schedule permitted, Fairbanks personally worked with Marilyn on stage movement, acrobatics, and fencing, all essential to playing the Peter Pan character. She couldn't have asked for a better instructor than the man who was very much a real-life Peter Pan.

In the fall, Marilyn went back to New York to start rehearsals. Jack came with her; he had decided that he could at least offer moral support and rearranged his own commitments in order to stay with his wife until *Peter Pan* opened in November. The play was booked into the Knickerbocker Theatre at Broadway and Thirty-eighth Street, so for convenience's sake they set up temporary housekeeping six blocks away at the Astor Hotel in a suite just down the corridor from Charles Dillingham's.

Marilyn was generally pleased with Dillingham's preparations for *Peter Pan*, especially when he told her that he expected to spend about $300,000 by the time he finished, which would make it one of the most expensive productions of any Broadway play or musical to date. Dillingham imported a crew of a dozen technicians from Germany to operate the steel-wire flying apparatus, which was considered technically superior to the one used by Maude Adams. A full musical-comedy-size orchestra would play a special background score composed by Milan Roeder. Jerome Kern and Buddy De Sylva, who wrote "Look for the Silver Lining," contributed a new song for Marilyn called "The Sweetest Thing in Life." Kern also composed a second number for her, "Won't You Have a Little Feather," with lyrics by Paul West.

What Marilyn didn't like was the bombastic, dictatorial style of the director, Basil Dean. He seemed to delight in tormenting his actors with withering barbs about their lack of ability and talent. Since Dean had directed many productions of *Peter Pan* in England, where it was an annual pantomime tradition, he knew exactly what he wanted and permitted no deviations. But his star wouldn't stand for it. "I've got to do it the way Marilyn Miller would do it or not at all," she told him; and supported by Charles Dillingham, who sat in on every rehearsal after that, she got her way.

The opening of *Peter Pan* on November 6, 1924, was somewhat overshadowed by the reelection of President Calvin Coolidge two days earlier. Whether by accident or design, it also was a week that started with Billie Burke making her musical comedy debut in Ziegfeld's *Annie Dear*. With Marilyn Miller going dramatic for the first time in *Peter Pan*, it looked as if the two ladies were out to steal each other's territory. The general critical consensus was that they both should have stayed where they belonged.

Dillingham seriously miscalculated by advertising *Peter Pan* as "glorifying glorious youth," which made it sound more like a Ziegfeld revue than a children's fantasy. Marilyn Miller was billed as "America's favorite," with her name printed in type larger and bolder than the title of the play. The newspaper reviewers, the majority of whom had seen Maude Adams's version, resented the vulgarization of the work into a star turn for a musical comedy queen.

"Marilyn Miller brought to the performance her youth and beauty and her knack of handling audiences," said Stark Young of the *New York Times*. "What she most lacked was pathos, something that might give the character the wistfulness of dreams and childhood. Her movements and certainty and her voice were almost too adequate for the elusive shadow that lies on every scene of Peter Pan's and makes them even more adorable. But she shared always with the role her own joy in it. In her region of art, she made Peter Pan her own and kept it young and glancing."

Percy Hammond said that as Peter, Marilyn was too professional for her own good, "more actress than fairy boy." Heywood Broun called her "a nice, jolly, material girl, with no nonsense about her. There are no legs in the universe to be compared to those of Marilyn Miller." Several days later, the *New York Times* said in an editorial that "although 'Peter Pan' was a prey to sad musings," the newspaper "still believed in fairies."

Audience response to *Peter Pan* was more favorable, especially when Marilyn flew out as far as the middle rows of the orchestra while hooked to a steel wire. A couple of times she got stuck when wires were crossed, breaking into roars of laughter—and the audience with her—while she waited to be rescued.

Peter Pan ran only 125 performances in New York, closing at the end of January 1925. As a result, Dillingham could only arrange a short road tour; theater owners weren't optimistic about the show's chances of survival against the by then widely distributed movie version. Dillingham lost his entire investment.

Unaccustomed to failure, Marilyn now wondered if she'd made the right move in affiliating herself with Dillingham. Perhaps she should have stayed with Ziegfeld, although his track record hadn't been very impressive lately either, what with the disastrous *Louie the XIV* with Leon Errol and *The Comic Supplement* with W. C. Fields.

Aware of Marilyn's discontent, Dillingham promised to do better the next time. He hadn't forgotten the circus idea that she had once mentioned to him. Jerome Kern, Otto Harbach, and Oscar Hammerstein had developed it to a point where they were ready to show Marilyn an outline.

It was all that she could have wished for and more, although it only slightly resembled Walter Catlett's original idea. The story centered around Sunny Peters, a bareback rider in an English circus, who falls in love with a wealthy young American. When she goes to see him off on his return voyage to the United States, she misses the last call to go ashore and becomes an involuntary stowaway. While aboard ship, Sunny is forced into a marriage of necessity with one of the passengers to avoid being arrested. All ends happily, of course, when she eventually divorces her husband and weds her true sweetheart.

Though the plot was as corny and as far-fetched as *Sally* and the other so-called "Cinderella" musicals that were popular throughout the twenties, Marilyn admired the way it found excuses for moving the action and musical numbers into spectacular settings—a circus with real animals, a luxurious ocean liner, the ballroom of a Long Island estate, and an outdoor fox hunt. Also, Jerome Kern had given Marilyn "Look for the Silver Lining" and other wonderful songs in *Sally*, so she couldn't imagine going wrong with him or lyricists Harbach and Hammerstein, who recently had collaborated with Rudolf Friml on the smash hit *Rose Marie*.

Most of all, she liked the title. If Marilyn Miller could be summed up in one word, that would be it—*Sunny*. She urged Dillingham to get going full blast.

Marilyn decided that she needed a vacation while *Sunny* was in preparation, so she and Jack sailed for Europe on the *Majestic*, which was then the world's largest ship. There were quite a few other celebrities on board, including the Dolly Sisters, Clifton Webb, and ex-Ziegfeld beauty Gertrude Vanderbilt. On the first night out, everybody attended a party in the suite of stage producer Harry Frazee, at which thirty-six cases of champagne were consumed.

Jack Pickford started lushing it up badly and spent most of the voyage nursing hangovers. While he was out of commission, Marilyn struck up a friendship with Ben Finney, a handsome *bon vivant* and world traveler two years her junior, who had just ended a torrid romance with movie star Barbara LaMarr. Finney, who was due to disembark at Cherbourg, fell in love with Marilyn and decided to continue on to Southampton, where she and Pickford were heading.

"I saw quite a bit of Marilyn in London while Jack continued to keep a fairly tight clutch on the bottle," Ben Finney said later. "Soon there were Winchellish items about us in the British press and lorgnettes were pointed at us when we entered a restaurant. So I decided finally, in fairness to everyone, that it was time once more for me to reach for my hat. I took the next boat train for Paris."

About ten days later, Marilyn and Jack also went to Paris. In Zelli's one night, whom should they run into but Ben Finney? "Marilyn gave me a big hug and a kiss, whereupon Jack slapped her. Whereupon I knocked him flat," Finney recollected.

"During the next week, Marilyn would visit her old friend Princess Vlora, the former Helen Kelly, nearly every afternoon and, by some coincidence, so would I. This was beautiful until I learned from my spies at the Ritz bar that Jack had hired a detective to have his wife followed," Finney said. "Once more I realized that

I was in a city not large enough for the three of us, or four, counting the private eye."

With Finney's departure, marital harmony was restored. Over the next few weeks, Marilyn filled three steamer trunks with new Chanel and Lanvin frocks. Jack bought her a pair of wirehaired fox terriers that they named Pan and Yvette. The new foursome went on to Aix-les-Bains, Lucerne, Zurich, Berlin, and London again, with plans to return to New York on the *Leviathan*. At the last minute they switched their tickets to the *Majestic* when they discovered they would have been sharing passage with Flo Ziegfeld, Billie Burke, and their daughter, Patricia.

Dillingham was in a panic when Marilyn returned to New York. After he'd scheduled *Sunny* to open at the New Amsterdam Theatre in late September, three other producers had selected opening dates just prior to his. As a result, there were to be four musicals by major composers premiering on Broadway in the space of a single week: Vincent Youmans's *No! No! Nanette!*, Richard Rodgers and Lorenz Hart's *Dearest Enemy*, and Rudolf Friml's *The Vagabond King*. Kern's *Sunny* would have to be extraordinary to escape being considered an anticlimax.

Dillingham's solution to the problem was to revert to a formula dating back to his Hippodrome days and to turn *Sunny* into a two-for-the-price-of-one spectacular, a combination book musical and superrevue. To justify spending $500,000, an unheard-of investment for a musical then, Dillingham was forced to raise the price of the best seats in the house from $3.50 to $5.

In support of Marilyn Miller, Dillingham assembled a cast that boasted a number of current headliners, including tap dancer Jack Donahue, an "eccentric" dance duo consisting of lanky Clifton Webb and tiny Mary Hay, and comedians Joseph Cawthorn, Esther Howard, and Pert Kelton. Cliff Edwards, better known as "Ukelele Ike," was given a specialty number—"Paddlin' Madelin' Home"—to show off his vocal and instrumental skills. George Olsen and His Music, the top dance band of the day, would appear in the play itself and also concertize during the intermission. Thrown in for good measure were the "Marilyn Miller Cocktails," eight long-legged precision dancers trained by Britisher John Tiller, whose "Tiller Girls" had been a hit of the 1922 *Ziegfeld Follies* (and were a forerunner of the Radio City Music Hall Rockettes).

Realizing that she was going to have strong competition, particularly in the dance division, Marilyn asked Fred Astaire, an old friend from vaudeville days, for assistance. After a moderately successful partnership that had started in childhood, Fred and his older sister, Adele, had recently become the toasts of Broadway in the Gershwins' *Lady Be Good.* Although he was too busy with his show to spend much time on *Sunny*, Fred Astaire choreographed Marilyn's big tap number, "The Wedding Knell," and also helped her to select the "boys" who'd dance with her.

From *Sunny* onward, the male chorus dancers of a Marilyn Miller show were always handpicked by the star herself, leading to many rumors over the years that she also slept with a large percentage of them. But Marilyn had a very good professional reason for being so particular. Handsome, talented partners heightened her own glamorous appeal and also set off a competitive spark that kept her performances fresh and exciting.

Whether Marilyn was selecting them for sexual purposes as well is really impossible to know. Although there are ex-chorus men still living who claim that they spent nights with Marilyn Miller, their word alone doesn't mean much; they could be merely basking in her glory.

A production as enormous and complex as *Sunny* created myriad problems, and the Philadelphia tryout at the Forrest Theatre didn't begin until September 9, 1925, leaving less than two weeks until the New York premiere. The need for further rehearsals and revisions was evident as performers flubbed their lines, a chorus girl skidded into the orchestra pit, and the first act had to be halted for fifteen minutes for a cumbersome scenery change.

Marilyn saw another omen of disaster in the fact that she was working in the same city and theater as she had been when Frank Carter was killed five years before. Her nervousness was borne out by the next day's newspaper reviews, which for all of the show's spectacular qualities described it as "pretty puny," "labored," and "struggling for humor that does not materialize." Marilyn's beauty and musical talents were unanimously praised, but the *Evening Bulletin* described her as "showing little ability as an actress, speaking her lines rather amateurishly." Kern's score was considered serviceable, but with "not a single catchy number or even haunting piece of melody throughout." If anything was going to save the show, it was song-and-dance man Jack Donahue: "Oh, Mr. Donahue, don't get sick or decide to retire! 'Sunny' needs you very badly," said the *Ledger*.

But a lot of expert doctoring could be done in twelve days, especially when Dillingham's creative team included not only Kern, Harbach, and Hammerstein, but also directors Hassard Short and Julien Mitchell, the guiding forces behind some of Ziegfeld's biggest successes.

Ironically, though six songs were dropped to speed up the show, no new ones were added, so the Philadelphia critics who panned the score must have been drunk, tone deaf, or both. Among the songs retained, "Who?" and "Sunny" became enormous popular hits almost overnight, and "Do You Love Me?," "Two Little Bluebirds," and "Let's Say Good Night Till It's Morning" were much requested dance band numbers for years afterward.

Marilyn Miller had the good luck of becoming permanently identified with both "Who?," which she sang as a duet with leading man Paul Frawley, and "Sunny," which was performed by Frawley and some of the chorus boys but was obviously *her* song. For the public hearing them played throughout the Roaring Twenties and well into the following decades, those two songs and "Look for the Silver Lining" signified only one person—Marilyn Miller.

Shortly after the Broadway opening, the show's featured dance band, George Olsen and His Music, recorded a single of "Who?" for the Victor label. It sold well over a million copies, which was a rarity in those days of wind-up Victrolas. In a few years time, Marilyn would often remark to friends that she wished she had a dollar for every one of the women who told her that their husbands proposed to them while listening or dancing to "Who?"

Oddly enough, Marilyn turned down a fortune in offers to make her own recordings of "Who?" and some of the other songs from *Sunny*. She felt the same way about phonograph records—and the burgeoning medium of radio as well—as she did about movies. Unless she could apply all her talents, she wasn't interested. She knew that she wasn't the greatest beauty, dancer, singer or actress, but when all her resources came into full play, something special happened that made her unique. She wasn't going to let the public see or hear Marilyn Miller at anything but her best.

That was certainly what the audience got when *Sunny* opened at the New Amsterdam Theatre on September 22, 1925. Dillingham spent a bundle on a grand entrance for Marilyn that topped anything in *Sally*. A drum major in resplendent uniform pranced onstage twirling a baton, followed by a sixty-piece brass band and a parade of clowns, acrobats, and what looked like the entire freak show of the Ringling Brothers–Barnum & Bailey Circus. To a burst of fanfare, Marilyn Miller appeared in a tutu of spangles and gossamer chiffon, riding bareback on a magnificent white horse. From then on, it was one ovation after another throughout the evening.

Whatever revising and tightening was done in Philadelphia worked miracles, because this time the critics were ecstatic. Jack Donahue was singled out for almost as much praise as Marilyn. Known in the trade as "the man with the laughing feet" and portraying the man whom Sunny marries temporarily to avoid getting arrested as a ship's stowaway, Donahue was very tall and darkly handsome, a striking contrast to Marilyn's blond daintiness. Tap-dancing together in the number "When We Get Our Divorce," they worked with machinelike precision, but with a buoyancy and grace that was not typical of Broadway "hoofers." Several critics were quick to announce the emergence of a new team worthy of comparison to the Astaires and the Castles.

Burns Mantle, the dean of New York drama critics, found *Sunny* superior in every way to *Sally*. Like Marilyn's earlier hit, it quickly became Broadway's hottest ticket. Receiving her customary 10 percent of the gross, her salary at house capacity averaged about $4,500 a week, considerably more than she'd earned during *Sally* because *Sunny* had higher admission prices.

Marilyn settled into her old dressing room at the New Amsterdam for what promised to be another very long engagement. If *Peter Pan* had raised any doubts about her future, they were forgotten now. Once again the star of the biggest hit in the history of Broadway's most fabled playhouse, she was as happy as she ever would be.

But marital problems were developing. During rehearsals for *Sunny*, Marilyn had gone to Jerome Kern's apartment one afternoon to hear some of his new music and, quite by accident, Ben Finney happened to be there. Jack Pickford was in Hollywood at the time, so Marilyn and Finney started keeping company again.

Apparently, word got back to Jack Pickford. The day before the New York opening of *Sunny*, Finney ran into a friend who told him that Pickford had just arrived in town and was gunning for him. "Later I happened to pass the Plaza Art Gallery where I saw in the window a cased pair of dueling pistols," Ben Finney said. "I bought them and had them delivered to Jack at the Ambassador Hotel. My card was enclosed and on it was written: 'My second, Jefferson Davis, will be around to see you in the morning.'"

Finney received no reply, but the next day he ran into Pickford in the Oak Room of the Plaza Hotel. Pickford greeted him cordially and laughed over the pistol gag. Then he said, "Ben, just to quell some of the nonsense that seems to be making the rounds about you and Marilyn, why don't you and I go to the opening together tonight?" Finney swallowed hard and went along with it.

"Jack had not told Marilyn of our joint expedition," Finney recollected. "And I had not been able to reach her before the opening curtain, so when she made her first entrance and saw Jack and me sitting there together in the first row, she damn near fell off the white charger she was riding! I often wondered if Jack planned it that way."

Marilyn circa 1917–1918. (Theatre Collection, Museum of the City of New York)

Family Portrait. Left to right, Marilyn, mother Ada, stepfather Caro Miller,
Claire, Ruth. (Billy Rose Theatre Collection, The New York Public Library)

Marilyn with first husband Frank
Carter. (Billy Rose Theatre Collection, The New York
Public Library)

Marilyn, age 12, as Sophie Tucker.
(Billy Rose Theatre Collection, The New York
Public Library)

Scenes from Sally *(1920).*

Marilyn with Jack Pickford in 1923, a year after their marriage.
(UPI/BETTMAN ARCHIVE)

Marilyn as Peter Pan (1924). (CULVER PICTURES)

*Marilyn with Jerome Kern,
composer of* Sunny. (Billy
Rose Theatre Collection, The New York
Public Library)

A First National Studios publicity still for the movie of Sunny. *Left to right,
Theodore Kosloff, Marilyn's dance instructor; Florenz Ziegfeld; Marilyn; Jack
L. Warner, in charge of production; and William A. Seiter, director (1930).*
(CULVER PICTURES)

Marilyn, as Barbara Hutton, in As Thousands Cheer, *with Chet O'Brien, in white tunic, whom she later married.* (Billy Rose Theatre Collection, The New York Public Library)

Marilyn with Florenz Ziegfeld (1928).
(CULVER PICTURES)

Marilyn with Adele and Fred Astaire, preparing for Smiles *(1930).*

*Marilyn with dance
partner Jack
Donahue.*

Marilyn as the IT girl of Hollywood. (CULVER PICTURES)

CHAPTER ELEVEN

CHANGES

MARILYN MILLER'S TRIUMPH IN *Sunny* marked the beginning of the end of her marriage to Jack Pickford. There was no way the relationship could survive the long separations caused by their ill-matched careers, let alone other problems that were developing.

Rumors that they were having troubles had started when Jack returned to California after the opening of *Sunny*. His departure was reported to be the consequence of a quarrel over Ben Finney, but Jack denied it. "That's all applesauce," he told Hearst columnist Louella Parsons, stating that the only reason he was back in Hollywood was to make two movies, *The Bat* and *Brown of Harvard*.

Marilyn refused to comment on the rumors, but she knew they were all too true. Married to Jack now for more than three years, she wondered how much longer the relationship could continue. She still thought he was a darling—clever, funny, extravagantly generous—but completely irresponsible and undependable.

They were not so much wife and husband to each other as partners for sex and companions for social occasions. When Jack wasn't fulfilling those roles during their times together, he was recovering from a hangover or off somewhere working up the next one. He would go out to buy cigarettes and not come home for several days.

135

Marilyn knew that Jack was taking drugs as well as drinking heavily, but there was nothing that she could say or do to stop him. In the beginning she tried, but he was like a little boy. He would pout for a while and then act up twice as badly as before. It was best to try to live around the problem and pretend it didn't exist.

Conversely, Jack could not tolerate Marilyn's flirtatious nature. If she even smiled at another man, he got upset. Yet he could not talk her out of her behavior any more than she could get him to stop drugs and drink. She was as much a spoiled brat as he was.

By that autumn of 1925, the relationship had evolved into a Twenties version of an open marriage, although Marilyn and Jack probably saw it as simply an arrangement that was preferable to getting divorced. Neither was eager to see their names involved in another public scandal, especially one that would give Flo Ziegfeld cause to gloat.

There were no set rules or regulations other than discretion. Play around if you must, but please don't talk about it. It was the old "What I don't know, won't hurt me" philosophy.

But in the gossipy world of show business it was very hard to keep such matters secret, and Marilyn was well aware of Jack's infidelities. While directing and starring in his last movie, *Waking Up the Town*, he'd been passionately involved with his beautiful though cross-eyed leading lady, Norma Shearer. Jack's affair with Bebe Daniels had also flared up again; among other things, they had become Hollywood's champion partners at bridge, which was a great fad at the time.

Marilyn's extramarital love life was conducted catch-as-catch-can. She needed male company, both as complement to her status as Broadway musical queen and for fulfillment of her need to be loved and appreciated. Sex was a necessary but functional aspect of her life. When Jack Pickford wasn't around to provide those services, there was never a shortage of substitutes. After a performance, Marilyn's dressing room would be crowded with handsome admirers all vying for the privilege of her intimate company. On the rare slow night, there were always plenty of men from the cast of the show to choose from.

Because Marilyn and Jack Donahue evidenced such rapport as a dance team in *Sunny*, it was widely suspected that they were having an offstage romance. Their close friends, however, didn't think so. Six years older than Marilyn, Donahue was believed to have only two mistresses—alcohol and dancing. He was notorious for his all-night "tap drunks," in which he and a few dancer cronies would get together with a case of bootleg scotch and challenge each other with tap routines until they could no longer stand up.

Moreover, for all his heavy drinking, Donahue was a devoted husband and father. He and his wife, vaudeville dancer Alice Stewart, had known Marilyn for years; the couple chose her as godmother and namesake for the youngest of their three daughters. Intimates considered it impossible that Marilyn would have betrayed that friendship and trust by having an affair with Donahue. Perhaps those defenders didn't know Marilyn as well as they thought they did and were attributing a moral fastidiousness to Marilyn Miller that existed only in the characters she played on stage.

There were never any innuendos about her relationship with Clifton Webb, the other leading dancer in *Sunny*. Webb had room in his life for only one woman, his mother, Maybelle, who'd been his constant companion for all of his thirty-four years. Webb was homosexual, but Maybelle occupied so much of his time that he could only manage fleeting encounters with chorus boys. Marilyn and Clifton used to swap information about the choristers' sexual orientations; it saved them the time and embarrassment of going home with the wrong type.

Marilyn and the Webbs became bosom pals. Clifton was a divine ballroom dancer—often compared to the late Vernon Castle—and Marilyn adored going out partying with him after the show, even

Clifton's real name, incidentally, was Webb Parmalee Hollenbeck. While looking for a more suitable professional name for her child prodigy, Maybelle happened to pass through Clifton, New Jersey, one day and *voila*!

though it always meant including Maybelle in their plans. Maybelle Webb was yet another formidable stage mother for Marilyn to deal with, but unlike Ma Pickford she was a delight, full of fun and with a zany belief in spiritualism and the occult.

In December 1925, Marilyn and the Webbs attended the re-opening of New York's ultraswank Rendezvous Club. Recently taken over by André Charlot, the London producer who was to the intimate revue what Ziegfeld was to the spectacular, the nightclub-cum-speakeasy was presenting the cabaret debut of Gertrude Lawrence, Jack Buchanan, and Beatrice Lillie. Marilyn wouldn't have missed it for the world, since a conflict in working schedules had so far prevented her from seeing the visiting Britons in *Charlot's Revue of 1926*, which had recently opened up across the street from *Sunny* at the Selwyn Theatre and was the talk of the town.

The scene at the Rendezous Club that night was reminiscent of a New York millionaire's private party. Besides Marilyn Miller and Clifton Webb, the formally dressed crowd included Gloria Swanson, Harpo Marx, Ethel Barrymore, Elsie Janis, Grace Moore, Irving Berlin, George M. Cohan, George Jessel, Gilda Gray, Alfred Lunt and Lynn Fontanne, plus more than a few Morgans, Vanderbilts, Rockefellers, Whitneys, and Duponts.

Marilyn took it all in her stride. Such get-togethers were typical of New York café society; she attended a couple of hundred of them every year. But what she wasn't prepared for was that evening's entertainment. Gertrude Lawrence's style and sophistication stirred Marilyn's envy. The hilarious Beatrice Lillie was Fannie Brice and Charlie Chaplin rolled into one.

As for Jack Buchanan, Marilyn fell in love with him instantly. His charm was entirely unlike that of any performer that she'd ever seen. He crooned his way cheerfully through his songs with perfect diction and a sort of catarrhal huskiness that made Marilyn tingle. He was no Fred Astaire as a dancer, but he knew how to tap his feet with an attractively casual air. The whole secret of his technique seemed to be complete naturalness and relaxation, reinforced by a sort of lazy zest.

But Jack Buchanan's main appeal to Marilyn was sensual. He wore his top hat, white tie, and tails as though he had been born in them. Good-looking rather than conventionally handsome, with fine blue-gray eyes and wavy dark brown hair, he was then thirty-five years old. His hollow cheeks and slim figure made him appear delicate and needful of mothering, a quality that Marilyn, like many women, found enormously sympathetic in a man.

As a friend of Jack Buchanan, Clifton Webb was all too delighted to play matchmaker when Marilyn expressed an interest in meeting him. Buchanan did not have to be pursued. He'd been drawn to Marilyn Miller since seeing her in *Sunny* on his first night in New York, but was reluctant to make a move because she was Mrs. Jack Pickford. Marilyn's assurance to Buchanan that it was a marriage in name only signaled the start of their affair.

Marilyn and "Johnny B" became so involved that they started talking about a professional as well as a personal relationship. Impetuously, Buchanan made a deal with Charles Dillingham for the British rights to *Sunny*, intending to produce it in London with Marilyn and himself as stars when they finished their present commitments. Marilyn could hardly wait to add the West End to her list of theatrical conquests.

London never happened. The affair lasted only three months, ending in the spring of 1926 when Jack Buchanan had to leave New York for the road tour of *Charlot's Revue*. With Marilyn tied to *Sunny*, there was no chance of the lovers meeting again for many months at the least. There were no regrets; it had been wonderful fun while it had lasted and they parted devoted friends. Later that year, with Britisher Binnie Hale starring opposite him instead of Marilyn, Jack Buchanan earned a fortune with his London production of *Sunny*.

It's doubtful that Marilyn would have dropped Jack Buchanan that easily if she hadn't had a replacement waiting in the wings who was equally charming and debonair. His name was Ben Lyon, and at twenty-five he was three years her junior. At that halfway point of the Roaring Twenties, Ben Lyon was a very romantic figure—an idolized movie star *and* a daring young aviator at a time when flying was the great American dream just coming true.

A prep school drop-out and former film extra, Ben Lyon's big break came in 1923 when Colleen Moore selected him to be her leading man in *Flaming Youth*. His engaging performance in the movie that started the whole "flapper" phenomenon elicited so much fan mail that First National Pictures signed him to a five-year contract. But his employers disapproved of his dangerous spare-time piloting activities and eventually exiled him to the film industry's Siberia—First National's eastern division studio in upper Manhattan—as punishment. Lyon, however, simply shifted his flying to Long Island's Roosevelt Field, which his friend Charles Lindbergh and many other pilots were using as a base for long-distance endurance tests.

Having watched Ben Lyon make celluloid love to such sex goddesses as Gloria Swanson, Pola Negri, and Barbara LaMarr, Marilyn was all too willing to be swept off her feet when he visited her dressing room one night after attending a performance of *Sunny*. Ben's roguish handsomeness and vibrant personality reminded her of Jack Pickford; but unlike her husband, he knew how to handle his liquor and didn't use drugs.

Marilyn and Ben had wonderful times together. On Sundays, if the weather was favorable, they made flying trips in his two-seater Ford monoplane. When she was working, he took her out almost every night to parties and nightclubs. Although it only took place once a month on a Saturday night, Marilyn's favorite outing was the post-showtime dinner dance called "The Mayfair," a gathering of the elite and successful at the Ritz-Carlton Hotel. Its Crystal Room had one of the world's most magnificent staircases, which every arriving guest had to descend in full view of the assemblage. Ziegfeld in all his glory could never have provided a better setting for a grand entrance, and Marilyn took full advantage of it when she paraded down arm-in-arm with Ben Lyon, both dazzling in their formal best.

As Marilyn was seen more and more in Ben Lyon's company,

the fact that she was married to another man did not go unnoticed by the gossip columnists. Was she getting ready to divorce Jack Pickford? Marilyn had no answer, but she would have been content to keep things as they were. Although she was in love with Ben Lyon, she could see no way of avoiding the same career conflicts that she'd had with Jack Pickford.

Sunny finally ended its New York engagement in December, 1926. The run of 517 performances was 53 less than *Sally* but its higher ticket prices resulted in the same gross—about $3 million. Even a subway strike and ten days of record heat during the summer had failed to dent business, and a lengthy cross-country tour was guaranteed. Marilyn approached it with mixed feelings, satisfied to go on collecting her 10 percent of the gross, but uncertain of what her next project would be once *Sunny* closed. Should she remain with Charles Dillingham or start shopping around elsewhere?

She knew that Dillingham would be in no rush to offer her a new show under her usual terms. He claimed to have lost $300,000 on *Peter Pan* and to be just about breaking even with *Sunny*, which had extremely high operating costs. For Marilyn this was Dillingham's problem, not hers. She was not about to lower her percentage deal just so Dillingham could make more of a profit. He would have to find other ways to economize.

An alternative presented itself on a raw December 9th when Marilyn, swathed in chinchilla, attended the cornerstone ceremonies for the spectacular art-deco playhouse that Flo Ziegfeld was building as a monument to himself at Fifty-fourth Street and Sixth Avenue. It was not exactly Broadway, but Ziegfeld considered it the future entertainment and convention center of New York, an opinion shared by his chief financial backer, William Randolph Hearst, who owned the neighboring Warwick Hotel.

Though Marilyn didn't relish sharing an outdoor podium with both Ziegfeld and Billie Burke, it was an important civic occasion and she had a legitimate reason for being there. As Vincent Lopez's band played "Look for the Silver Lining," Marilyn deposited a copy of the opening night program from *Sally* in a bronze box of mementos to be cemented into the new theater's foundation. Emcee Will Rogers told the immense crowd of onlookers: "In case you never knew what they do with old newspapers, it's all explained today. They put 'em in cornerstones."

Afterward, while Marilyn and Will Rogers were strolling across Sixth Avenue together to attend a reception at the Warwick, he told her that he thought it was very unfortunate that she and Ziegfeld had parted company. If they hadn't, Marilyn might be starring in *Rio Rita*, which was to be the Ziegfeld's inaugural production in February. Marilyn doubted this; she knew enough about *Rio Rita* to realize that she was neither vocally nor physically suited to the title role, which was being played by the sultry prima donna Ethelind Terry. But Marilyn guessed what Will Rogers was really driving at and suspected that Flo Ziegfeld had put him up to it. Still, returning to Ziegfeld's management seemed a logical move to make if she couldn't resolve her situation with Dillingham.

Marilyn decided that it was worth looking into, even if it did seem like eating crow. The new Ziegfeld Theatre reaffirmed its namesake's position as the foremost musical showman of his time, as well as the biggest of the big spenders. Further, the main cause of Marilyn's personal difficulties with Ziegfeld—Jack Pickford— was virtually out of her life and unlikely to return in any significant way, if at all.

Marilyn held several private meetings with Ziegfeld before she left New York to tour with *Sunny*. Two months later, in February 1927, Ziegfeld announced that he'd signed Marilyn Miller to a new five-year contract, calling her "unquestionably the outstanding musical comedy star of the world." Without mentioning Jack Pickford by name, Ziegfeld said, "It was only through a misunderstanding that Miss Miller left my management, and I am looking forward with great pleasure to producing her next play later in the year." To avoid raising any doubts about the future of *Rio Rita* at the new theater, he noted that Marilyn's show would open at the New

Amsterdam, where she had had continued successes dating back to the 1918 *Follies*.

Charles Dillingham didn't sound terribly unhappy when he learned of Marilyn's defection back to Ziegfeld: "I've seen them come and I've seen them go, and I am still producing plays after twenty-five years. Charming as she is, I shall probably be able to stand the loss of Miss Miller in my shows." Dillingham said that the only production he had planned for the coming season was a musical version of *Trilby*, which would require "a much stronger voice than Marilyn Miller's."

Marilyn always denied it, but some of her friends believed that before Ziegfeld would take her back under his management, he made her promise him she would divorce Jack Pickford. That the couple were separated didn't satisfy Ziegfeld. His vanity demanded the kind of public vindication that only a front-page divorce suit would provide. Without having to say it himself, he wanted the world to know that Florenz Ziegfeld was right all along: Jack Pickford must be scum or sweet Marilyn Miller wouldn't be divorcing him.

Whether or not Ziegfeld made it a condition of their deal, it was true that Marilyn didn't initiate divorce proceedings against Jack Pickford until after she signed her new contract with the producer. Even then she moved slowly and reluctantly, as if being forced against her will to choose between two things that were equally distasteful. She didn't want Ziegfeld to have the upper hand, and though her passion for Jack Pickford was long over, she was still too fond of him to cause him any more trouble with embarrassing disclosures about his private life.

Marilyn could easily have sued him for divorce on grounds of adultery. She knew that he was romantically involved with an actress with whom he had worked, but she chose to disregard the other woman, who was married to another well-known person. Acting on the advice of attorney Dudley Field Malone, Marilyn finally decided to seek a Parisian divorce. The French capital had a reputation among wealthy Americans as a place to obtain "easy" decrees. Although the Paris courts were noted for their severity with French nationals, an American or other foreigner could obtain a divorce after six months residence and on the same grounds that were permitted in their home state or country.

The system was an invitation to fraud. There were certain hotels in Paris where, after only a few weeks residence and considerable greasing of palms, one could obtain a domicile certificate testifying to the six months requirement. Also, there were court clerks who, in return for a hundred francs, would not ask for verification of the applicant's home address. In that way, for example, a New Yorker could claim to be a resident of some other state and take advantage of divorce laws that were far less stringent than his or her own. The great majority of divorces granted to Americans in Paris cited desertion or incompatibility as the cause. There was no need to sue over adultery, cruelty, alcoholism, impotence, or other reasons that could prove embarrassing to the participants when they became matters of public record.

In May 1927, Marilyn arranged for her friend Mary Eaton to replace her for the balance of the *Sunny* tour and started making arrangements for the trip to Paris. Her steady beau, Ben Lyon, was between movie assignments and decided to go with her, traveling separately for the sake of appearances. Lyon wanted Marilyn to marry him in Paris the moment that she was free, but she wouldn't commit herself until the divorce papers were safely in her hands.

Meanwhile, Jack Pickford thought it might facilitate the process if he went to Paris as well to assist Marilyn with the legal proceedings. That was the last thing she wanted, but there was nothing she could do to stop him. She dreaded to think of the repercussions when it became known that she was in Paris with both her lover and her soon-to-be ex-husband.

It didn't take long for the press to catch on. When Jack Pickford sailed from New York in June on the *Berengaria*, he told pierside reporters the reason for his voyage and described it as an amicable divorce. "Marilyn and I are perfectly friendly and there is nothing to argue about," Pickford said. "She's the loveliest girl I have ever known. She has a marvelous character and is not only agreeable but a dandy person. I shall stay in Paris until this unfortunate matter is settled."

Three days later, Marilyn departed for Paris on the *Ile de France*, cautioning newsmen that she had nothing to say except that she'd just finished an exhausting eighteen months with *Sunny* and was heading for a combination vacation and shopping spree. That same afternoon, Ben Lyon was discovered boarding the *Leviathan*, also bound for France. When told that Marilyn had sailed only hours earlier on the *Ile de France*, Lyon beamed at reporters and said, "How interesting." Lyon was accompanied by his mother and sister, leading to speculation that they all were on their way to a wedding.

By the time the *Berengaria* docked at Cherbourg, Jack Pickford was seriously ill, a combination of seasickness and his usual over-indulgence in booze and drugs. His sister and traveling companion, the alcoholic Lottie Pickford, was also wretchedly hung over, so they had to hire a private ambulance to take them to Paris. Hardly the most dignified arrival for the advance guard of an American divorce action, it did not go unnoticed by Parisians who were campaigning for an end to foreigners' open defilement of the city's legal system.

Marilyn's own behavior when she got to Paris did not help the situation. After deliberately avoiding reporters for several days, she finally told one of them, "One of my purposes in coming abroad was to file a divorce suit, but I have been too busy thus far to do anything about it." Since Marilyn's activities seemed to consist solely of shopping, having a good time with lover Ben Lyon, and paying cheer-up visits to the still convalescent Jack Pickford, her statement caused outrage in the chambers of the Palais de Justice. The president of the Tribunal of the Seine called for an immediate investigation into the whole matter of foreign divorce cases. In the meantime, petitions of "doubtful character" would be refused a hearing.

To no one's surprise, Marilyn soon announced that she'd given up the idea of getting a divorce. In the company of Ben Lyon, she frolicked on the French Riviera for a week and then returned to New York with him on the *Olympic*. As they were disembarking, Marilyn told reporters that she had no plans to marry Lyon: "How could I? Wouldn't that be bigamy?" Admitting that the couple had an "understanding" about their future, Ben Lyon declined to disclose the details.

In August, Marilyn sailed back to France alone on the *Berengaria* and quitely filed for divorce with the Versailles Tribunal. Her petition was accepted on the condition that there would be no publicity until the decree was actually granted. Early in November, she officially became the ex-Mrs. Jack Pickford. Mentioned as the reasons for the divorce were an incompatibility of temperaments and the impossibility of a reconciliation. Marilyn announced that she would never marry again. She was, according to the gossip columns, "wed indissolubly" to her career.

Attesting to the overwhelming success of *that* marriage was Marilyn Miller's selection as one of the most popular female stars of her time in a public poll conducted by I. Miller, the women's shoe manufacturer and retailer, at the end of 1927. It was a very prestigious honor, designed to be a permanent memorial. Sculptor A. Stirling Calder was commissioned to make full-length marble statues of the winners to fill four golden niches on the exterior of the new I. Miller Building at the northeast corner of Broadway and Forty-sixth Street.

Marilyn won in the musical comedy category, with her statue depicting her in the role of *Sunny*. The three other winners were Ethel Barrymore for drama, shown as Ophelia in *Hamlet*; Rosa Ponselle for opera, as Vincenzo Bellini's Norma; and, ironically, Marilyn's former sister-in-law, Mary Pickford, for films, as *Little Lord Fauntleroy*. More than half a century later, the four statues still stand majestically over a much-changed Times Square.

CHAPTER TWELVE

PRINCESS ROSALIE

THE RECENT DIVORCÉE STARTED her new Ziegfeld contract with *Rosalie*, which opened at the New Amsterdam Theatre on January 10, 1928. Alexander Woollcott, the fattest as well as the most celebrated stage critic of the time, vividly described the event for readers of the *New York World*:

> There comes a time once in every two or three years when the vast stage of that playhouse begins to show signs of a deep and familiar agitation. Down in the orchestra pit, the violins chitter with excitement and the brasses blare.
>
> The spotlight turns white with expectation. Fifty beautiful girls in simple peasant costumes of satin and chiffon rush pell-mell onto the stage, all squealing simple peasant outcries of "Here she comes!" Fifty hussars in fatigue uniform of ivory white and tomato bisque march on in columns of four and kneel to express an emotion too strong for words.
>
> The lights swing to the gateway at the back and settle there. The house holds its breath. And on walks Marilyn Miller!

Preoccupied with her divorce, Marilyn had been little involved with the preparation of *Rosalie* until she had reported for rehearsals, although Ziegfeld kept assuring her that it would provide plenty of opportunities for dancing, which was always her main concern. The idea for the show originated with writer William Anthony McGuire, a frequent collaborator of Ziegfeld's, who needed to raise money to pay off a gambling debt and sent the producer a forty-two-page telegram outlining a plot for a musical comedy. It was inspired by Queen Marie of Rumania's famous visit to America in 1926, and Ziegfeld probably would have thrown it away except for the fact that McGuire had shrewdly named the heroine *Rosalie*. That was also the name of Ziegfeld's mother, and he couldn't resist informing her immediately that he'd decided to produce a show in her honor! To keep it a family project, Ziegfeld persuaded his sister, Louise, the wife of a rich Detroit industrialist, to put up most of the financing as her contribution toward mama's glorification.

Since William Anthony McGuire was an alcoholic and quite undependable in his working habits, Ziegfeld hired Guy Bolton to collaborate on the book. As one of the authors of *Sally*, Bolton knew what was best for Marilyn Miller, and the following story evolved. At a ball in Paris, where she's masquerading as a peasant, Princess Rosalie of the tiny European kingdom of Romanza meets and falls in love with a dashing lieutenant in the U.S. Army Air Force. When he trails Rosalie to Romanza and discovers that she's of royal blood, he returns to his base at West Point convinced that his suit is hopeless.

The plot thickens when Princess Rosalie arrives in the United States on an official visit. During a guided tour of West Point, she again meets the lieutenant and romance flares anew. After Rosalie has gone back to Romanza, the lieutenant decides that he can't live without her. Undaunted by their different worlds, and inspired by the recent historic flight of Charles Lindbergh, he wings across the Atlantic for a reunion with Rosalie and the inevitable happy ending. The problem of her royal position is resolved when her father, King Cyril, abdicates and Romanza becomes a democratic republic.

When Ziegfeld came to selecting the music for *Rosalie*, he found himself in a desperate spot. Composer after composer rejected his offers because they already had more commissions than they could handle. Finally, Ziegfeld invited two of the best to a meeting in his office and asked them to share the assignment: George Gershwin, who was currently working on *Funny Face*, and Sigmud Romberg, who was preparing *New Moon*.

Ziegfeld told them: "Gentlemen, it is hopeless to argue with me. Both of you had better agree now. It will save a world of argument." When the two men reluctantly bowed to his hurricane force, he added: "And remember, gentlemen, I have to have the music in three weeks. Not a day later."

Actually, it wasn't that much of a chore for either Gershwin or Romberg, since they were both so prolific that they had scads of old melodies and songs stored away that had never been used or had been discarded from other shows. By the time Marilyn started rehearsals, Gershwin and Romberg had submitted about a dozen songs each. Gershwin was especially anxious for Marilyn to do "The Man I Love," originally written with brother Ira for Adele Astaire in *Lady Be Good*, but dropped during the tryout. Marilyn thought it was gorgeous but not for her. As a slow ballad, it had to be performed with little or no bodily movement, which was definitely not Marilyn Miller's style. She later regretted the decision, for "The Man I Love" became one of the Gershwins' most popular songs after torch singer Helen Morgan added it to her nightclub repertoire.

By opening night, *Rosalie* had seven songs by the Gershwins and eight by Sigmund Romberg and his lyricist, P. G. Wodehouse. For the most part, the Gershwin numbers were used in the American scenes, the Romberg in the European, a nice juxtaposition given the composers' native origins. By letting "The Man I Love" slip through her fingers, Marilyn was left with no songs that became hits outside the show. The only song that did—the Gershwins' "How Long Has This Been Going On?"—was performed by the peppy ingenue, Bobbe Arnst.

At Marilyn's insistence, Ziegfeld had signed Jack Donahue as a costar, and *Rosalie* consolidated their reputation as a peerless dance team. Their admiration for one another's talents seemed to inspire them to do some of their best work in the Gershwin duets "Oh Gee! Oh Joy!" and "Let Me Be a Friend to You."

Rumors die hard and it again was suggested that the two stars were having an affair. Ironically, Jack Donahue was never Marilyn's lover even onstage. In *Rosalie* as in *Sunny*, Donahue played a sort of guardian angel and devoted friend to both the heroine and the hero. Her love interest in *Rosalie* was Oliver McLennan, an Australian tenor making his American debut.

As a nod to the highly successful *No! No! Nanette*, the show was originally titled *Rah! Rah! Rosalie*. But Ziegfeld shortened it to just *Rosalie* when someone pointed out to him that the longer version was an open invitation to critics calling it "Bah! Bah! Rosalie." It turned out to be good advice.

Just two weeks prior to the opening of *Rosalie*, Ziegfeld had dazzled Broadway with *Show Boat*, which critics hailed for its revolutionary integration of music with a realistic plot, hoping that it would spell an end to the empty-headed, semirevue style that had predominated throughout the decade. Consequently, Ziegfeld sabotaged himself with *Rosalie*, which was a throwback to the old form. Reviewers blasted it for its many inanities, such as turning West Point coeducational so that Marilyn and fifty chorus girls could dress up as cadets for a rousing tap number.

But Marilyn Miller had a tremendous and loyal following, and she captured the audience from the very first night of *Rosalie* when she overcame a momentary mishap. There was a scene in which a royal flunkie had to carry a huge cat on a plush pillow. The actor tripped coming down some steps and the cat escaped into the wings. The recapture took ten minutes. Marilyn was laughing so hard that the audience also became hysterical. She finally sat down at the rim of the stage and joked with them until the performance resumed.

Although compared unfavorably to *Sally* and *Sunny*, *Rosalie* still had enough magic in the names of Miller, Donahue, Gershwin,

Romberg, and of course Ziegfeld to keep the New Amsterdam filled for months before catching up with the advance box-office sales and broker "buys."

Working for Ziegfeld for the first time in five years, Marilyn offered him no encouragement when he started to make romantic overtures. Standing outside her dressing room, he would ask, "Will my Princess Rosalie deign to see me?" Unless she had business to discuss with him, Marilyn would tell him to get lost and order the maid to shut the door in his face.

Never one to give up easily, Ziegfeld ordered his publicity agent, Bernard Sobel, to prepare an elaborate scrapbook of *Rosalie* mementos, including press clippings, photographs, and watercolor sketches of Marilyn by a staff artist. With gold-edged pages and bound in antique leather, it cost $200 to assemble. Told it was a gift from Ziegfeld, Marilyn tossed it into the bottom of her wardrobe closet and never looked at it again.

When *Rosalie* eventually started to flag at the box office, Ziegfeld changed his wooing into quarreling. "That was one of the unpleasant aspects of Ziegfeld's nature," Bernard Sobel said later. "He could harass his stars and staff if things went wrong. He was so persistent that Marilyn, who was famous for her smile, broke down in tears one night. 'I can entertain them when they come into the theater, but I can't go out in the streets and drag them in,' she said."

Sobel thought that Ziegfeld had no reason to complain about Marilyn's dedication to her work. Hours before a performance, she would come to the theater, put on her practice clothes, and run down to the bare stage to practice her tap and ballet routines. During performances, she often suffered blinding sinus headaches, yet she gave not the slightest sign of discomfort. The audience would have been astounded had it been aware of the iron determination that kept that delicate, pink and white body floating through air.

Marilyn was relieved when Ziegfeld made no new attempts to interfere in her romantic life. Only when Jack Pickford suddenly threatened to descend on her was there cause for concern. Slipping

out of a sanitarium where he was being treated for delirium tre-
mens, Pickford took a thirty-one-hour plane trip from Los Angeles
to New York to plead with Marilyn for a reconciliation. Telephoning
her from several stopover points along the way, he sounded so
unbalanced that in desperation Marilyn called Ma Pickford for
advice on what to do. When Jack Pickford arrived in New York,
there were two private detectives waiting at the airport to take him
straight back to California.

The main man in Marilyn's life was still Ben Lyon, but unfortunately for their love affair, he was now making more films in
Hollywood than he was in New York. To fill the void, Marilyn was
keeping company with John Warburton, an investment counselor
whose family was prominent in Philadelphia high society.

Although romance wasn't involved, Marilyn had also become
very attached to Edward Graham, a powerfully built chorus boy
who had acquired the nickname "Mecca" after playing an oriental
slave in the sensuous "Tsin" allegory in the *Greenwich Village
Follies of 1920*. For all his butch appearance, Mecca was a gentle
homosexual who worshipped Marilyn. They became friends while
working together in *Peter Pan*, and she always found a place for
him in subsequent shows. Mecca also served as a social escort when
she needed one and was a kind of body servant as well, carrying
Marilyn on and offstage in his muscular arms if she was suffering
one of her headaches.

Several months into the run of *Rosalie*, Marilyn and Ziegfeld started
to consider ideas for her next show. William Anthony McGuire,
who must have been drunk at the time, suggested musicalizing the
1918 hit *East Is West*, which had starred Fay Bainter. How the
tragic hobble-footed Chinese heroine, Ming Toy, could have suited
a glitzy, always smiling toe-dancer like Marilyn Miller is incon-
ceivable, but Ziegfeld was enthusiastic enough to ask George and
Ira Gershwin to write the music. Fascinated by the exotic setting
and the sensitive love story of racial miscegenation, the brothers

had composed half the score when Marilyn suddenly told Ziegfeld that it was too serious a subject for her and she didn't want to do it. The show was scrapped, but out of the wreckage came one of the Gershwins' most enduring songs, "Embraceable You," which turned up three years later in the non-Ziegfeld *Girl Crazy*.

Marilyn did express keen interest in another of Ziegfeld's ideas, so the Gershwins and McGuire were assigned to develop that one instead. It was to be called *Show Girl*, based on J. P. McEvoy's hugely popular novel and magazine serial about the rise to fame of chorine Dixie Dugan. Marilyn liked it because of its similarity to *Sally*, with the ignoble heroine eventually becoming a Ziegfeld star in a spectacular dance finale.

Meanwhile, *Rosalie* was nearing the end of its run at the New Amsterdam, closing at the end of October 1928, to make way for Ziegfeld's new Eddie Cantor–Ruth Etting musical, *Whoopee*. The 335-performance, 42-week engagement was considerably shorter than the 71 weeks of *Sally* and the 65 weeks of *Sunny*, but the show still grossed a very substantial $1.5 million. Marilyn's 10 percent of the take averaged out to a salary of about $3,500 a week, or $1,000 a week more than her minimum guarantee of $2,500.

Her connection with *Rosalie* was far from over, since Ziegfeld had booked an extensive road tour well into the spring of 1929. Because of another commitment, the romantic lead, Oliver McLennan, was leaving the show, so Marilyn, as was her contractual right, started to audition replacements. She finally settled on a tall, dark, and handsome Britisher, Archie Leach, who'd been starting to make a reputation for himself in Arthur Hammerstein productions. But Hammerstein hated Ziegfeld and just for spite made a deal for Leach with the Shuberts instead. Marilyn lost contact with the young actor, but was delighted to see him turn up in movies several years later under the new name of Cary Grant.

Right after New Year's, Marilyn received a big surprise when *Rosalie* started a twenty-week engagement at Chicago's Illinois Theatre. Waiting for her in her dressing room one night was a note that said: "I am in the city on business and would like to see you. Please leave one ticket for tomorrow night at the box office." It was signed "Edwin J. Reynolds."

Marilyn's emotions were in a turmoil. In all her thirty years, her father had never surfaced. She had often fantasized about his appearance and what direction her life might have taken if he hadn't deserted his family when she was an infant. When he came backstage to visit after the performance, Marilyn greeted the stranger hesitantly. His hand reached out for hers and he kissed her lightly on the cheek. "Hello, daughter," he said shyly. Reynolds told Marilyn that he'd followed her career with pride, but that he could never work up enough courage to arrange a meeting until now.

Marilyn dined with her father several times while he was in Chicago, but it was too late to develop a relationship that existed only on a birth certificate. On his last night in town, Reynolds attended *Rosalie* once more and sat in a front-row seat. When Marilyn was taking her curtain calls, she waved at him and saw that he was crying. He waved back and blew her a kiss.

She never saw her father again, but they kept in touch with an occasional letter. Reynolds had remarried and resided in Bayou Liberty, Louisiana, about twenty miles from New Orleans. What he had done with his life after leaving Ada and their four children was a mystery. If Marilyn knew, she never talked about it.

Later that month, she had another unexpected visitor. Herman Starr, the president of First National Pictures, was passing through Chicago en route to New York following production meetings on the West Coast. When he telephoned to ask if he could drop by her suite at the Drake Hotel, Marilyn thought it would be merely a social call, since Starr was a close friend of Ben Lyon.

But Starr had come to talk business—big business. Would Marilyn be interested in making some movies for First National? Say maybe at $100,000 for the first and even more for subsequent ones?

Marilyn was *very* interested.

◆ Chapter **THIRTEEN**

GOING HOLLYWOOD

THE MOST MUSICAL YEAR in the history of motion pictures was to be 1929. Hollywood's sound revolution had advanced to a point where "talkies" were no longer considered a novelty or passing fad. Moreover, the most successful were such musicals as *The Jazz Singer*, *The Singing Fool*, and *Broadway Melody*. The noisier and more tune-filled the movies were, the more the public seemed to like them. "All singing! All dancing! All talking!" became the motto for an entire industry. Musicals were ground out nonstop. Not even dramatic pictures could escape the insertion of a song or two.

But at the same time, the studios had to face the reality that within their ranks there was an acute shortage of silent stars who had good speaking voices, let alone musical abilities. It was a bit like asking a stock company of deaf mutes to put on Wagner's *Ring* cycle. It couldn't be done.

The obvious solution was to turn to the Broadway theater for a whole new roster of players. It seemed only natural that Marilyn Miller, the queen of musical comedy, should be among the first to be recruited. As an advertising blurb soon put it, "The screen has robbed the stage of its most prized possession!"

Having rejected all movie offers for years, Marilyn wasn't going to be rushed into accepting one now. Before she would sign with First National, she made sure that all the conditions were right. Her biggest stage success, *Sally*, was to be the vehicle for her debut. She was to have approval of the director and main supporting cast. To convey as much of the real Marilyn Miller as possible, photography had to be in color rather than black and white.

By April, the contract was ready for Marilyn to sign. First National would pay her $100,000 for *Sally* and had an option for one additional picture at $150,000. Marilyn received $5,000 immediately and was to get the balance in six weekly installments while *Sally* was being made. If the production of *Sally* took longer than scheduled, she was to receive an additional $16,000 a week for a maximum of three weeks.

The agreement was contingent on the approval of Flo Ziegfeld, who still had Marilyn under contract for the stage. Since he stood to share in the $30,000 that First National was paying for the rights to remake *Sally* (it had already done a silent version in 1925), Ziegfeld raised no objections, provided that production didn't begin until Marilyn finished the *Rosalie* tour.

The deal also gave Ziegfeld an excuse to drop Marilyn from his plans for *Show Girl*, which was due to open in July. Too much of a gentleman to tell her so, Ziegfeld thought Marilyn was getting a bit old to play a struggling young chorus girl. He replaced her with his latest protégée, nineteen-year-old Ruby Keeler, then better known as Mrs. Al Jolson. Marilyn lost nothing in the reshuffling except a chance to introduce Gershwin's "An American in Paris" ballet (since Ruby Keeler was only a tap dancer, the number was assigned to Harriet Hoctor). *Show Girl* lasted only 111 performances.

Early in June, Marilyn arrived in Los Angeles to start work on *Sally*. Whether it was the effects of a torrid heat wave that was gripping the city or simply a severe case of "going Hollywood," she immediately showed signs of a swollen ego. Hal Wallis, then general studio manager for First National Pictures, said later that Marilyn "wouldn't get off the train at Pasadena until we sent a Rolls Royce to meet her. She insisted on a new wardrobe, including a chinchilla coat, which cost thousands even in those days. Her dressing room had to be completely remodeled with paneled walls, French antiques, and a sunken bathtub fit for Cleopatra."

Marilyn's attitude may have been a coverup for the deep insecurities she was feeling at the time. Except for a silent screen test, she'd never made a movie before, nor did she know the first thing about microphone or camera techniques. Yet if she swept onto the set behaving like anything less than a queen who was completely in control of the situation, she would be exposed for the novice that she really was.

In fact Marilyn's inexperience did not become a major problem because everybody connected with *Sally* was groping their way through. There was not only the cumbersome Vitaphone sound system to contend with, but also the far-from-perfected Technicolor process, which tended to turn blues into greens and human complexions bilious. Under such primitive conditions, working days were very long—ten, twelve, or more hours, often well into the night.

What made it even more frustrating was that Vitaphone and Technicolor were technically incompatible. Vitaphone was recorded by a gramophone needle cutting into a large wax disk. Technicolor required lighting ten times as bright as black-and-white photography. The intense heat generated would melt the Vitaphone disks, not to mention the dehydrating effect it had on the actors and crew. A completely new ventilating system had to be installed by opening vents in the roof and floor of the sound stage. That created still another problem: the noise of the fans was being picked up by the microphones.

Filming of the musical numbers was also fraught with complications. A sixty-member Vitaphone Orchestra was required to be on the set all the time so that the music could be recorded directly on the sound track while the action was being photographed. The

technique of recording the sound separately and then synchroniz-
ing it to the picture had not yet been developed.

According to Hal Wallis, there were difficulties with Marilyn's
voice. "On stage, her personal magnetism blinded audiences to
her lack of vocal talent. She actually had a very thin voice and we
immediately understood why she had never made a recording,"
Wallis said. "Her contract specified that nobody must dub her.
The sound department did everything but stand on its head to
make her sound vocally exciting, but it didn't work."

First National's obvious intention with *Sally* was to prove to the
public that movies had finally reached a point of technical development where they could surpass anything done on the stage. The
indoor set representing the formal garden of a Long Island millionaire's estate was the largest and most costly ever built at the
Burbank studio, including lily ponds, two working fountains and a
tremendous dance floor for the production numbers. There were
100 dancing girls and boys in the cast, 40 showgirls and 36 ballerinas
trained by Albertina Rasch, plus 250 dress "extras" for the crowd
scenes.

The director was John Francis Dillon, recommended to Marilyn
by Ben Lyon, whose first big success had been Dillon's silent
Flaming Youth. For her leading man, Marilyn selected Alexander
Gray, who had played the same role with her during the original
road tour of *Sally* and was another new First National contractee.
Marilyn wanted Leon Errol to recreate his original role of the
Grand Duke, but when he proved unavailable she settled happily
for First National's star comedian, Joe E. Brown. Others prominent
among the thirty-five principals were T. Roy Barnes (replacing
Walter Catlett), a close friend of Marilyn's since they had worked
together in *The Passing Show of 1914*; comedienne Pert Kelton,
who'd been with her in *Sunny*; and Ford Sterling, one of the
original Keystone Cops and the man who started the custard-pie-
throwing tradition.

Oddly enough, where First National stinted was the music. Only
two of the original Kern songs, "Look for the Silver Lining" and

"Wild Rose," were used. In addition, three new songs were written by First National's contract team, Al Dubin and Joe Burke: "Sally," "If I'm Dreaming," and "All I want to Do, Do, Do Is Dance." This was becoming a standard practice in Hollywood. Whenever films were made of stage musicals, the studios usually opted for new songs and often whole new scores. The copyrights were assigned to their own music publishing companies, thus enabling them to collect royalties that they wouldn't have from the original songs.

Five songs were a big drop from the twelve in the stage production of *Sally*, but then the movie was about ninety minutes shorter in length. There would have been no room left for the story if the same number of songs had been used in the film.

Marilyn hated the whole regimen that was an essential part of filmmaking. When she was working on the stage, she rarely got out of bed before noon. In Hollywood, she had to be up at dawn and at the studio two hours in advance of shooting so that makeup artists and hair stylists could prepare her for the cameras.

When her presence wasn't required on the set, Marilyn had to grant press interviews or pose for publicity and advertising photographs. If she'd been a starry-eyed beginner, she might not have minded it so much, but well established and pushing thirty-one, she thought it unnecessary and beneath her dignity. What was to be gained from dragging her out to Malibu Beach to model the latest one-piece bathing suit fashions for *Photoplay*? Granted, she did have a beautiful body, but would anyone believe Marilyn Miller's advice that "an hour or so with a medicine ball each day and you'll never have to worry about your figure. More eighteen-pound medicine balls and less eighteen-day diets are what this country needs."

But what bothered Marilyn most was the restriction on her social life. Often she had to work until ten or eleven at night, which meant going straight home to sleep if she was to arrive back at the studio early the next morning looking fresh and rested. It didn't take her long to find a way to rectify that problem. Have an affair with the head of the studio and you could do pretty well as you damn pleased!

The man she set her sights on was Jack L. Warner, vice-president in charge of production for the family-owned Warner Brothers Pictures, which took control of First National in 1928 and ran it as a separate division. Jack Warner's influence over Marilyn's career was equivalent to Flo Ziegfeld's, but with one essential difference. In furtherance of her own interests, she could let herself become Jack Warner's mistress, something that she could never do with Flo Ziegfeld.

For one thing, Jack Warner didn't make Marilyn's flesh crawl. He was only six years older (Ziegfeld was her senior by nearly thirty years), and although he was no John Gilbert or Ramon Novarro, Warner dressed impeccably, had a dynamic personality, and was great fun to be with. A frustrated comedian, he kept Marilyn laughing with old jokes and stories about his experiences as a boy soprano, singing during the reel-change intervals in his brothers' nickelodeons.

Even more to the point, Marilyn was impressed by the power that Jack Warner wielded in Hollywood. He and his brothers were largely responsible for the introduction of talking pictures and still held the lead over their competitors. Marilyn had no way of telling if she'd succeed as a movie star or not. Having such an influential "friend" certainly couldn't hurt her chances.

Jack Warner was then ripe for plucking. Married for thirteen years and the father of a twelve-year-old son, he was separated from his wife but reluctant to get a divorce because she was demanding several million dollars in Warner Brothers stock as a settlement. Warner had been involved in many affairs with studio actresses, but when Marilyn Miller came along, she had an appeal far beyond the ordinary performer. Hollywood always had something of an inferiority complex about itself. Anyone who came from the "legitimate" theater was held in awe, but a Broadway musical comedy star *and* a Ziegfeld beauty was Venus herself.

Who made the first advance is not known, but after Marilyn and

Jack Warner spent a few nights together, it was decided that she should move from the Beverly Wilshire Hotel to La Ronda, an ultraexclusive celebrity hideaway that bordered on Beverly Hills and Hollywood. There Marilyn could entertain Warner in complete privacy and comfort. Her duplex apartment had a parlor, dining room, and kitchen on the ground floor, and two bedrooms and a lavish bath upstairs.

Once she had Jack Warner under her power, Marilyn took great liberties working at First National. She rarely bothered to learn her lines, so the script girl was forced to print them in chalk on a blackboard to one side of the camera. To make matters worse, she was slow to respond to studio "calls." She once kept the *Sally* unit waiting three days for her to show up to do one song.

Jack Warner wasn't the only man Marilyn was involved with at the time. One was a previous lover, Jack Buchanan. As luck would have it, Buchanan was also working at First National, appearing opposite the saucy French singing comedienne Irene Bordoni in an adaptation of her recent Broadway hit *Paris*. With bachelor Buchanan, Marilyn could step out to parties and nightclubs without causing gossip, which she couldn't do with her other Jack of the moment.

Marilyn was also spending a lot of time with Alexander Gray, her leading man in *Sally*. Six months earlier, his wife had been killed in an automobile accident, and he had yet to get over the shock. It was an experience so similar to her own with Frank Carter that Marilyn tried to help Gray come to terms with his loss. Often, after work, she took him back to her apartment and let him pour out his sorrows over cocktails. Sometimes he stayed the night.

Marilyn's romance with Ben Lyon was over, but they remained on friendly terms. Ironically, Lyon had become engaged to Bebe Daniels, who had been Jack Pickford's mistress for a time when he was still married to Marilyn. Having lost interest in both men, Marilyn bore Daniels no animosity, and the two women plus Lyon were often seen gallivanting around Hollywood together. As for Jack Pickford, he was getting ready to marry another Ziegfeld alumna, showgirl Mary Mulhern, who would divorce him two years later on charges of physical and mental cruelty.

The production of *Sally* was completed in nine weeks, three weeks over schedule. How much of that delay was caused by Marilyn and how much by the problems with the Vitaphone and Technicolor processes is unknown, but Marilyn did collect $50,000 in overtime pay, which was cheerfully okayed by none other than Jack Warner himself.

Publicity boasted that *Sally* cost $1 million—a figure often used to impress the public in those days of 35¢ admission prices. But according to First National's production files, it was exactly $619,195.25. Included in that amount was Marilyn's salary of $149,998, roughly $17,000 a week or $2,750 a day (studios were then on a six-day week). Since Marilyn had never earned more than $5,000 a week in the theater, it was small wonder that she wanted to keep Jack Warner as a friend.

But all good things must come to an end—at least until the next time. When Marilyn finished *Sally*, she went back to New York to confer with Ziegfeld about a new show. Although First National intended to exercise its option with Marilyn for another picture, it couldn't do so until Ziegfeld had a turn at her services.

As it turned out, Ziegfeld had nothing to offer Marilyn for the moment. Although he was working on two projects, there was no place for Marilyn Miller in either of them. To keep the Ziegfeld Theatre occupied after the quick flop of *Show Girl*, he'd hurriedly contracted with British producer Charles Cochran to put on Noel Coward's recent West End success *Bitter Sweet*. Ziegfeld also was supervising the production of *Glorifying the American Girl*, a celluloid revue that Paramount Pictures was shooting at its Long Island City studio. Were Marilyn not already signed to First National, Ziegfeld would have starred her in it; instead, he used Mary Eaton.

To keep Marilyn occupied, Ziegfeld told her to arrange a meeting with Noel Coward to see if he might have some ideas for a show that would interest her. Coward was in New York for the rehearsals of *Bitter Sweet*, and was proving so meddlesome that Ziegfeld was looking for any excuse to get him out of his hair for a few hours.

In 1920, as a struggling young playwright on his first visit to America, Noel Coward saw *Sally* six times, finally working up enough courage one night to go backstage and introduce himself to Marilyn. They'd been friends ever since, but had never considered collaborating because their styles seemed incompatible. Marilyn Miller stood for glitzy Broadway extravaganzas, whereas Noel Coward was synonymous with sophisticated plays and romantic musicals that were close to operettas.

Yet if Ziegfeld favored it, Marilyn and Noel were willing to put their heads together. Coward had vivid childhood memories of an early American musical that he'd seen done in London called *The Belle of New York*. Marilyn seemed perfect for the part of the heroine, a Bowery mission worker who reforms a wastrel playboy; but the plot would have to be revamped and a whole new music score written. Why not update it to contemporary Manhattan and weave in some racier, more sophisticated romantic and comedy elements that would make the prim and proper original unrecognizable?

Marilyn was all for it. And if Marilyn Miller and Noel Coward were happy, Flo Ziegfeld was too. He told Coward to submit a story outline as soon as possible; if he liked it, they had a deal.

Unfortunately, no one figured on the stock market crash of October 29, 1929. Like thousands of other investors, Flo Ziegfeld was wiped out, although in his case it might have been avoided if his switchboard operator hadn't stayed home sick on Black Tuesday!

Ziegfeld had taken his secretary and his entire office staff to testify in a court action in which he was being sued for nonpayment of a bill for a $1,600 electric sign. His broker, Edward Francis Hutton, continually called Ziegfeld's office to advise him to cut his losses by selling out, but there was no reply. Efforts to reach him at all his usual haunts were to no avail. Who expected to find Flo Ziegfeld in Foley Square instead of Times Square? He lost $2 million in stocks, most of it bought on margin.

Marilyn Miller was luckier. Although she had a substantial investment in stocks, she owned them outright and suffered only a paper loss, which was eventually recouped. Purchased on the advice of steady beau and investment counselor John Warburton, her holdings were all in the "blue chip" category, including Goldman-Sachs, National City Bank, Pennsylvania Railroad, Bethlehem Steel, Chase Bank, and United States Steel. With another $200,000 in cash and jewelry stored in a safe-deposit box, she had no financial worries.

What did worry Marilyn was the future of her career. Although Ziegfeld was able to go through with the production of Noel Coward's *Bitter Sweet* (the funding had been taken care of before the crash), there was no telling how long it would be until he recouped some of his losses and could consider new projects.

The prospects for Marilyn aligning temporarily with a Ziegfeld competitor were equally dismal. Charles Dillingham had also gone bankrupt, and the Shuberts and Arthur Hammerstein, the most active producers of musicals, were on the verge. There wasn't much that Marilyn could do but adopt a hopeful attitude that conditions would soon improve. In the meantime, she would concentrate on moviemaking.

_____

CHAPTER FOURTEEN

Nothing to Smile About

ADVERTISING FOR SALLY PROCLAIMED Marilyn Miller "the new sweetheart of the screen!" In December 1929, her first movie had its world premiere at New York's Winter Garden, where fifteen years earlier she had made her Broadway debut in *The Passing Show of 1914*. It was an ironic comment on where Marilyn Miller and show business in general were heading. Long one of the leading legitimate theaters, the Winter Garden had been turned into a talking picture house in 1928 with Al Jolson's *The Singing Fool*.

Sally was launched initially as a so-called "road show," presented twice daily at $1 and $2 a ticket. First National was careful to inform the public that that was a bargain in comparison to the $6.60 being charged for current stage attractions. The *New York Times* seemed to concur when it described *Sally* as "without doubt the most beautiful picture that has come to the screen."

Critics were divided about Marilyn's performance. Those who'd seen her in *Sally* on the stage nine years before were disappointed; nothing that she did in the film equaled their vivid memories of that magical experience. On the other hand, more than one critic who'd never seen the theatrical *Sally* called Marilyn "a burst of

165

Technicolored sunshine." The public seemed to agree: business was "socko," according to *Variety*.

Although First National held an option for another picture at the same fee, Jack Warner chose to disregard it. Instead he gave Marilyn a new contract for two pictures at $200,000 each! Whatever his personal motives, he could afford to be generous. Thanks to its pioneering efforts in sound films, Warner Brothers made more money in 1929 than any other company in the industry's history, and had a 745 percent increase over its own profits of the previous year.

Given the success of *Sally*, Jack Warner wanted Marilyn to get started on another film as soon as possible (to say nothing about the resumption of their affair). Although they'd already discussed *Sunny* as a follow-up, he wondered if she'd rather do *The Hot Heiress*, an original script by Herbert Fields with songs by Richard Rodgers and Lorenz Hart.

Afraid to take a chance on an untried property that concerned a millionaire's daughter on the make for a steel riveter, Marilyn decided to stick with *Sunny*. Also, she knew that the sale of the movie rights to the play would benefit Charles Dillingham, who'd been wiped out in the stock market crash. She still felt guilty over his dropping a bundle on *Peter Pan*. Thanks to Marilyn's inside tip, Dillingham was able to run the price of *Sunny* up to $130,000, which seemed a gold mine, even though he had to share it with Jerome Kern, Otto Harbach, and Oscar Hammerstein II.

Hollywood also came to the rescue of Flo Ziegfeld, who signed a contract with Samuel Goldwyn to coproduce film versions of some of his Broadway hits, starting with Eddie Cantor in *Whoopee*. With part of the money from that deal, Ziegfeld could start planning the next stage venture. He knew it would have to be with Marilyn Miller. Not only did he have a commitment with her, but her name was insurance against box-office failure. All her shows, except for the nonmusical *Peter Pan*, had been winners.

But Ziegfeld being Ziegfeld, he realized that the new show would have to be something extraspecial if it was going to compete successfully against the flood of musicals now pouring out of Hollywood. After Marilyn Miller, whom did musical comedy audiences adore more than Fred and Adele Astaire? Putting the three of them together in one show, with a few other top names and a major composer, seemed a surefire formula for a hit. Marilyn loved the idea and so did the Astaires, who'd long been hoping for a chance to work in a Ziegfeld production.

The only snag was that Ziegfeld didn't have a book to hang the show on. The nearest thing to it in his active file was the plot outline that Noel Coward had given him before returning to England, which was entitled *Tom, Dick and Harry* and hardly sounded like a vehicle for Marilyn Miller and Fred and Adele Astaire. Still, Coward had written it with Marilyn in mind, so it was better than starting from scratch. Ziegfeld handed it over to a close friend, the novelist and short story writer Louis Bromfield, to see what another distinguished author could do with it. Fortunately, there was no urgency because the principals were going to be busy elsewhere for many months to come. Marilyn and Ziegfeld were on their way to Hollywood for their separate movie commitments, and the Astaires were appearing in *Funny Face* in London.

Before leaving for California, Marilyn invited a few friends from the New York press corps to her suite in the Sherry Netherland Hotel to tell them that she'd become engaged to Michael Farmer. Her new fiancé was conspicuous by his absence, having sailed to Europe on the *Aquitania* a few days earlier. But Marilyn's friends Clifton and Maybelle Webb were present to confirm the fact if the large square-cut diamond ring on her finger wasn't sufficient proof.

Marilyn said that she had first met Michael Farmer in Paris in 1927 while she was filing for divorce from Jack Pickford. "We spent one afternoon together and then I didn't see him again until this past winter in New York. We began to go around together. I had never forgotten him—his handsome face, the way he has of commanding attention whenever he enters a room, a café, a theater, the fun we've had together.

"We are friends, too, even before we are sweethearts," she continued. "We like the same things, the same places, the same people. We should be happy—but even if we should not be, no matter what has happened to me in the past, or what might happen to me in the future, I could never be disillusioned."

Not even the Webbs could tell if Marilyn was serious or not. Clifton Webb said later that he thought it was all a publicity stunt: Marilyn needed to glamorize her private life now that she was a Hollywood star, and Michael Farmer didn't care how his name was used as long as it was spelled correctly. It may also have been Marilyn's way of telling other women to keep away, that Michael Farmer was her exclusive property.

He was, after all, one of the most "eligible" of the current crop of high-society playboys, as well as one of the most mysterious. Except that he called himself Michael Farmer, no one knew who he was, where he came from (probably England or Ireland), or how he got his money (most likely from playing stud to wealthy women). Dark-haired and about thirty years old, Farmer was reputed to be the best-looking man in Paris, where he lived when not traveling with the international set. Dressed elegantly and always accompanied by two miniature poodles, he held court nightly at Bricktop's, the late-hours club run by the redheaded black American entertainer whose real name was Ada Smith.

With Marilyn working in New York or Hollywood, her "engagement" to Michael Farmer seemed to be conducted mainly by long-distance telephone. Those were the days, of course, when transatlantic calls were not commonplace, but Farmer thought nothing of picking up the phone at Bricktop's and buzzing Marilyn just to play music and sing to her. Sometimes he would be joined by his friend Cole Porter. Marilyn was often the first person in America to hear Porter's latest compositions.

Whatever other sweet tidings Michael Farmer whispered to Marilyn long distance is unknown, but she was soon telling Louella Parsons that, when she married Michael, they would raise a family and live in Europe at least six months of the year.

* * *

In May, Marilyn was back in Hollywood for the filming of *Sunny*. From Lita Grey, the second but now ex-Mrs. Charlie Chaplin, she rented a Beverly Hills mansion that she delighted in calling "my Lita Grey home in the West." It fulfilled her requirements for privacy—Jack Warner was still a frequent visitor—and also had a tennis court, swimming pool, and small gymnasium where she could exercise and practice every day.

After a year of inactivity (she hadn't worked since completing *Sally* the previous summer), Marilyn desperately needed to get back into condition. She started training daily with Theodore Kosloff, her ballet master from the early Shubert days, who ran a school in Hollywood and was also to choreograph her hunting ball number in *Sunny*.

As Marilyn took her place at the barre on the first day, she attempted to turn her feet into first position and failed. She struggled on, watching herself in the mirror on the opposite wall. She tried a plié, bending her knees outward. An audible creak of her bones brought an expression of pain to Kosloff's face as well as hers. He sent her home to recuperate. Her calf and thigh muscles were so sore that she could barely get down the stairs to the street.

After Swedish massage and applications of hot towels, Marilyn's legs started to feel better. The next day she worked ten minutes with Kosloff, the following day fifteen minutes. In a month she was on point again and dancing about as well as could be expected for a part-time ballerina who was nearing her thirty-second birthday.

Marilyn had expected Jack Donahue, who starred with her in *Sunny* on the stage, to repeat his role in the movie version. But a near lifetime of alcoholism and overwork had finally caught up with Donahue and he could not pass the screen test. He looked a wreck, which was especially sad because his dancing was virtually unimpaired. As a compromise, Jack's younger brother, Joe Donahue, a close look-alike and his theater understudy, replaced him in the film of *Sunny*.

Not too many months later, Jack Donahue died of kidney failure. He was only thirty-eight years old. Marilyn was devastated. Not only had she lost a cherished friend and performing partner, but she knew it was the end of a tradition that dated back to the beginnings of vaudeville. There would never be another "hoofer" quite like Jack Donahue. No doubt his death also gave her a sense of her own mortality.

As a favor to another longtime friend, Marilyn saw to it that Lawrence Gray was hired for the romantic lead in *Sunny*. No relation to Alexander Gray of *Sally* (they were similar types, causing the public much confusion), Lawrence Gray was Marion Davies's latest paramour. They'd recently made two pictures together, but Davies thought it was time that Gray started working elsewhere lest her producer and benefactor, William Randolph Hearst, should catch on to the affair. Since Lawrence Gray was quite handsome, Marilyn was all too happy to request him for *Sunny*, but out of loyalty to old chum Marion, she kept it a strictly professional relationship.

By the time *Sunny* started production in June 1930, the public was rapidly becoming irritated by the torrent of musicals that had continued unabated for nearly two years. In 1929 alone, there were about seventy-five musicals, which averaged out to more than one a week. That was almost 20 percent of the four hundred features that were released by the ten largest Hollywood companies that year.

It was Jack Warner's theory that what the public liked least about musicals were the long production numbers that slowed the story and the tendency of the players to break into song and dance at the slightest provocation. As a result, *Sunny* would depart even farther from its original stage version than *Sally* had. There were only two songs (Kern's "Who?" and "Sunny"), two production numbers, and no big supporting cast or choruses of singers and dancers. Publicity stressed the adjective *intimate* rather than *spectacular*.

Marilyn didn't object to the changes. She was getting paid more for *Sunny* than she was for *Sally*, yet had far less to do in the way of strenuous dancing and singing. What didn't please her was *Sunny* being photographed in black and white instead of color. But First

National had had an unsatisfactory experience with *Sally* and its other Technicolor films. Aside from the bluish-green garishness of the screen image, the special prints were four times as expensive as black and white, tended to buckle in projectors, and were easily scratched. Use of the process was being avoided until cost and technical improvements could be made.

With the absence of color photography, Marilyn found working conditions on *Sunny* much more pleasant. The torrid heat generated by the extra lighting, as well as the long delays while camera crews argued over what color scheme to use in each scene, were no longer a problem. As for the sound recording, there had been tremendous advances since *Sally*. An orchestra was no longer required on the set, since the musical track could now be recorded separately. *Sunny* also benefited from a new soundproofing device called "the blimp," a special casing for the camera that eliminated the need for a stationary isolation booth and permitted a return to the more fluid camera movements of silent days.

Although *Sunny* was a less elaborate production than *Sally*, it ended up costing nearly $100,000 more. One of the reasons was the costlier rights to the original play, but the biggest factor was Marilyn's salary. With $25,000 worth of overtime thrown in, it amounted to $225,000. Jack Warner obviously still thought that she was worth every penny of it.

In September, Marilyn was back in New York for conferences with Flo Ziegfeld about her show with Fred and Adele Astaire. William Anthony McGuire was writing the book and Vincent Youmans, composer of *No! No! Nanette* and *Hit the Deck*, was working on the score with lyricists Clifford Grey and Harold Adamson.

Well aware that she'd be getting some keen competition from the Astaires in the dance department, Marilyn coaxed Ziegfeld into hiring Theodore Kosloff to choreograph her big ballet number and Ned Wayburn, another important collaborator since her Shubert days, to be the show's overall director. However, the title, *Tom, Dick and Harry*, had to be changed. After ten years, the public had come to expect Marilyn Miller in a musical in which she was the title character. It had been a lucky charm for her, and she wasn't about to break tradition. Ziegfeld saw the sense in that and agreed.

But Ziegfeld had the Astaires' egos to contend with as well, so it was essential that William Anthony McGuire find a title that would satisfy all three stars. The result was the double-edged *Smiles*. Although it would be the name of Marilyn's character, a deluge of smiles was what the show intended to provide for everyone who saw it.

Picking up where Noel Coward's and Louis Bromfield's outlines left off, McGuire's plot concerned a sad-faced teenage orphan (shades of *Sally*) who is whimsically named Smiles when adopted by four soldiers—American, English, French, and Italian—at the end of World War I. Ten years later, Smiles and her four benefactors are living in New York, where she has blossomed into a beautiful Salvation Army lass working among Bowery derelicts.

Two rich socialites, Bob Hastings and his sister Dot, are out slumming one night and stumble into Smiles's mission, which starts a long series of comic and amorous misadventures punctuated by an oriental costume ball on a Long Island estate, a fashion show in a swank Paris hotel, and a formal garden party on the roof of a Manhattan town house. In the end, Smiles must marry either Bob Hastings or the American ex-soldier, who is the youngest of her four benefactors.

In the first draft of the script, Smiles picked Bob Hastings, who, of course, was being played by Fred Astaire. But during rehearsals it soon became obvious that Marilyn Miller and the slight, gangly Fred Astaire were physically and romantically a poor match. Writer Ring Lardner, serving as script consultant while William Anthony McGuire was off on a drinking spree, told Ziegfeld that the audience would never believe that Marilyn would choose Fred over tall, dark, gorgeous Paul Gregory, who was cast as the former doughboy. The ending was changed, at least in the play. For rumors were circulating that Marilyn Miller and Fred Astaire were having an offstage romance.

More likely, they were just old friends enjoying each other's companionship. Fred Astaire was then thirty-one years old; sister Adele, born only nine days after Marilyn Miller, was thirty-two. Marilyn had known them both since they were all child vaudevillians, often crossing paths in their travels but never appearing on the same bills. Since becoming stars, they had continued to move in the same social circles as favorites of the rich and highly placed.

While *Smiles* was trying out in Boston, rehearsals and performances kept everybody indoors so much that Marilyn finally said to Fred Astaire one night, "Let's take a ride someplace after the show. Let's escape and get some fresh air." And so they did, Fred, Adele, Marilyn, and Mecca Graham, the chorus dancer who was her close and devoted friend.

They were driving along for about half an hour, singing, joking, and laughing, when they reached the bridge that crossed the Charles River to Cambridge. Midway across, they stopped to admire the view, and Marilyn and Fred got out to see if there might be any boats passing on the river below. They were leaning against the railing with their backs to the roadway when two policemen came up behind them, grabbing Fred by the collar of his coat.

"You're not going to do it, buddy," one policeman said, while his partner took Marilyn by the arm. Marilyn and Fred tried to explain who they were, but the policemen wouldn't listen. The bridge had been the site for a number of suicides in the past, and the police had orders to grab anyone who stood there. As a result, several single and dual jumps had been prevented. Marilyn and Fred finally talked their way out of it and invited the cops to be their guests at *Smiles* at the Colonial Theatre. "We got even with them," Fred Astaire said in retrospect, although that wasn't the intention then.

To make the long rehearsal hours more endurable, Marilyn and Adele Astaire were always playing pranks. Once, prior to the New

York opening, they were still working at 3:00 A.M. when they heard Ziegfeld order his secretary, Goldie Clough, to get James Stroock of Brooks Costume there immediately. Since Goldie didn't know Stroock's home telephone number (he'd hardly be at the showroom at that ungodly hour), she had to go up to the Ziegfeld Theatre's executive office by way of the fire escape to get it because the elevator wasn't running.

In pitch darkness and crawling on her knees part of the way, Goldie finally made it to the office. As she was groping for the light switch in the hall, she felt a hand go up her skirt and pinch her bottom so hard that she screamed. When she turned the light on, she saw Marilyn and Adele rolling on the floor, hysterical with laughter.

But smiles became increasingly rare as the show drew closer to its premiere. Except for the Astaires' dancing and the opulent staging by Joseph Urban, the Boston critics were unimpressed by the show. Having enjoyed a virtual love affair with reviewers over the years, Marilyn was mortified when the *Evening Transcript* insisted that she could "merely sing, dance, pose and prattle according to her abilities, which do not increase." The critic added that Marilyn "belongs to an older order of such musical comedy pieces." Her need to have "a sentimental, prettified, glamorous 'vehicle'" clashed with the requirements of the "light, dry, sophisticated Astaires," who were hailed as thoroughly up-to-date.

After that panning, Marilyn became very difficult to deal with; the cast was cautioned by the stage manager to keep their distance. Whether it was Marilyn's own fault or that of the material that she had to work with, she decided that her performance would be impeccable by the time of the New York opening. In the meantime, she wanted certain changes made. She claimed that the musical director, Paul Lannin, was throwing her off balance and would have to be replaced. She hated the lyrics of two of her songs and demanded they be rewritten or dropped. Ziegfeld promised her that everything would be done to her satisfaction.

It was, but at the cost of Ziegfeld's friendship with the composer,

Vincent Youmans, who refused to go along with the changes and threatened to withdraw his music from the show. Ziegfeld finally was forced to get a court injunction against Youmans, claiming that withdrawal of the music on such short notice would mean closing *Smiles* and throwing more than two hundred people out of work.

Frank Tours, who had worked with Marilyn as far back as the *Follies*, took over as conductor, and Ring Lardner, who'd already done some polishing of McGuire's book, was asked to doctor the two songs that Marilyn disliked. One of them, *Rally Round Me*, which Marilyn sang in the first act with a group of Salvation Army "lassies," required little more than altering a line that began "I used to shirk my work."

Marilyn refused to budge on the second number, "Time on My Hands," which had lyrics by Harold Adamson and Mack Gordon. It was supposed to be a duet with Paul Gregory. She loved Gregory's singing it to her, and she loved dancing to the melody alone, but she would not sing the refrain. She never explained why; maybe she was just being obstreperous. But new words were written by Ring Lardner, and for Marilyn Miller at least, "Time on My Hands" became "What Can I Say?" But only in its original version did "Time on My Hands" become a perennial favorite.

With tickets priced at a record $22 each (reverting to a normal $7.70 top the next day), *Smiles* opened at the Ziegfeld Theatre on November 18, 1930, to one of the most fashionable audiences in Broadway history. The combined upper-crust followings of Marilyn Miller and the Astaires accounted for more ermine coats and orchid corsages than had ever been seen in one place before. Forty-seven photographers and newsreel cameramen roamed the lobby and auditorium, tracking down celebrities like human prey. Outside on Sixth Avenue, ten thousand spectators were held behind barricades by 250 policemen.

Individually and collectively, Marilyn and the Astaires brought the house down a dozen times that night, but with so many friends and admirers in the audience it was difficult to tell how genuine the response was. The trio had the stage to themselves in just one number, "Anyway, We've Had Fun," and Marilyn and Fred were paired in "I'm Glad I Waited," the only song from the show besides "Time on My Hands" that became a Youmans standard. Other highlights were Marilyn's "Crystal Lady" ballet in an oriental setting, Fred's "Say, Young Man of Manhattan" tap dance, and the Astaire duets, "Be Good to Me" and "If I Were You, Love."

According to first-nighter Walter Winchell, Marilyn stopped the show eighteen or nineteen times. "The greatest and most marvelous and grandest and stupendous and most beautiful and most thrilling and most colossal and most wonderful show that ever has been produced in the whole wide world," Winchell breathlessly raved in the next morning's *Daily Mirror*. Not mentioned, of course, was the fact that Winchell's employer, William Randolph Hearst, was one of the owners of the Ziegfeld Theatre.

The non-Hearst critics were not so impressed. All three stars were generously praised—Percy Hammond of the *Herald Tribune* said Marilyn was "gracious, unaffected, sprite-like and show-worthy"—but the libretto was blasted. Hammond called it "dreary," the *Telegram*'s Robert Garland "mechanical," the *Daily News*' Burns Mantle "dull," the *Evening Post*'s John Mason Brown "cumbersome," and the *New Yorker*'s Robert Benchley "dumb." Benchley probably summed the whole evening up best when he wrote, "Considered as the Golden Calf brought in on the Ark of the Covenant, it was a complete bust."

On the strength of Marilyn's and the Astaires' past successes, agencies and brokers had purchased enough tickets in advance of the opening to keep *Smiles* running for about eight weeks. But once the unfavorable press reviews appeared, box-office sales plummeted, and Ziegfeld made a last-ditch effort to turn *Smiles* into a hit by replacing some of the weaker musical numbers. When Vincent Youmans could not come up with any additional songs that pleased him, Ziegfeld purchased a few from Walter Donaldson, including "You're Driving Me Crazy," which didn't save *Smiles*, but went on to become one of the most popular songs of the decade.

Ziegfeld's dilemma was compounded by a weekly payroll of

$23,000 for the cast alone. In lieu of percentage deals, Marilyn was getting $5,000 a week and the Astaires $4,000 (a bargain at $2,000 each). Also receiving big salaries were leading man Paul Gregory, the featured comedians Eddie Foy, Jr., and Tom Howard, and the special guest artist, harmonica virtuoso Larry Adler, then all of sixteen years old. There were twenty supporting actors, plus a chorus of sixty-six showgirls, singers, and dancers (including a struggling ski-nosed newcomer named Leslie "Bob" Hope).

On December 1, Ziegfeld posted a notice backstage that *Smiles* would continue on a week-to-week basis. Marilyn, the Astaires, and the other principals accepted a 25 percent salary cut, which helped slightly, but Ziegfeld still had to seek outside financial help as well. Due to the economic depression and his own recent series of flops, the only backing he could get was from underworld characters like "Waxy" Gordon, "Dutch" Schultz, and "Legs" Diamond.

Marilyn may have put the stamp of fate on the whole sad business of *Smiles* when she became ill and missed a number of performances, with understudy Caryl Bergman taking her place. The official explanation from Ziegfeld's office on January 3, 1931, was that Marilyn merely had a cold and would return to *Smiles* the next day. But it was a full week before Marilyn came back. In the meantime, Broadway gossipmongers were equally divided as to whether she was recuperating from an abortion (none other than Ziegfeld himself was supposed to have impregnated her) or from a nervous breakdown.

The latter was nearest the truth. Being in a flop show can devastate a performer, especially if she's been accustomed to the kind of success Marilyn Miller had experienced. She felt a mixture of mortification and inadequacy. She wanted to forget it had ever happened. All the extra strain and tension made her migraine headache attacks even worse, and she went to an ear, nose, and throat specialist for relief. He performed a minor but delicate drainage operation on her sinuses that was supposed to make her less susceptible to such suffering in the future.

Marilyn's return to *Smiles* didn't improve the box-office revenues. In mid-January, Ziegfeld finally admitted defeat and closed down after the sixty-third performance. *Smiles* was the costliest failure of his career; he lost over $300,000 and again found himself close to bankruptcy.

Unlike Ziegfeld, Marilyn's embarrassment over *Smiles* was more psychological than financial. She still had a movie contract, plus scads of money in savings and investments, so she could afford to coast along awhile without a weekly paycheck. But the damage to her professional reputation was inestimable.

By an unfortunate coincidence, Marilyn's film of *Sunny* opened while *Smiles* was dying its slow death, and the movie also took a box-office nosedive. What made its failure harder to comprehend was that Marilyn and *Sunny* both received favorable reviews. Some critics preferred it to *Sally* and predicted an even bigger success.

But the movie public's apathy toward musicals had become so widespread that *Sunny* played to half-empty theaters when first released. By the time it reached the neighborhoods, it was sharing double bills with less prestigious but more exploitable First National films such as *Gorilla* and *The Truth About Youth*.

It was curious that during that period of economic depression both stage and movie audiences were turning away from musicals, which were designed to cheer the spirits and provide a pleasurable escape from reality. Perhaps musicals were too inconsequential and too costly, a luxury one could easily live without while money was scarce. Or maybe it was the content of musicals—the performers, stories, songs—that the public had tired of rather than the form itself.

Whatever the reasons, Marilyn Miller's professional world was crumbling around her. Whether she could survive the consequences, only time would tell.

CHAPTER FIFTEEN

THE NEW "IT" GIRL

"MARILYN CAME TO OUR apartment the day after the closing of *Smiles* and practically collapsed in tears," Fred Astaire said later. "It was a shattering disappointment for all of us. We were fond of Flo Ziegfeld and felt bad for him, as well as for ourselves."

The future looked dismal. Marilyn and the Astaires were exhausted, mentally as well as physically. Since they had no immediate commitments, they decided to travel to Europe together to revive their spirits. Marilyn had some catching up to do with Michael Farmer, as did Adele with Lord Charles Cavendish, who'd been courting her since they had met in London the previous year. "Minnie," as Adele called her worrywart brother, planned to go hunting in Scotland.

Before departure, there was a sense of relief when the Astaires signed a contract with producer Max Gordon to appear in a new revue in June called *The Band Wagon*. Marilyn also had an offer of sorts from Flo Ziegfeld for a new edition of the *Follies*, provided that he could raise the funding. Marilyn told him she'd think about it, but she wasn't keen on the idea. Returning to the *Follies* after a decade of stardom in her own vehicles seemed an open admission that her best days were behind her.

Marilyn and the Astaires sailed from New York on the *Bremen*. By the time they reached Southampton, where Fred disembarked to go to Edinburgh, the international grapevine was buzzing with talk about a shipboard romance. Marilyn and Fred Astaire were in love and engaged to be married, the Associated Press reported.

There may have been an initial bit of truth to the story; a mutual friend of theirs said later that Fred was smitten with Marilyn, but that he couldn't get to first base with her because she considered him too much of a fuddyduddy. But the gossip was chiefly a prank of Marilyn and Adele's, designed to rile Fred and to provoke a jealous reaction from Marilyn's fiancé, Michael Farmer.

The "news" reached Michael Farmer in Paris before Marilyn and Adele arrived. As Farmer circulated among his chums at Bricktop's that night, he was in an angry mood, claiming that he'd been double-crossed and swearing vengeance if Marilyn and Fred Astaire really had become engaged.

What followed resembled the plot of a screwball comedy. After checking into the Ritz Hotel with Adele Astaire, Marilyn deliberately avoided Farmer for two days. Finally, when someone tipped him off that Marilyn and Adele were having a nightcap in the Ritz bar, he rushed there by taxi from Bricktop's for a confrontation. According to Farmer, the women jumped up from their table when they saw him approaching, ran out of the hotel by a side entrance, and drove off in a taxi.

Farmer pursued them in another cab. In Montmartre, they caused such a commotion that spectators leaped into cars and taxis to follow the progress of what became a wild, all-night chase through the deserted streets of the city.

At dawn, Farmer returned to Bricktop's, bedraggled and alone. Marilyn and Adele somehow had managed to give him the slip. Toward evening, he learned that they'd left Paris for London by plane in spite of a snowstorm over the English Channel. Lacking their courage, Farmer took the boat train to London and eventually caught up with them in the bar of the Savoy Hotel. This time nobody ran. Marilyn and Farmer hugged and kissed and collapsed in each other's arms laughing.

A week later, Farmer was back at Bricktop's boasting to Cole Porter that his engagement to Marilyn was still very much on and that they'd made it binding with three days of nonstop lovemaking. It was the nearest thing to a honeymoon that Marilyn and Michael Farmer would ever have. That summer, he became involved with another glamorous American visitor to Paris named Gloria Swanson and married her.

Returning to New York in March 1931, Marilyn found the Broadway theater industry suffering terrible financial problems. The Shuberts were in receivership, more than half the theaters were shuttered, some never to reopen, and *Variety* reported as many as five thousand actors unemployed.

Flo Ziegfeld had nothing for Marilyn but the *Follies*, which was being funded by the tottering Erlanger Theatre Corporation as a last-ditch effort to save itself from bankruptcy. Ziegfeld spoke of turning it into a virtual three-ring circus complete with elephants, and Marilyn wisely turned it down. Despite a cast headed by Helen Morgan, Harry Richman, and Ruth Etting, it turned out a box-office disaster, marking a sad end to Ziegfeld's presentation of the *Follies* for all time.

Marilyn and Ziegfeld discussed other possible projects, including a revival of *Sally* and a new musical based on *When Knighthood Was in Flower*, in which Marilyn would portray Mary Tudor, already done on the stage by Julia Marlowe and in films by Marion Davies. But as Ziegfeld rambled on grandiosely, Marilyn realized that he was losing his grip on reality and living in the past. Without wanting to hurt him by saying it to his face, she doubted that they'd ever work together again, and she turned out to be right.

With Ziegfeld all but written off, and with no other stage producers contending to hire her, Marilyn headed west to Los Angeles for conferences with her remaining champion, Jack Warner. It took

five days to get there on two crack trains—the Twentieth Century
Limited to Chicago and the Santa Fe Super Chief the rest of the
way. But Marilyn wasn't in any rush and her deluxe compartment,
the gourmet food, and impeccable service kept her well insulated
from the drab sights of depression America that were passing outside the window. It also gave Marilyn an opportunity for a fling
with Maurice Chevalier, who by sheer coincidence happened to
be occupying the compartment right next door.

Marilyn's arrival in Hollywood started rumors that First National
had summoned her there to negotiate an end to her contract. With
movie musicals continuing to be box-office poison, the studios were
dropping high-salaried Broadway stars from their rosters even faster
than they had signed them up at the start of the talkie boom.
Consequently, more than a few eyebrows were raised when it
became known that effective May 1, 1931, Marilyn Miller would
start a new three-year contract with First National at $8,000 a week!

The potential value of Marilyn's new contract was more than a
million dollars. For the first year, she had a guarantee of forty
weeks of work for a maximum of three pictures. The second year,
her salary would be $10,000 a week, and the third year $11,000 a
week. Those figures placed Marilyn Miller among Hollywood's
highest-paid stars, who then included Greta Garbo, Constance
Bennett, Ann Harding, Kay Francis, John Gilbert, Norma Shearer,
William Powell, Ruth Chatterton, George Arliss, Will Rogers, Janet
Gaynor, Wallace Beery, and Ronald Colman.

Despite the box-office failure of *Sunny*, it would seem that First
National believed that Marilyn Miller still had a tremendous future
in movies. That was not the case, however. Darryl F. Zanuck, Jack
Warner's head of production, tried to talk him out of the deal, but
there was no arguing with Warner. It was among the first of a series
of disagreements that eventually caused Zanuck to quit Warner
Brothers–First National to form an independent company that
through a merger with Fox Films became known as 20th Century-
Fox.

What methods of persuasion Marilyn used on Jack Warner to

obtain such a lucrative contract can only be guessed at. But in addition to the obvious sexual ones, she more than likely made a strong appeal to his protective side, begging him to come to the rescue of her faltering career. Marilyn didn't need the money as much as she did the prestige and publicity that went with it. Her professional reputation was badly tarnished by the flops of *Smiles* and *Sunny*, but a million-dollar movie contract was proof that Marilyn Miller still had what it takes.

Jack Warner could go along with it because it made Marilyn dependent on him. Warner Brothers–First National was well protected by option clauses. There was no way that Marilyn could last six months, let alone three years, if Jack Warner became dissatisfied with the relationship for personal or business reasons.

Selecting Marilyn's first film under the new contract presented a problem. Given their current unpopularity, it would have been financial suicide to do another musical. Besides, there were only two of Marilyn's original Broadway vehicles left that hadn't been filmed: *Rosalie*, which Ziegfeld had sold to International Pictures, and *Smiles*, which was unthinkable under any conditions.

Marilyn thought she saw an opportunity for herself when Greta Garbo walked out of MGM in a contract dispute and it looked as if she'd have to be replaced in the upcoming *Grand Hotel*. Marilyn wanted Jack Warner to loan her to MGM. With her dancer's discipline and the role's similarity to experiences in her own life, she believed that she could play the disillusioned ballerina in *Grand Hotel* as well as anyone. Jack Warner, who had serious doubts about Marilyn being able to handle such a heavy dramatic part, was saved the embarrassment of having to propose it to MGM when Garbo decided to go back to work.

Darryl Zanuck finally found a vehicle for Marilyn in a German film entitled, in the English translation, *Her Majesty Love*. Since the advent of talkies, European-made pictures, so popular during the silent era, had virtually disappeared from American screens because of the language barrier, playing only a handful of theaters in the biggest cities in subtitled versions. The Hollywood studios soon realized that some of those neglected films could be a rich source of material if done over in English with American stars. What also made those European films worth considering was that they had been pretested, in the same way that a Broadway play was before Hollywood bought it. If they received favorable reviews and did good business in the American "art" theaters and in their country of origin, it was virtually guaranteed that some Hollywood studio would bid for the remake rights.

Zanuck was especially attracted to *Her Majesty Love* because it was a stage hit in Germany before being turned into a film, which seemed a double guarantee of success. Also, the film was splendidly directed by Joe May with a sophisticated touch reminiscent of Ernst Lubitsch, whose frothy *The Love Parade* and *The Smiling Lieutenant* were enjoying a great vogue all over the world at that time. Zanuck thought that the direction and camera work in the German *Her Majesty Love* couldn't be improved upon, which meant that First National could save on production costs by copying it almost scene by scene and shot by shot. For an obvious reason, Zanuck assigned William Dieterle, a new long-term contractee from Germany, to be the director.

Zanuck considered *Her Majesty Love* suitable for Marilyn Miller because it gave her a musical context without actually being a musical. Like the Lubitsch films, the stress was on comedy and romance, with a few songs and a modicum of dancing carefully integrated into the action.

In *Her Majesty Love*, Marilyn would portray Lia Toerrek, a barmaid in a Berlin nightclub who falls in love with a wealthy man-about-town. His snobbish family is appalled and forces him to sign an agreement to the effect that he'll be disinherited if he ever marries her. That doesn't prevent him, however, from taking as his wife the Baroness von Schwarzdorf, whom Lia becomes when she marries a titled roué, walking out on the latter before the union can be consummated.

The plot was reminiscent of *Sally* and *Sunny*, and Marilyn agreed to do it, provided that she was given a voice in the casting of the other principal roles. She saw an opportunity to work with some old friends, which she thought would help her give a better and more relaxed performance than in her previous films.

For leading man, Marilyn requested her former lover Ben Lyon, but not to rekindle an old flame (he was happily married to Bebe Daniels and they were expecting their first child). Marilyn knew that the chemistry would be right, and Lyon also was conveniently under contract to First National. Bald-headed comedian Leon Errol, whose nervous gestures and accordion legs had contributed so much hilarity to the original stage production of *Sally*, was assigned to portray the philandering Baron von Schwarzdorf.

Jack Warner blew his stack when Marilyn wanted W. C. Fields to play the part of her father. Except for one sound two-reeler based on one of his vaudeville routines, Fields hadn't made a movie since the silent *Fools for Luck* in 1928. Hollywood considered him washed up, not only because his pictures were unpopular, but also because of his alcoholism and his complete disregard for prepared scripts, which made him almost impossible to control.

But Marilyn, whose friendship with Fields dated back to the 1918 *Follies*, considered him one of the funniest men alive. She believed that silent movies did him an injustice, not being able to capture his raspy voice and ad-libbed wisecracks—the essence of his artistry. With much reluctance, Jack Warner finally gave in to Marilyn's badgering. Thanks to her, it was the beginning of the most successful phase of W. C. Fields's career.

The start of production of *Her Majesty Love* was postponed when Marilyn fell during a rehearsal, injuring her right knee. While she was recuperating—lying flat on her back in bed for three weeks— rumors started that she would never dance again. That proved untrue, but Marilyn's dance numbers in *Her Majesty Love* were reduced to just one, a tango with Ben Lyon, in which he was as much a crutch as a partner. Because she was still convalescing, Marilyn's movements throughout the film seemed rather clumsy and bizarre for one normally so graceful.

To make up for the time lost by Marilyn's accident, William

Dieterle directed *Her Majesty Love* with a speed and ferocity that left her a nervous wreck by the end of a working day. Not helping her mood was W. C. Fields, who kept goosing her off camera just before she had to go on. She would jump and spew obscenities at him.

In one scene, Fields infuriated Marilyn and Dieterle by improvising bits of business that weren't in the script. He smashed dishes against the wall and spilled the contents of salt and pepper shakers into Marilyn's hair. She stormed off the set, but later excused Fields for his behavior when this scene of a formal dinner party turned out to be the highlight of the film. Beginning with a simple request from a man at the other end of the table to pass an eclair, the action had Fields flipping pastries with impeccable accuracy onto a plate fifteen feet away, juggling china, and entertaining the snooty guests with details of his barbering business and daughter Marilyn's work as a barmaid.

For movie audiences, *Her Majesty Love* was to mark the birth of a *new* Marilyn Miller. Jack Warner believed that her earlier film publicity had been too dignified, too much in awe of her status as a first lady of the Broadway theater. The drab shop girls and bored housewives who bought most of the movie tickets weren't interested in that—they wanted glamor and fantasy, Warner told his publicists. Marilyn Miller would have to be transformed into a sex goddess in order to take her place next to Garbo, Dietrich, Shearer, Crawford, and the rest.

A tall order, but the First National publicity department tried its best, deciding that Marilyn Miller would be the new "it girl" of Hollywood. The designation wasn't original, but it had worked miracles for Clara Bow, whose silent stardom had been eclipsed by the advent of sound. Articles started appearing in fan magazines that described Marilyn Miller as an expert on love: "She knows the gain and the loss, the pain and the pleasure. She has had love to keep, or to toss away. She has loved and she has been loved," declared *Screen Secrets*.

Marilyn told a *Motion Picture* reporter, "I couldn't work, I wouldn't want to live, if I were not in love. That is how important it is to me. Why I would be nothing more than a mechanical doll, wound up and going through the motions. You *have* to love, you have to have someone to work for, someone to please, someone who cares, in order to make any of it worthwhile. Love is not only important. It is the only importance. It is life to me."

She added: "I could never lose my faith in men, in love, or in life. Because I might have unfortunate experiences proves nothing. The world is wide and an individual is no solution to any problem. As a matter of fact, I have had no unhappy experiences through men. Save death. Men have always been marvelous to me, treated me perfectly, been generous and sweet. I *love* love. It's all that really matters."

Gladys Hall wrote in *Photoplay*: "No American girl of our times has known the attentions that Marilyn Miller has known. When she is in Hollywood, New Yorkers are constantly phoning her. When she is in New York, Hollywood men burn up the wires. When she is abroad, the radiogram people wax wealthy. Cross country phone calls aren't cheap, but five dollars a word is a bargain on the other end of the wire. She is said to have more sex appeal in one of her gay little laughs than all the smoldering Negris and Garbos in the world. Men may bow at those startling altars, but they want to marry Marilyn."

Of course, Marilyn's romantic publicity never mentioned her affair with Jack Warner. Perhaps to placate Warner's feelings, publicists made sure that there was no mention made of any men except those in her past, such as Frank Carter, Jack Pickford, Ben Lyon, and Michael Farmer.

Whether Jack Warner knew it or not, Marilyn had fallen in love with a fledgling screenwriter, Charles Lederer, who was the nephew of her great friend Marion Davies. Marilyn kept running into Charlie at Marion's Santa Monica beach house or at the Hearst Castle at San Simeon, where she was a frequent weekend guest. A romance developed that sputtered on and off for a couple of years.

Charles Lederer was then twenty-five, eight years younger than Marilyn, although he looked older than his years because he was prematurely balding. He'd just finished collaborating on the screenplay of *The Front Page* and belonged to what was known as the "Algonquin Round Table West," comprised of Dorothy Parker, Ben Hecht, Charles MacArthur, Herman Mankiewicz, Robert Benchley, and other New York literary lions who'd succumbed to Hollywood contract offers.

Marilyn was attracted by Lederer's brilliant intellect, a quality rare in the men she'd been involved with, and by his refreshingly inverted sense of values; he sensed he could get a better perspective on the human condition from standing on his head than from reading philosophy books. Like his Aunt Marion and Marilyn herself, he had a prankish sense of humor and delighted in deflating pomposity of any kind.

Marilyn sometimes became the target of Lederer's mischief, but it only endeared him to her more. According to their mutual friend Ben Hecht, Marilyn once tried to convince Lederer that he was the only man in her life. Knowing better, Lederer told her that was so much "horse shit"—and to prove that he meant it, he had a truckload of fresh horse manure dumped outside the windows of Marilyn's apartment.

Ben Hecht also remembered a dinner scene between Marilyn and Lederer in an exclusive restaurant. Marilyn was reading the riot act to Lederer for something he'd done or not done. As she came to the end of her lecture, Lederer, who'd been listening to her seemingly spellbound, got up and handed Marilyn his trousers. He'd removed them surreptitiously while she was talking. "Here," Lederer said, "you wear these," and walked boldly out of the restaurant in his undershorts.

Hecht and most of their other friends considered the affair juvenile and inconsequential. But it was fun while it lasted, which was probably all that Marilyn and Lederer ever intended it should be.

A much more serious relationship was developing between Marilyn and a handsome hunk of movie actor named Don Alvarado, whom she had met through her friend Bebe Daniels. Alvarado had been Daniels's lover during a lull between Jack Pickford and Ben Lyon, which gave the two women a lot in common and made for a classic example of Hollywood bed swapping.

Two years younger than Marilyn, the wavy-haired, mustachioed Don Alvarado's real name was Joe Page. Formerly a dance instructor, he broke into films as a stand-in for Rudolph Valentino. After Valentino's sudden death on the operating table in 1926, Alvarado helped to fill the movies' incessant demand for Latin lovers, a demand filled by such as Ramon Novarro, Antonio Moreno, Rod LaRocque, Gilbert Roland, Ricardo Cortez, and Duncan Renaldo.

Don Alvarado starred or was featured in *The Bridge of San Luis Rey*, *Rio Rita*, *The Loves of Carmen*, and a dozen other films, playing opposite such leading ladies as Bebe Daniels, Constance Talmadge, Dolores Del Rio, Lily Damita, Fay Wray, Loretta Young, and Constance Bennett. His off-screen affairs with some of those women was the cause of his divorce from dancer Ann Boyar, by whom he had a daughter.

Marilyn became acquainted with Don Alvarado when they started double-dating with Bebe Daniels and Ben Lyon. Alvarado was a masterful ballroom dancer; he and Marilyn could knock the crowd dead when they stepped out on the floor together at the Cocoanut Grove or the Montmartre. Marilyn also soon discovered that Alvarado was a stallion in bed. His violent, almost brutal lovemaking was a rapturous new experience for her.

Their romance started slowly, but quickly seethed. Louella Parsons reported that Marilyn and Alvarado were "engaged," a Hollywood euphemism for sleeping together, but no date was set for a wedding. Alvarado shuddered at the mere mention of the word because he was burdened with heavy alimony and child-support payments from his first marriage.

And Marilyn was more concerned about her career than about

taking a third plunge into matrimony. Until she knew for certain whether she was going to become a full-time movie star or be commuting back and forth to Broadway, she intended to avoid any personal commitments that she might regret later. The answer would come sooner than she expected.

◆ CHAPTER SIXTEEN
_____

THE END OF AN ERA

ADVERTISED AS "THE GAYEST LAUGH SHOW ON EARTH," Marilyn Miller's *Her Majesty Love* became one of the saddest box-office failures of the year when released in December 1931. Two months later, her three-year, million-dollar First National contract was terminated, with Marilyn receiving $75,000 as a settlement.

It was a shattering blow to her ego and to her professional standing, not to mention her pocketbook. And there was nothing that she could do about it. Jack Warner was suddenly unavailable; he wouldn't even return her telephone calls.

Surprisingly, the cause of it all, *Her Majesty Love*, was not a bad movie. It received generally favorable reviews as light, pleasant entertainment. Some critics even called it Marilyn's best film work so far. What made the public stay away is uncertain. Perhaps they weren't conditioned properly, mistaking the film for another of the big song-and-dance extravaganzas that were still out of favor. Perhaps the film was too continental and sophisticated, too faithful to the German original. Hal Wallis, who was then a Warner–First National executive, attributed the failure to Marilyn herself. "The magic she had onstage, that indefinable charm that made up for her tiny voice and moderate acting talent, utterly vanished on camera," he said later.

Although Wallis may have been correct, there were also technical factors beyond Marilyn's control. Every studio had a particular visual style to its films and Warner–First National's was gritty and low-keyed. Had Marilyn been photographed and lighted in the soft, diffused glow of Paramount or the bright intensity of MGM, her impact on the screen might have been closer to what it was on the stage.

Another strike against her was that Marilyn Miller had been in the public spotlight for a very long time. Although she'd been making movies for only three years, she'd been known as a theater star for seventeen, since before World War I. She had to contend with the fact that the public was fickle in its loyalties and eventually became bored with familiar names and faces, especially when they were cast in overfamiliar roles. There were newer and younger stars coming along who had a fresher appeal and fascination for the movie public. She had among her rivals Joan Crawford, Marlene Dietrich, Barbara Stanwyck, Bette Davis, Joan Bennett, Katharine Hepburn, Carole Lombard, Claudette Colbert, Jeanette MacDonald, Ginger Rogers, Jean Harlow, Irene Dunne, and Jean Arthur.

Yet the death blow to *Her Majesty Love* and Marilyn Miller's movie career may have been nothing more than the Great Depression. In 1931, it finally caught up with the movie business, which was the last industry in the United States to suffer hard times. In the year that followed, ticket sales dropped even more precipitously, for a total loss of fifty million admissions a week in two years.

Her Majesty Love contributed to Warner Brothers–First National's loss of $12 million for the fiscal year ending in August 1932. Warner Brothers' common stock, which sold as high as $80 in 1930, would fall to 50¢ a share by that time. Needless to say, before that ever happened, economies had to be made and people let go if the company was to survive.

If *Her Majesty Love* had been pulling in crowds, Jack Warner might have been able to keep Marilyn under contract, but there was no way now that he could justify her tremendous salary to his brothers Harry and Albert, who ran the business end of the company. They ordered Jack to drop Marilyn Miller as quickly and as inexpensively as possible.

How does one go about dismissing a star employee who also happens to be your mistress? Certainly not gracefully, especially if one is reneging on a million-dollar promise to her at the same time. The negotiations must have been murderous for Marilyn to have accepted $75,000, which was less than 10 percent of the amount still outstanding on her contract. Yet in those depressed times, $75,000 bought a lot of apples. Marilyn probably decided it was far better than nothing, which was what she might have ended up with if she'd taken legal action. There was a good chance that there might not even be a Warner Brothers left to sue if the recent bankruptcies of Paramount and RKO Radio were any indication.

An interesting theory about all this was later put forth by Marion Davies, who believed that Marilyn would have received a much bigger settlement from Jack Warner if she hadn't been two-timing him with Don Alvarado. According to Davies, Warner didn't know he was sharing Marilyn with the other man until Alvarado's ex-wife, Ann, maliciously brought it to his attention. Whether Marion Davies guessed right or not, there was a surprising development several years later when Jack Warner divorced his wife of many years and married Ann Alvarado.

Once her contract was settled, Marilyn went back to New York. There was no reason to remain in Hollywood. Since all the studios were cutting back on production, she saw little chance of affiliating elsewhere, given her recent record of flops. As for her affair with Don Alvarado, it would continue, subject to the usual separations caused by two disparate careers.

Marilyn was again at a professional crossroads. It was apparent that her future rested in the theater rather than films, but she had no real control over her destiny. She wasn't a writer or a sparker of ideas. She had to weigh the offers that were made to her and try to select what she thought was most suitable. Fortunately, she had no immediate money problems, so she could still afford to be choosy.

Broadway was suffering worse financial problems than Hollywood, and it looked as if Marilyn might have a long wait. The banks were taking over the operation of theaters as their owners continued to default on mortgages. The 1931–32 season brought only 152 productions, of which 121 flopped and only 16 were hits. Musicals and revues, which cost more to put on and required higher admission prices, were the biggest disaster area. Producers lost $2 million on the season.

Flo Ziegfeld welcomed Marilyn back to New York by sending her to see his latest extravaganza, *Hot-Cha!*, which teamed Bert Lahr and the Mexican spitfire Lupe Velez in a nonsensical story about a bullfighter and a nightclub entertainer. Marilyn was appalled. The show was dreadful, and Lupe Velez, suffering from a hangover, made the evening worse by delaying the opening curtain half an hour. During intermission, Marilyn went backstage to lecture Lupe about professional behavior, only to find the star's dressing room locked. The stage manager told Marilyn that Lupe's sister was giving her an enema to sober her up.

When Marilyn telephoned Ziegfeld the next day to report the incident, he didn't sound bothered. All he wanted to know was whether they could get together to discuss a new show. Marilyn thought he was balmy, but just to humor him she agreed to come to his office at the Ziegfeld Theatre. When she arrived, Ziegfeld had already departed for the day. His secertary, Goldie Clough, said he had scooted out by the rear fire escape to avoid creditors and process servers who were waiting for him in front of the theater.

Goldie started to cry as she told Marilyn of Ziegfeld's struggles to remain in business and of his increasingly bizarre behavior. Letters were left unopened and unanswered for months. Clocks and watches were barred from the office because they reminded him of death. Now sixty-three years old, Ziegfeld was taking rainbow-colored hormone pills that he hoped would restore his virility. To test their effectiveness, he was covorting with chorus girls right there in his office, and on weekends, he took whole squads of them home for orgies while Billie Burke was in Hollywood making a movie.

Marilyn shed no tears over the revelations, but they were sad confirmation that she'd never work for Ziegfeld again. When they finally did manage to meet, she was shocked by his drawn appearance and faltering voice. He had little to offer Marilyn but promises. He was closing *Hot-Cha!* after a disastrous run and trying to raise money for a revival of *Show Boat* with most of the original cast. He asked if Marilyn would be interested in making a guest appearance on the weekly radio show that he was going to be hosting for Chrysler Motors. She said she'd think about it.

With financing from the underworld-connected realty tycoon A. C. Blumenthal, Ziegfeld did manage to get *Show Boat* back on Broadway for a short run, but it was the last thing he ever did. Early that summer, he was stricken with pleurisy, and Billie Burke took him to California to recuperate. Ziegfeld rallied briefly, had a relapse, and died in Cedars of Lebanon Hospital in Los Angeles on July 22, 1932.

Marilyn learned of Ziegfeld's death from a reporter for the *Daily News*, who telephoned her for a eulogistic statement to be included in the obituary. She was too shaken by the news to say anything, and she refused all subsequent calls from the press.

She also declined an invitation from radio station WOR to appear with other Ziegfeld stars on a memorial program that was broadcast nationally on July 24. Listening to it in her hotel suite, she broke down crying when Paul Robeson sang "Ol' Man River."

Marilyn wept even harder when she read a letter written by her friend and former *Follies* colleague Will Rogers, which was published in that day's *New York Times*:

> Our world of "make believe" is sad. Scores of comedians are
> not funny, hundreds of "America's most beautiful girls" are not

gay. Our benefactor has passed away.

He picked us from all walks of life. He led us into what little fame we achieved. He remained our friend regardless of our usefulness to him as an entertainer. He brought beauty into the entertainment world. The profession of acting must be necessary, for it exists in every race, and every language, and to have been the master entertainment provider of your generation, surely a life's work was accomplished.

And he left something on earth that hundreds of us will treasure till our curtain falls, and that was a "badge," a badge of which we were proud: "I worked for Ziegfeld."

So goodbye, Flo, save a spot for me, for you will put on a show up there some day that will knock their eye out.

Marilyn did not attend Ziegfeld's funeral. Neither did the majority of his friends and coworkers, because it was held in Hollywood rather than New York. Everyone deplored Billie Burke's decision to bury Ziegfeld at Forest Lawn Memorial Park, a continent away from his beloved Broadway. The epitaph selected by the widow for his memorial was a verse from Shakespeare's narrative poem "Venus and Adonis":

> For him being dead, with him is
> Beauty slain;
> And Beauty dead, black chaos
> Comes again.

Whether or not Marilyn Miller noticed any significance in that for her own life, it pretty well summed up the career dilemma that she was facing at that time. Flo Ziegfeld's death marked the end of a theatrical era of which Marilyn Miller was an integral part. Could she survive in a world without Ziegfeld, one in which her kind of gaudy, banal musical seemed not only an anachronism but too risky a business proposition? The trend was toward revues such as *The Band Wagon*, dramatic musicals such as *Show Boat*, and satires on the order of *Of Thee I Sing*, which in 1931 was the first musical comedy to win a Pulitzer Prize.

Marilyn appeared to miss the significance of those developments, holding out for another star vehicle along the lines of *Sally* and *Sunny*. Clifton Webb wanted her to join him in *Flying Colors*, third in a series of sophisticated revues with music by Howard Dietz and Arthur Schwartz, but she wasn't interested. Neither could Cole Porter tempt her with *The Gay Divorce*, which was to be Fred Astaire's first solo show since his sister had given up her career to marry Lord Charles Cavendish. Even less appealing to Marilyn was Earl Carroll's invitation to be in his next edition of the *Vanities*, where the star turns were little more than time fillers between production numbers featuring nearly naked show girls. She also turned down an offer of $8,000 a week to head the stage show at the six thousand-seat Roxy movie cathedral. At four performances a day, it seemed too much hard work and confirmation that her theatrical career was over.

As 1932 drew to a close, Marilyn had been off the Broadway stage for two years and absent from movie screens for almost a year. Her public visibility was limited to a busy social life. She went to all the theatrical first nights and movie premieres and frequented the night spots, particularly the Cotton Club, Texas Guinan's, and Palais Royal. She never lacked handsome young escorts, many with names in the Social Register.

It was an easy, carefree existence. Despite her professional inactivity, Marilyn Miller was still considered a very big star. She could coast along on that popularity indefinitely. She lived in considerable luxury at the Sherry Netherland Hotel, then under the same management as the Waldorf-Astoria. Her secretary, Belle Harris, came in during the day to take care of the mail, arrange appointments, and look after business matters. Marilyn's maid, Carrie Wallace, not only coddled her and cooked for her, but also made many of her clothes. Carrie could see a dress in a magazine

or a designer's salon and copy it for Marilyn at a fraction of the
cost. Carrie's husband, Sam, was Marilyn's chauffeur, taking her
around town in a black Rolls Royce that had a separate driver's
compartment with a convertible roof.

For all her wealth, Marilyn believed in sharing it. She was known
as one of the softest touches in show business. During those depression years especially, people she'd worked with who were down
on their luck were always contacting her for money, and she never
disappointed them. Once while she was out shopping, an
ex-Ziegfeld dancer came up to her with a tale of woe. Marilyn was
so moved that she took off her $3,000 mink coat and gave it to the
girl.

Marilyn's main romantic interest was still Don Alvarado.
Hollywood suddenly had a surplus of Latin lovers, which enabled
him to spend more time in New York with Marilyn. Some of her
friends thought that he was her paid gigolo. At the very least,
Alvarado was getting free room and board while he was staying
with her at the Sherry Netherland.

They had a very intense and passionate relationship. Marilyn
seemed to enjoy being roughed up by Don Alvarado, who had a
fiery temper. Marilyn's maid used to put a special makeup,
Leichner's Formula #2 and #5, over the black and blue bruises
so that they wouldn't show when she went out in public. He once
hurled a diamond-and-ruby bracelet, a gift from Flo Ziegfeld, into
the toilet and flushed it. Luckily, the bracelet got caught in the
drain pipe, and a plumber managed to retrieve it.

Gossip had it that Marilyn and Alvarado were headed for the
altar. Clifton Webb jested that the only reason the couple hadn't
been married yet was that Marilyn could never wake up early
enough to get to the license bureau before it closed. Not that she
was lazy. But her sinus headaches were most severe during the
morning hours and tended to wear off by late afternoon. Besides,
she'd usually been out all night partying.

In December, Marilyn and Alvarado unintentionally made headlines through a misadventure that started when they attended a bon-voyage party for movie director Allan Dwan on the *Bremen*. The liner sailed while Marilyn, Alvarado, and five other guests were still on board. Nobody panicked because on similar occasions in the past they were able to disembark with the ship's pilot at Sandy Hook. What they didn't know was that the pilots' union had recently taken a vote to end the practice. When the *Bremen* reached Sandy Hook, Marilyn and the others were told that their next stop would be Cherbourg, France.

The group was classified as stowaways until arrangements could be made for their billeting. Marilyn and Alvardo were carrying only $10 between them, so she sent a radiogram for funds to her friend and former mother-in-law, Carrie Carter, in New York. "On board the Bremen without clothing" began the message that startled Mrs. Carter at breakfast the next morning. Eventually the mess was straightened out and everybody obtained cabins.

Marilyn tried to make the best of the situation. When the *Bremen* docked at Cherbourg, she decided that she'd go to Paris to visit Jack Pickford, who was seriously ill in the American Hospital there. For several months, her former husband had been communicating with her through friends, begging her to come to his bedside. Convinced that he was dying, he wanted to see her one more time.

Marilyn didn't feel up to it. Told that Jack looked like a shriveled old man, she preferred to remember him as the handsome devil that he had been. But now that she was in such close proximity, she really had no excuse. Unfortunately, she was without her passport. The French authorities refused to admit her into the country without one. The more she cursed and pleaded with them, the more adamant they became. She stayed on board.

By the time the *Bremen* reached Southampton, Marilyn's nerves had gotten the best of her. She was feeling too ill to return to New York by the next ship. Acting on the advice of the *Bremen*'s doctor, British immigration gave her special permission to debark for no more than a week, to rest and seek medical treatment. Claiming to be her fiancé, Don Alvarado was allowed to accompany her to London, where they stayed at the Ritz Hotel until sailing for home on the *Europa*.

When they arrived in New York five days later, the couple had been away for almost three weeks. When a dockside reporter asked her about her future plans, Marilyn said, "My dear, how can one tell what one is going to do tomorrow?"

Jack Pickford died in Paris on January 3, at the age of thirty-six, an ominous start for the year 1933. It was in the same hospital where his first wife, Olive Thomas, had died under mysterious circumstances in 1920. The cause of his death was ambiguous. The official medical explanation was "multiple neuritis, which finally affected the brain center," but friends believed it was the result of his almost lifelong addiction to drugs and alcohol, plus syphilis in its tertiary stage.

Marilyn had loved Jack and she mourned him deeply, but not without remembering Flo Ziegfeld as well. Rivals for Marilyn's affections and, for the most part, bitter enemies, they'd died within six months of each other. Who could say which of them had triumphed in the end? Ziegfeld had a much longer life and his achievements would become a major chapter in theatrical history, but Marilyn believed that he'd never really been happy in his personal relationships. Jack Pickford's career was insignificant, but he had had fun and packed a lot of living into his thirty-six years. He died, Marilyn was told, with a contented smile on his face.

As the weeks and months passed, Marilyn became even more aware of her own mortality. Before too long, she would turn thirty-five, and the prospect terrified her. A glance in the mirror told her that she still was a beautiful woman, but she could no longer pass for an ingenue. If she was ever going to revive her career, it would have to be soon.

But the outlook continued to look grim. Even though the new president in the White House was promising a return to prosperity, it seemed a long way off. Business at the Broadway legitimate theaters was so sluggish that, for the first time in history, every show running, including the so-called "hits," was selling tickets at cut-rate prices.

In April, Marilyn was disheartened by an invitation to attend the rededication of the Ziegfeld Theatre as Loew's Ziegfeld, a second-run movie house. Marilyn considered it a desecration of the Ziegfeld tradition and refused to participate in the ceremonies, castigating Eddie Cantor, Jimmy Durante, and other former Ziegfeldians who did. She couldn't help remembering a telegram that Will Rogers had sent to Ziegfeld on the opening night of the showplace in 1927: "Hope you never hang a movie screen in your theater."

A few weeks later, Marilyn heard that the New Amsterdam Theatre was being foreclosed by the Dry Dock Savings Bank and faced a fate similar to the Ziegfeld's. Before that happened, she decided to make a pilgrimage to the theater that had housed her biggest successes.

Since it was late afternoon when she arrived, only the stage doorman was on duty. Marilyn hadn't worked at the New Amsterdam in five years and they were strangers to each other. She had to slip him a $10 bill before he would let her wander backstage.

Entering her old dressing room, Marilyn sat there recalling an opening night, when it had been overflowing with flowers and gifts from admirers. Then she walked out on the empty stage. A solitary janitor's lamp threw off the only light. She moved down front and looked out on the empty auditorium, imagining for a few seconds that every seat was occupied by the enthusiastic, well-dressed patrons of the Ziegfeld days.

Marilyn danced a few little steps and stopped, realizing that she was fantasizing opening-night triumphs that might never happen again. She slumped down and sobbed, then took hold of herself, ran out of the New Amsterdam, told her chauffeur to take her home, and cried for the rest of the night.

CHAPTER SEVENTEEN

THOUSANDS CHEER AGAIN

MARILYN MILLER RETURNED TO the Broadway stage in September 1933, thanks to an admirer who, as a teenage theater fanatic, had often sneaked into the New Amsterdam's second balcony to watch her in *Sally*. Her benefactor was Moss Hart, by then a promising twenty-eight-year-old playwright collaborating with Irving Berlin on a revue called *As Thousands Cheer*.

On a warm evening in June, Marilyn found herself seated next to Moss Hart at a dinner party given by her bicoastal beau, Charlie Lederer. Although Marilyn was unaware of it, Hart and Irving Berlin had been considering her for their show, but had finally ruled her out. "We thought the parade had passed for Marilyn," Moss Hart said later. "We wanted someone refreshing, vibrant, youthful."

But Hart suddenly had to revise his opinion. "Marilyn was beautiful. I could not remember when she was more beautiful," he continued. "All the thrill of the days when I saw this lovely dream girl on the stage came back to me. I think I had been very much in love with her, and very much in awe, too. She was so gay that night. She seemed the most alive person in the place. She talked about many things. Her eyes danced and I fell in love with her all over again. I thought maybe I should wire Irving Berlin, who was in Bermuda at the time. Perhaps we were making a mistake in not considering her."

Marilyn happened to tell Hart about her recent backstage visit to the New Amsterdam. He was deeply moved: "I knew what she was getting at. This was the great Marilyn Miller and she was through. Still in her early thirties, beautiful, wealthy—and she was through. The magic of her name lingered, but as far as the theater was concerned, Marilyn Miller was a has-been."

Moss Hart didn't wait to cable Irving Berlin. He phoned him long distance and said, "Irving, maybe I'm wrong, but Marilyn Miller is our lady." Berlin thought a moment and replied, "Maybe you're right."

Marilyn's joining *As Thousands Cheer* wasn't as straightforward as Moss Hart made it sound. She had second thoughts and needed a lot of persuading before she finally signed the contract.

As Thousands Cheer was to be a witty satire on current events and famous people, hardly the typical Marilyn Miller show. She was afraid that the public as well as the critics might not accept her in that context. She also questioned her right to take on an assignment for which she felt unqualified. If it hadn't been for her friend Clifton Webb, who'd already accepted one of the starring spots, she probably wouldn't have done it. Webb had a number of hit revues to his credit, including *The Little Show* and *Three's a Crowd*, and promised to help Marilyn get ready. Well aware that she was a wonderful clown and mimic, he kept telling her that she was underestimating her talent.

Marilyn had some ego readjusting to do as well. Not only was she accustomed to playing title roles, but in every one of her shows since 1920 with the exception of *Smiles*, she had received 10 percent of the weekly gross against a hefty guarantee. The most that Irving Berlin would offer her was top billing over the other stars and a flat $2,500 a week.

With no alternate proposals on the horizon, Marilyn capitulated, telling Irving Berlin that he was an even better businessman than he was a composer. Berlin himself was getting 40 percent of the gross, 20 as composer and 20 as coproducer and coauthor. He also was an equal partner with Sam H. Harris in the ownership of the Music Box Theatre, which was to house the show.

Berlin and Harris had lined up an impressive cast for *As Thousands Cheer*. In addition to Clifton Webb, Marilyn's other costar would be Helen Broderick (mother of future movie actor Broderick Crawford), the caustic-tongued comedienne who was considered in a class with Fannie Brice and Beatrice Lillie. Given featured billing below the title, but with her name in type the same size as the stars, was singer Ethel Waters. Forced to contend with the racial prejudices of the time, the producers weren't quite sure how much prominence they could give Waters without losing some of their potential audience. It was still the biggest opportunity yet given a black woman in a predominantly white Broadway production.

Appearing with such a talented group, Marilyn knew that she would have to work harder than in many years. Worse, she had to lose about ten pounds if she were going to get back into top physical condition. Rehearsing and dieting during that sizzling late summer of 1933 was an ordeal that brought Marilyn to the verge of a nervous breakdown. On August 12 and again on September 15, she spent several days in Doctors Hospital, recovering from what her personal physician, Frank Berner, described as "overwork."

But whatever suffering Marilyn had to go through was worth it, she admitted later. When *As Thousands Cheer* opened at the Music Box on September 30, the audience did just that, cheering her to the rafters. When Moss Hart went back to her dressing room to offer congratulations, Marilyn hugged him and started to cry, but this time they were tears of happiness.

Marilyn would have been the first to concede that *As Thousands Cheer* was by no means a solo triumph. Clifton Webb, Helen Broderick, and Ethel Waters, Irving Berlin's music, Moss Hart's sketches, Hassard Short's staging, Charles Weidman's choreography, and Irene Sharaff's costume designs all contributed to making what many critics hailed as the best Broadway revue they had ever seen. The great modern dancer José Limón, who appeared in the show, probably summed it up best when he said, "There had never been a revue as slick, as classy, as chic, as tuneful, as literate, as handsome, as sophisticated, as expensive, and as successful. From now on there was nowhere else to go except down, or perhaps in a new direction."

As Thousands Cheer was meant to be topical. All the sketches, songs, and dances were presented as if they were items in the latest edition of a newspaper. A trick lighting effect similar to the one used on the Times Tower in Times Square flashed headlines across the stage in banner form to introduce each number. Not all of them were humorous. Audiences gasped when "UNKNOWN NEGRO LYNCHED BY FRENZIED MOB" brought on Ethel Waters as a newly widowed southern mother singing "Supper Time."

That dirgelike number never failed to stop the show, causing some friction between Waters, Marilyn, and Clifton Webb. Not that the last two were jealous, but they had to follow "Supper Time" with a flippant dance number, "Our Wedding Day." Finding it hard to be cute and amusing right after Waters's grim, overwhelming plaint, they wanted "Supper Time" cut or moved to another part of the show. But Irving Berlin and Sam Harris decided it would remain as it was.

Consequently, Marilyn and Webb got into a friendly duel with Ethel Waters almost nightly over who could stop the show the longest. Waters had a slight edge, because Irving Berlin had also given her "Heat Wave" to perform. But Marilyn and Webb usually came out the winners with the revue's big "take home" song, the one that the audience was whistling and humming when leaving the theater. It was called "Easter Parade," exquisitely staged and costumed in various shades of brown to resemble a living version of the rotogravure section of a Sunday newspaper.

Marilyn used to refer to "Easter Parade" as her "Broadway Rose" number after Irving Berlin told her how he came to write it. While sitting in Lindy's Restaurant one day, he spotted through the window an eccentric, bedraggled character known as "Broadway Rose." She was wearing a grotesque hat burdened down with frayed artificial roses, carrots, a fern or two, and some dangling shoelaces. Berlin said to himself, "You're in your Easter bonnet, hey girl?"

Feeling an idea coming on, Berlin went home, wrote some lyrics and matched them to the tune of a 1917 discard of his called "Smile and Show Your Dimple." After Marilyn and Webb introduced it in *As Thousands Cheer*, "Easter Parade" became Berlin's biggest-selling hit until "White Christmas" came along nine years later.

A new Marilyn Miller emerged from *As Thousands Cheer*. Still dancing and singing as winningly as ever, she was, as Clifton Webb said, "now out of the pink-and-white baby-faced class." Her comic gifts, almost dormant since her *Passing Show* and *Follies* days, came to the forefront. She and Clifton Webb portrayed two of the most famous couples of the day: Joan Crawford and Douglas Fairbanks, Jr., squabbling over the publicity rights to their divorce; and Barbara Hutton and Prince Mdivani, debating their future together in the Irving Berlin song "How's Chances?"

In "The Funnies," Marilyn was a long-haired tot dressed in Alice in Wonderland fashion, cavorting with Sunday comics characters like the Katzenjammer Kids, Mickey Mouse, Jiggs and Maggie, Popeye, Skippy, and the Toonerville Trolley folk. In "Noted Playwright Returns to England," Marilyn, Webb, and others played cabin staff on the *Normandie*. Having just finished five days of catering to the whims of Noel Coward, they all start to behave like characters from his plays.

The revue was awash with other celebrity roles, including Clifton Webb as Mahatma Gandhi and John D. Rockefeller (receiving Rockefeller Center for a ninety-fourth birthday present); Helen Broderick as Mrs. Herbert Hoover and Aimee Semple McPherson; and Ethel Waters as Josephine Baker, singing "Harlem on My Mind."

Overnight, *As Thousands Cheer* became the hottest ticket in New York. To no one's surprise, it had one of the longest runs in the history of revues, chalking up four hundred performances and playing to absolute capacity for most of that time, a remarkable achievement for that economically depressed period of 1933–34. After nineteen years as a Broadway star, Marilyn Miller's future never looked brighter.

Delighted though she was with her newfound success, Marilyn would have enjoyed it more if she had someone to share it with. For the moment, there was no special man in her life. Don Alvarado was gone, back in Hollywood, where he soon found a new mistress to batter. When *As Thousands Cheer* came along, Marilyn's private life took a decidedly second place as she went into training. Not until after the opening did she begin to feel pangs of loneliness.

Helping to fill the void was Jimmy Donahue, the twenty-year-old millionaire playboy whose cherubic face reminded Marilyn of the children in the Campbell's Soup ads. One of the heirs to the Woolworth fortune, he was first cousin of Barbara Hutton, whom Marilyn just happened to be impersonating in *As Thousands Cheer*. But her friendship with Donahue predated that, starting around the time he was kicked out of prep school at fifteen and became one of the youngest fixtures of New York café society.

Because Jimmy Donahue was homosexual, his relationship with Marilyn was strictly platonic, but she found him amusing company, a big spender, and an excellent dancer. When they went out night-clubbing, they never failed to attract attention with their hot rumbas and fancy adagios.

Another bond between Marilyn and Donahue was a mutual interest in the men and "boys" of the chorus. It was Donahue who first called Marilyn's attention to Chester and Mortimer O'Brien, twenty-four-year-old fraternal twins who were dancing in the chorus of *As Thousands Cheer*. Donahue had been following the twins' careers with interest since seeing them in *Fine and Dandy* and *Face the Music*, but he couldn't get anywhere with them sexually. He wished Marilyn better luck.

She was strongly attracted to Chet O'Brien, the more outgoing and better looking of the pair. Chet was also one of the assistant stage managers, which gave Marilyn an excuse to get to know him without starting unnecessary gossip among the rest of the company. She was concerned by the fact that she was more than ten years older than Chet. According to the social conventions of the time, it was bad enough that she was a star and he just a member of the chorus. The substantial age difference would make her seem even more of a sex-driven monster.

A romance developed when Marilyn began to request Chet as her partner during practice sessions. Claiming that he was the best dancer in the show, she wouldn't settle for anyone else. "Chet used to confide in me and tell me of his aspirations to be a star," Marilyn said later. "I found myself liking him an awful lot. He told me he'd admired and wanted to meet me years before he ever started working on the stage. I'm not quite sure how it happened, but before I knew it, I had fallen in love."

They started going out together after the show, not every night, because Marilyn was usually exhausted after a performance, but a couple of times a week. There were plenty of parties and nightclub openings to choose from, but any gathering held by Jules Glaenzer of Cartier's headed Marilyn's list of priorities. The guest list was a Who's Who of the entertainment world, business, and high society.

The repeal of Prohibition at the close of 1933 brought an end to speakeasies. They were replaced by grandiose nightclubs featuring lavish floor shows and "name" bands, and Marilyn had a hard time deciding whether Chet should take her to the Casino de Paree, the Manhattan Casino, the Palais Royal, the Hollywood, the Central Park Casino, or the Paradise, not to mention the Cotton Club in Harlem or the brand new Rainbow Room on the sixty-fifth floor of the RCA Building in Rockefeller Center. Unless she was a guest of the management or making it a threesome with Jimmy Donahue, Marilyn always had the bills sent to her home. She didn't expect Chet to pay, nor did she want to embarrass him by settling up in front of him.

* * *

But not everything went well for Marilyn. After *As Thousands Cheer* had been running several months, her sinusitis flared up, bringing with it migraine headaches and spells of nausea and vomiting. Marilyn missed several performances, returned for a time, and then had a relapse which kept her out of the show for two weeks in February 1934. Although she wasn't docked for those absences, Marilyn endorsed her paychecks over to her understudy, Peggy Cornell, to whom she felt they rightly belonged.

By the spring, Marilyn was still feeling ill and wondering how much longer she could continue in *As Thousands Cheer*. Her doctor advised her to stop working and take a long rest, but Chet O'Brien talked her out of it. He said that Marilyn should keep on for as long as she could, that she was integral to the success of the revue, and that she would be blamed for putting 150 people out of work in hard times if it closed as a result of her departure. Veteran trouper that she was, Marilyn saw a point in the "show must go on" adage and agreed to stay.

Two incidents changed her mind. One night as she was whirling into the wings at the end of a dance number, she tripped and crashed into wispy Clifton Webb, nearly knocking him over. Webb called Marilyn a "fat cow," she fired back an obscenity or two, and a bitter argument was under way between the two longtime friends. Chet O'Brien went to Marilyn's defense and, in front of the small crowd that had gathered, berated Webb for being a homosexual and patronizing "rough trade."

Not surprisingly, Clifton Webb complained to Sam Harris, demanding that Chet O'Brien be fired. Marilyn told Sam Harris that if Chet went, she went too. Everybody stayed.

A few weeks later, trouble of another sort developed when Marilyn's rich friend Jimmy Donahue decided to play a joke on her that could only be accomplished with the help of Chet O'Brien in his capacity as an assistant stage manager. While Marilyn was impersonating his cousin Barbara Hutton, Donahue thought it would be a riot if he surprised her by walking on in the middle of the skit.

Donahue created a stir, but not in the way he intended. When he minced on stage in a princely uniform, Marilyn broke up laughing, but the audience was not amused and a few people started to boo. Donahue hastily retreated to the wings, where the house manager and a security guard were waiting to escort him to the exit as soon as he changed out of costume.

Chet O'Brien's job was once again in jeopardy, and this time the case against him was much more serious than in the Clifton Webb incident. A performance had been disrupted and patrons irritated. Furthermore, it was suspected that Chet had accepted money from Donahue, although he vehemently denied it.

Marilyn made no threats of quitting in order to prevent Chet from being fired. Although she refused to believe that he'd taken a bribe, she knew that he was wrong in permitting Donahue to go onstage. She would not make a fool of herself by pretending otherwise and going to her lover's defense.

Instead, Marilyn decided that she would not renew her forty-week contract, which was due to expire in July. Sam Harris did not try to dissuade her; he thought it was a wise decision because of her health. Dorothy Stone, the multitalented daughter of theater grand mogul Fred Stone, was signed as Marilyn's replacement.

By the time Marilyn left, *As Thousands Cheer* had played 320 performances, 31 of which she had missed because of illness. The revue ran for another ten weeks at the Music Box and then went on an extensive road tour of more than a year.

Marilyn's departure from *As Thousands Cheer* came exactly twenty years from the time she first achieved theatrical stardom in *The Passing Show of 1914*. And in two more months, when she turned thirty-six, it would be thirty-one years since she had started working professionally. She wondered whether these were signals to quit while she was at a high point. She knew it would be extremely difficult to land another assignment as good as the last one, even if her health permitted her to go on working.

Financially, she had no worries. She could afford to take it easy for a while in the company of her handsome young lover. Renting a house in a secluded section of Great Neck, Long Island, Marilyn settled down with Chet for a long summer's idyll that by fall would turn into something more permanent.

CHAPTER EIGHTEEN

THE STAR AND THE CHORUS BOY

"MARILYN MILLER MARRIES CHORUS BOY" read the headline in hundreds of newspapers across the United States on October 4, 1934, three days after the event actually happened. The patrician *New York Herald-Tribune* couldn't resist telling its blue-blooded readership that the groom was not listed in *Who's Who in the Theater*.

Hoping to avoid just such backbiting from the press, the couple tried to keep the wedding secret, Obviously they failed; in fact, their attempts at concealment were so mismanaged that Marilyn and Chet must have been drunk on more than just love at the time. In filling out the application for the license, Marilyn gave Memphis, Tennessee, as her birthplace and said that her permanent residence was the Beverly Wilshire Hotel in Los Angeles.

Marilyn did seem to know what she was doing, however, when she claimed to be thirty instead of thirty-six. It made her appear to be only five years older than Chet O'Brien, rather than eleven. But her vital statistics were well known, and news accounts were quick to point out the lie, which in the end caused her more embarrassment than the truth would have.

The wedding was held in the town of Harrison in Westchester

County, not far from the New York City line. As might be expected of a late riser like Marilyn Miller, it did not take place until nearly midnight. Two hours before that, a chauffeur-driven Rolls Royce carrying Marilyn, Chet O'Brien, and Marilyn's niece, Lois Montgomery, pulled up in front of the town clerk's office, which, of course, had long closed for the day. A watchman told them that if it was an emergency they could find the clerk, William Wilding by name, at a barn dance that was being held upstairs above Ford's Garage, home of the Harrison Volunteer Fire Department.

Dressed up as a country bumpkin in overalls, a faded waistcoat, and fake whiskers, Clerk Wilding could not be persuaded to leave the festivities when Marilyn sent her chauffeur to tell him that she wanted to obtain a marriage license. She and her companions had no choice but to go to the dance themselves to plead their case. Stopped at the door, they each had to buy a ticket for 50¢ before they were allowed entrance.

Wilding finally capitulated. Still wearing his party costume, he went back to his office and issued Marilyn and Chet a license. Although her niece had come along to serve as a witness, the couple still needed someone to perform the ceremony. It was discovered that the justice of the peace had already retired for the night, but the prospect of officiating for Marilyn Miller dragged him out of bed. He considered it such an honor that he offered to donate his $10 fee to one of the local churches. Marilyn had no preference, but Chet O'Brien did and the money went to the Roman Catholic St. Gregory's.

Marilyn's decision to marry for the third time was dictated as much by social convention as by feelings. In that more prudish time, couples were not supposed to live together unless they were married to each other. They might try it temporarily, as Marilyn and Chet had that summer, but they couldn't go on indefinitely without causing a scandal and irreparably damaging their reputations. Marilyn's was already badly tarnished. There were many in the press who disapproved of her past record of broken engagements, in which she trysted openly with such "fiancés" as Ben

Lyon, Michael Farmer, and Don Alvarado, but never got around to marrying them.

But although Marilyn's marriage to Chet O'Brien may have satisfied one rule of public morality, it violated others and she was never allowed to forget it. She had taken a husband who was not only much younger than herself, but who also ranked very far below her professionally. The press, which claimed to be the voice of the people, could only interpret that in one way: Marilyn Miller was a fading star who had to buy love, and Chet O'Brien was a conniving chorus boy who was only using her to advance himself. As long as they remained married, Marilyn and Chet were stuck with this stigma, accurate or not.

For a few months, the newlyweds dropped out of the public spotlight. Weary of living in hotels, Marilyn leased a floor-through apartment in a town house at 46 East Sixty-fifth Street and hired decorator Thorval Anderson to completely redo it. Also tired of the same old Rolls Royce that she'd been driving around in for years, she allowed Chet to talk her into selling it and buying a $9,600 customized Cadillac limousine. Equipped with a sixteen-cylinder engine, it was bigger than any car on the streets of New York at that time.

In December, after reading too many innuendos about her marriage in the gossip columns, Marilyn decided to fight back by proving to the world that her husband was immensely talented and not a fortune hunter. Chet O'Brien had been asked to stage the dances for a new intimate revue called *Fools Rush In*, but the young producer, Leonard Sillman, was short of the necessary funds.

Impressed by Sillman's recent success with *New Faces of 1934*, Marilyn arranged a meeting with him to offer financial assistance. Thinking not only of her husband, she told Sillman that if just a few careers were helped or started by the show, it would be well worth her investment. Borrowing Sillman's fountain pen, she made out a check for $25,000 and handed it to him.

Marilyn also considered the investment in *Fools Rush In* as a first step toward becoming a producer—packaging shows and probably appearing in some of them as well if her health permitted her to continue performing. With the great stage impresarios of the past dying off—that summer, Charles Dillingham had been the latest to pass away—Marilyn realized that she, and the theater in general, were rapidly running out of magicians. New ones were needed. And why not Marilyn Miller? If George M. Cohan and Fred Stone could do it, so could she, even though very few women had tried up to then.

The rehearsals for *Fools Rush In* were "a notch above the annual graduation exercises at the booby hatch," Leonard Sillman said later. William A. Brady, the elderly and hard-drinking impresario who was the other principal backer, detested Marilyn Miller, and the feeling seemed mutual. They sat at opposite sides of the theater offering advice to Sillman and shouting insults at each other. According to Sillman, Marilyn was chugging beer from a gallon jug and Brady's lips seemed permanently attached to a quart bottle of rye. The two backers agreed on only one thing, firing one of the leading actors, who kept turning up late and inebriated.

Fools Rush In opened on Christmas night, 1934, at the Playhouse Theatre. To bring Leonard Sillman luck, Marilyn lent him a multidiamond horseshoe pin to wear, which had been Dillingham's gift to her on the opening night of *Sunny*. Sillman lost it, or at least said that he did. Marilyn suspected that he hocked it to pay some of his bills after he read the terrible reviews.

As Walter Winchell put it, "Fools rushed out even faster than they rushed in." Broadway didn't get much of a chance to appreciate the talents of choreographer Chet O'Brien or of the cast, which included Imogene Coca, Richard Whorf, and Leonard Sillman himself. The revue ran only fourteen performances. In a futile, last-minute effort to keep it running, Marilyn's millionaire chum Jimmy Donahue placed additional display ads in all the newspapers, charging them to the F. W. Woolworth account. But business was so bad that Leonard Sillman couldn't meet his closing week payroll. Marilyn, who didn't want a group of starving actors and workers on her conscience, wrote Sillman another check for $8,000 and decided that she wouldn't become a producer after all. The $33,000 she had spent wasn't going to break her, but it was still a very painful and expensive lesson.

After the last performance, Marilyn insisted on taking Chet O'Brien and Leonard Sillman out on the town. "We'll show those sons of bitches how to take failure," she said. Before they entered the "21" Club, she took Chet by one arm and Sillman by the other. "Chin up and a big smile!" she told them.

"That was precisely how we invaded those sacred portals on the black night of our despair," Sillman later remembered. "After '21' we went to the Stork Club, then to El Morocco. All night long Marilyn insisted we laugh and carry on as if we'd just had the biggest hit since 'The Student Prince.' It was such an uncommon thing to do, such a courageous thing. But then Marilyn Miller was no common, or cowardly, creature. She was beautiful offstage and onstage and inside and out."

The theater was slowly recovering from the depression, and 1935 would be its best year since the 1929 crash. Marilyn received a number of offers for new shows, but rejected them all. Earl Carroll wanted her for his *Sketch Book* revue, George White for his latest *Scandals*. Her old mentors the Shuberts asked her to consider joining Beatrice Lillie and Ethel Waters in the Howard Dietz–Arthur Schwartz revue *At Home Abroad*. But too much strenuous dancing was involved and Marilyn let the assignment go to the up-and-coming Eleanor Powell, who went on to major stardom in movies as a result of it. Billy Rose, who fancied himself the new Flo Ziegfeld, hankered after Marilyn for a circusy Rodgers and Hart musical spectacle called *Jumbo* at the vast five thousand-seat Hippodrome. But she wasn't keen on the idea of playing third fiddle to Jimmy Durante and a live elephant.

In the spring of 1935, Marilyn's hopes for reviving her career turned toward Hollywood. Metro-Goldwyn-Mayer had announced plans for an extravaganza based on the life of Florenz Ziegfeld. Not unnaturally, Marilyn thought that she should be in it. She was still sensitive about her experience at Warner Brothers–First National; but after a moratorium of several years, the studios had started grinding out musicals again. The Ziegfeld film seemed the perfect way to prove that Marilyn Miller could be a movie star after all.

Marilyn left New York for Los Angeles in May. Although it was now possible to travel coast to coast in a twelve-passenger DC-1 airliner in about thirty hours, she stuck to the train because flying aggravated her sinus condition. When she left Grand Central Station on the Twentieth Century Limited, it was without Chet O'Brien. He had started out ahead of her, driving the ostentatious Cadillac limousine that Marilyn would need to get around Hollywood. Lest it be assumed that her young husband had become her lackey, she intended to hire a chauffeur locally for the duration of her stay.

The Ziegfeld film was the brainchild of his longtime writing associate William Anthony McGuire. He first sold the idea to cost-conscious Universal Pictures, but when the estimated budget started to exceed $1 million, Universal got cold feet and allowed him to take the project to spendthrift MGM.

Since Marilyn had worked with McGuire on most of her Ziegfeld shows, he was the first person she contacted when she arrived in California. McGuire was friendly, but not very encouraging. If it was up to him, he said, Marilyn Miller would be one of the main characters in the picture, but Ziegfeld's widow, Billie Burke, had script approval. Knowing how much she disliked Marilyn, McGuire doubted that Burke would stand for her receiving much prominence.

McGuire turned out to be correct. MGM had trouble enough convincing Burke that the film should cover Ziegfeld's first marriage to Anna Held. Any references to personal problems involving Ziegfeld and Marilyn were forbidden. But Burke had no objections to Marilyn Miller being represented in recreations of one or two of her old Ziegfeld musical numbers. Whether Marilyn wanted to appear as herself or have another actress portray her should be her decision. Burke had selected Myrna Loy for her own part, with William Powell as Ziegfeld and Luise Rainer as Anna Held.

Marilyn sought advice from another Ziegfeld colleague, Fannie Brice, who'd already agreed to play herself in a supporting role. Marilyn said that she wouldn't appear in anything but a star part, but Brice told her she was *mishuga*. Having gone through a similar disappointment in the early days of talkies, Brice reminded Marilyn that neither of them was getting any younger. Whatever Hollywood offered them, they should grab. Brice was receiving $50,000 for *The Great Ziegfeld* and thought that Marilyn should be able to command the same. That wasn't bad recompense for what shouldn't amount to more than two weeks work.

Marilyn had no agent, preferring to do her own bargaining. When she opened negotiations with Hunt Stromberg, the producer of *The Great Ziegfeld*, he was more receptive than she expected. What she didn't know was that Stromberg was having trouble lining up authentic Ziegfeld stars. Eddie Cantor and Will Rogers had already turned him down, although they'd consented to actors impersonating them. Without too much haggling, Marilyn was able to get a promise of the $50,000 she was demanding.

She overplayed her hand, however, when it came to discussing billing. Marilyn Miller had to be listed as one of the stars, with her name equal in size to the biggest in the cast. Stromberg refused, claiming it would give a false impression of her contribution to the film, which he envisioned as not much more than a glorified walk-on. He explained to her that William Powell, Myrna Loy, and Luise Rainer were to be the only stars. She would have to settle for featured billing along with Fannie Brice and other Ziegfeld alumni who were appearing as themselves, including Leon Errol, Ann Pennington, Gilda Gray, and Harriet Hoctor.

Marilyn told Stromberg to take his $50,000 and "shove it." She said that she'd earned more money for Ziegfeld than any star who ever worked for him. If she wasn't going to get the credit and attention that she thought she deserved, MGM would have to do without her. Stromberg pleaded with Marilyn to reconsider, but she was adamant. The deal was off.

Two days later, Hunt Stromberg telephoned Marilyn and offered her $10,000 if she'd permit another actress to portray her. Before hanging up on him, Marilyn threatened to sue MGM for $1 million if they so much as mentioned her name in the film or in any of the publicity and advertising.

Marilyn's trip to Hollywood did have one positive outcome. Marion Davies told her about a wonderful new Beverly Hills ear, nose and throat specialist who might be able to help her sinus problem. Marilyn promptly made an appointment to see him. The results of the examination were distressing, yet encouraging.

As the doctor rather bluntly explained it, Marilyn had chronic sinusitis and there was no permanent cure for it. Because of inadequate treatment in the past, irreversible damage had occurred in the tissues lining the sinus and also in the underlying bone. Removal of those structures was obviously impossible, but surgery could be performed to improve the drainage of mucus that was causing much of her discomfort. If she had the operation and kept up a regular program of maintenance afterward, the doctor thought that Marilyn would not only feel better than she had in years, but also be far less likely to suffer prolonged attacks that would prevent her from working.

Not bothering to seek a second opinion, Marilyn checked into a hospital in Los Angeles as soon as arrangements could be made. The operation would cost $3,000, which seemed an exorbitant sum for medical treatment in 1935, but the penalty of being a celebrity. She thought it would be worth every penny if it alleviated her condition.

Performed under a general anesthetic, the surgery took several hours. Since it was all internal, there was no disfigurement except a swollen face, which subsided after a week in the hospital. Upon her release, Chet O'Brien took Marilyn to Lake Arrowhead to recuperate at the Arrowhead Springs Hotel, an exclusive resort controlled by a consortium of movie stars and studio executives.

The operation appeared to be a success. Marilyn was feeling well and raring to go when she returned to Los Angeles. While Chet O'Brien drove the Cadillac back to New York, she decided to stay another week to catch up with old friends.

One night, she received a telephone call from Carole Lombard to join an informal gathering at her house on Hollywood Boulevard. She had no idea Lombard was counting on her to entertain. The guests were mainly nonperformers, including Lombard's lover, screenwriter Robert Riskin; director Walter Lang and his wife, "Fieldsie," who was Lombard's secretary and best friend; Alice Terry, the retired silent film star; and gossip columnist Lloyd Pantages, whose family connection to the Pantages theater circuit made him one of the few journalists permitted an inside view of Hollywood private life.

"As soon as Marilyn stepped in the door, she became the life of the party," Lloyd Pantages said later. "Though she apologized for being out of practice, she put on a real show all her own for the sake of the rest of us. We pushed back the rugs and the furniture. With a Victrola providing the music, Marilyn danced and sang, doing numbers from her shows and demonstrating the differences between the new-fangled steps and the old-fashioned. She went from ballet to the black bottom. I don't believe any type of dancing was overlooked. She was having enormous fun and so were we.

"After a time, of course, she became tired," Pantages continued. "For hours afterward we all sat around and chatted. Marilyn was unhappy about not being in *The Great Ziegfeld*. Although she didn't come right out and say it, I think she was humiliated by her overall failure in movies. Things like that really mattered to people who had grown up in show business, especially to a grand trouper like Marilyn Miller. For her, I fear, life was starting to lose its zest, but you'd never know it from looking at her. She glowed even in the dark."

* * *

In August, Marilyn and her husband went to stay at the Balsams Hotel in the White Mountains of New Hampshire to escape the torrid New York City weather, although she was there more to work than to play. Marilyn was determined to start a new show before the end of the year, and she had plenty of exercising and practicing to do first to get back into shape. The fifteen thousand-acre resort had all the facilities and healthy outdoor environment that she required.

While Marilyn and Chet were playing golf one day, a caddy brought them the tragic news that Will Rogers had been killed in a plane crash at Point Barrow, Alaska, along with the famous aviator Wiley Post. Marilyn was horrified, and collapsed in tears when she heard the report confirmed on the radio. Of all the people she had known in show business, Marilyn regarded Will Rogers as the gentlest, the wittiest, and the most benevolent. His death at fifty-five was the bitterest affirmation yet that the golden days were over.

By autumn, Marilyn was more optimistic and determined to revive her career. For the first time ever, she signed with an agent, Louis Shurr, considered one of the shrewdest in the business. Another of his clients, Bob Hope, was itching to do a show with Marilyn. She was eager if they could find the right script; she admired the former chorus boy for having survived the flop of *Smiles*. Three years later, Hope had achieved stardom in Jerome Kern's hit musical *Roberta*.

Marilyn was also looking for a vehicle that she could do with Ray Bolger, whom she considered the best dancer to come along since the late Jack Donahue. Bolger had, in fact, gone to Hollywood to portray a character patterned after Donahue in *The Great Ziegfeld*, so any collaboration with Marilyn would have to wait until the film was completed.

In the meantime, Louis Shurr was dickering with producers about teaming Marilyn with the comedians William Gaxton and Victor Moore, who had worked together so memorably in *Of Thee*

222 • The Other Marilyn

I Sing and *Anything Goes*. Making the final decision difficult was the demand for composers, which by far exceeded the supply. There was a long waiting line for the likes of Kern, Porter, Gershwin, Berlin, and Youmans, who were now dividing their energies between the stage and movies.

In October, Mr. and Mrs. Chester O'Brien celebrated their first wedding anniversary, a thumb in the nose to the gossipmongers who had predicted that the marriage of star and chorus boy wouldn't last more than six months. Looking for a new angle to exploit, they wondered if the couple might be getting ready to start a family.

Since Marilyn had turned thirty-seven the previous month, it seemed unlikely that she intended to make her next production a baby instead of a Broadway show. But she may have been pregnant briefly. Chet O'Brien later claimed that she was, but that she had a miscarriage in the early stages.

Behind her back, Marilyn's friends referred to Chet O'Brien as her "kept man" rather than as her husband. He was lover, companion, nurse, errand boy, and training coach all combined in one. Coming from a poor shanty Irish background, he was a stranger to Marilyn's world of wealth and luxury. She taught him table manners and social etiquette, developed his poise, and showed him how to dress. In the process, she spent a small fortune on him.

It was later revealed that during her marriage to Chet O'Brien, she had written him checks totaling $56,329 to cover his personal expenses. Marilyn also spent $88,567 to keep the two of them housed, fed, and entertained. Their combined living expenditures averaged out to about $2,000 a week, which in depression 1935, was twice what a third of American families earned in an entire year.

Maintaining such extravagance was impossible. As 1935 drew to a close, Marilyn hadn't worked for eighteen months. With no money coming in, except from a trust fund she'd set up for herself, unpaid bills were starting to accumulate. Whenever her secretary, Belle Harris, tried to discuss the matter, Marilyn would tell her not to worry. She was still a big star capable of earning a lot of money. A new show was bound to come along soon.

For a time it looked as if one had arrived. A chance to appear with Ray Bolger materialized when producer Dwight Deere Wiman offered Marilyn one of the leading roles in a musical comedy called *On Your Toes*, with a score by Richard Rodgers and Lorenz Hart, who were also collaborating on the book with director George Abbott.

The role of a temperamental Russian ballerina would give Marilyn a further chance to display the comic talents that had won her so much acclaim in *As Thousands Cheer*, but she had doubts about the dancing requirements. Her last demanding ballet work had been in *Smiles*. After an interval of almost six years and at age thirty-seven, she knew it would be foolhardy to believe that she could get herself back into condition for such a strenuous assignment, let alone carry it out eight times a week. She reluctantly declined the part, which finally went to Tamara Geva.

It was a crushing disappointment for Marilyn, and undoubtedly contributed to her failing health. The symptoms were the same as before her sinus operation of the previous spring: headaches, nausea, lack of energy. When Chet took her out nightclubbing, a few sips of champagne could make her sick. Several times, she threw up at the table, though usually she managed to get to the ladies' room first. She would tip the matron $20 to help her clean up and look presentable again.

Although columnist Walter Winchell saw Marilyn become ill one night at the Stork Club, he was too fond of her to write about it. On a previous evening, Marilyn had dispatched Chet O'Brien to Winchell's table to pass him $50 in cash to give to a destitute show girl mentioned anonymously in that day's column. Later, Marilyn sent over a note: "Please don't say where it came from." Winchell never told Marilyn that the girl she was helping had once been in the chorus of *Smiles*.

Nightclubs were off-limits to Marilyn as her health gradually deteriorated. So were the dance practice sessions she'd been having almost daily with Chet O'Brien. There came a time when he asked Marilyn to perform a simple "truck" step, which should have been automatic for her, and she had great difficulty.

Looking for a quick remedy, Marilyn consulted one of the currently fashionable "miracle" doctors, W. Lawrence Whittemore, who prescribed a series of insulin treatments. Although insulin then as now was used mainly for diabetes, some doctors believed it had properties that helped alleviate emotional distress. Dr. Whittemore thought that Marilyn's main problem was a bad case of nerves over her career and that she needed building up.

Beginning on January 22, 1936, a nurse came to Marilyn's apartment every evening after dinner, injected her with insulin, and remained by her bedside until the next morning. The injections tended to cause disorientation, restlessness, and brief coma, and Marilyn required constant observation until they wore off.

The nurse, Helen Roff, later gave an opinion of Marilyn's condition and the benefits of the treatment: "When I was first called in, she seemed like a very sick, weak, discouraged person. She did not improve. She appeared to be getting weaker."

Roff also said that Chet O'Brien didn't seem to understand the seriousness of his wife's illness. "He didn't pay much attention to it. I never saw him in her bedroom. Sometimes I saw him having dinner with her when I arrived. He slept elsewhere. My best recollection is that he flitted in and out of the apartment."

Early in March, Marilyn's sisters, Ruth Sweeney and Claire Montgomery, came to visit from out of town. On March 12, Marilyn was taken to Doctors Hospital, where she was registered under the name of Mrs. Chester O'Brien to avoid publicity. But the press found out anyway and Dr. Whittemore was forced to make an announcement about her condition. He said that Marilyn was suffering from overwork and needed a complete rest, a ludicrous diagnosis, but probably the only explanation he could give under the circumstances. He was certainly not going to admit that he had made a colossal blunder by treating Marilyn with insulin, thereby putting her life in jeopardy.

When she entered the hospital, Marilyn was alert and able to receive visitors. She took a turn for the worse on March 20, going into a coma. Eleven days later, she was still unconscious. Dr. Whittemore announced that she had developed a "toxic condition" with fever running as high as 107 degrees.

On April 1, Marilyn was reported "much improved" and by April 6 "almost out of danger." During that night, her temperature soared to 108 degrees. At 9:27 A.M., on April 7, 1936, she died. Chet O'Brien and her sister Claire were at her bedside. Several minutes before death, Marilyn opened her eyes. A nurse told reporters later, "She said not a word. She smiled, a rich, deep comfortable smile, and then closed her eyes and passed away."

Before the day was over, the statue of Marilyn Miller that overlooked Broadway from the facade of the I. Miller Building was draped in black.

♦ CHAPTER NINETEEN

NO SILVER LINING

IN AN EDITORIAL HEADLINED "REGRETS FROM ALL," the *New York World-Telegram* said:

> Now that Marilyn Miller is dead, at the untimely age of thirty-seven, anyone who ever saw her must feel a poignant, personal loss.
>
> Hers was the superlative gift of beauty. Thousands of other pretty girls are available to the casting directors of Broadway shows. But few have the quality, as she did, of projecting her loveliness across the footlights, of delighting her audiences with the sense of her sweetness, innocence and good humor.
>
> Temperament certainly was in her makeup, too. Florenz Ziegfeld and other managers occasionally were scorched by her fire, although she and Ziegfeld were reconciled and she went back again to his management. But there was never a flurry between her and the public, which responded like a child to her beauty.
>
> In her short life, she had all that Broadway stardom can give, and no other musical star outshone her. We hope it made her happy, for she certainly gave great pleasure to many others.

What killed Marilyn Miller five months before she was due to celebrate her thirty-eighth birthday? The official explanation given by Dr. Whittemore was that she died from hyperpyrexia (abnormally high fever), due to a toxic condition following a long history of sinus infection and osteomyelitis of the jaw.

No autopsy was conducted, nor was it required by law. Since Marilyn's face would have to be cut open and put back together again, Chet O'Brien and her sisters saw no purpose to it and decided that she should go to her final rest with her beauty unimpaired.

But the New York City Board of Health death certificate filled out by a house physician at Doctors Hospital was at variance with Dr. Whittemore's explanation. The house doctor said that he was unable to state definitely the cause of death, but that the diagnosis of Marilyn's illness was acute cerebral edema (swelling of the brain) and acute toxic psychosis, with chronic sinusitis as a contributory or secondary factor.

In layman's terms, the most accurate interpretation was probably given by Marilyn's sister Claire Montgomery, who said that Marilyn died as the result of incompetent medical treatment. The doctor who performed the sinus operation on Marilyn the previous year had cut too closely to the membranes that surround the brain, leaving it very vulnerable to infection. When an infection did develop, Dr. Whittemore's insulin injections only succeeded in making her condition worse.

In Marilyn's final days, a brain specialist, Dr. Foster Kennedy, was called in, but the infection had already spread too far for him to operate. In this era before antibiotics, nothing could be done.

When a famous star dies young, nobody believes the cause is really medical. The press had a field day with stories of Marilyn Miller dying of a broken heart, of Marilyn's burning herself out through overwork and fast living, and of her being unable to cope with the fact that she was fast approaching forty.

The broken heart theory stemmed from Marilyn's disappointment at being denied satisfactory parts in the movie *The Great*

Ziegfeld and the play *On Your Toes*, both of which, ironically, opened to great success on Broadway within a week of her death. Although Marilyn had warned MGM not to mention her name in conjunction with *The Great Ziegfeld*, her death provided the premiere with this publicity anyway. Critics couldn't avoid mentioning the coincidence of the two events, nor the fact that two fictional characters in the film—a Ziegfeld protégée called Mary Lou and a star named Sally Manners—seemed to be patterned after the real and stage Marilyn Miller.

If a broken heart did contribute to Marilyn's death, it was unlikely that her distress over *The Great Ziegfeld* and *On Your Toes* was the main cause. Some of her close friends believed that she simply lost the will to carry on. Hollywood had passed her by and Broadway seemed about to. Her marriage was a farce and her health was failing. Any one of those factors was enough to break a woman's heart; the combination was certainly lethal.

There was a widely circulated rumor that Marilyn wanted to die before she was forty. The theatrical columnist Arthur Pollock supplied a possible explanation: "Perhaps it was because she had in her acting always a certain childlike charm and youthfulness and thought that as an actress she would be nothing at all when she grew old enough to lose those qualities. Maybe she was right.

"Marilyn Miller was always a dainty, graceful little thing, pretty as a picture, charming because of her grace and pictorial quality," Pollock said. "She guessed wisely perhaps that after forty all would be gone. And then what would there be left?"

Marilyn must have had some inkling that she was dying. While she was still conscious in the hospital, she told Chet O'Brien: "Make sure that I'm treated like Barbara Hutton." A $5,000 silvered copper casket, and a lavish funeral that might have been produced by Ziegfeld himself assured that she was.

More than three thousand people, many of them show business celebrities, crowded into St. Bartholomew's Protestant Episcopal Church on Park Avenue to attend the services. Outside, another five thousand persons so crowded the surrounding area between Fiftieth and Fifty-first streets that a hundred policemen were required to keep traffic lanes open. The previous day, twenty-five thousand people had trooped in single file past her coffin while it lay open in the chapel. Although Marilyn Miller hadn't appeared on the stage for two years or the screen for five, the huge turnout demonstrated the undiminished affection the public held for her.

A dozen enormous floral pieces, including a gigantic star of pink roses sent by ex-sister-in-law Mary Pickford, adorned her casket. Banks of smaller bouquets filled the wide spaces surrounding the altar. Ten cars were required to transport all the flowers to the cemetery afterward.

Barbara Hutton's cousin Jimmy Donahue offered to donate $1,000 to St. Bartholomew's if the organist would play a medley of songs identified with Marilyn Miller, such as "Look for the Silver Lining," "Who?," and "Easter Parade." But the rector, George Paull Sargent, considered it in poor taste and said no. The processional was Handel's Largo. During the half-hour-long service, a mixed choir of sixty voices sang "Abide with Me," "I Heard a Voice," and "Hark! Hark! My Soul."

Marilyn was buried at Woodlawn Cemetery, in the templelike, white marble mausoleum that she had built for her first husband, Frank Carter. She had survived him by sixteen years. Now they were reunited; and in accordance with Marilyn's wishes, the crypt was sealed forever.

The full tragedy of Marilyn Miller's last years did not become apparent until her will was filed for probate on April 17, 1936. The principal beneficiary was her mother, Ada Miller, who was to receive $150 weekly for the rest of her life from a trust fund. Marilyn also bequeathed $25,000 outright to her father, Edwin D. Reynolds, and $15,000 to her close friend and first mother-in-law, Carrie Carter. The residuary estate was to be shared by Marilyn's two sisters and her niece, Lois Montgomery.

An unusual clause in the will expressed the wish that Marilyn's despised stepfather, Caro Miller, should not benefit from any of the monies that her mother received. The couple had remarried in 1930, and neither attended Marilyn's funeral.

Since no mention was made of Marilyn's surviving husband, newspaper accounts said that Chet O'Brien had been "cut out" of her will. That was not exactly true, because the document was executed in 1931, two years before Marilyn even met O'Brien; but since she had never bothered to amend the will after becoming involved with him, perhaps it amounted to the same thing. To no one's surprise, Chet O'Brien soon filed suit in New York Supreme Court for half of Marilyn's estate, which he claimed was his dower right by law.

Meanwhile, Marilyn's attorneys started to settle her affairs to determine how much the estate was worth. Her household furnishings, including a specially built bed upholstered in rose-pink silk, were auctioned off at Silo's on Vanderbilt Avenue, realizing only several hundred dollars. Her Cadillac limousine was sold for an equally paltry amount. Marilyn's liquid assets ultimately totaled a mere $40,000. However, there were debts (unpaid bills and funeral expenses) that amounted to $50,000, so her will was something of a mockery; the substantial bequests to Edwin Reynolds and Carrie Carter could not be paid. But there was still the matter of a $78,000 trust fund that Marilyn had set up for herself in 1935. She had been receiving weekly payments from the income and principal. By the time she died, there was only $60,000 left in the trust, and this now became the estate's principal asset. Chet O'Brien demanded half of it, much to the oppositon of Marilyn's sisters and her mother.

For years afterward, Marilyn Miller's name kept popping up in the news as Chet O'Brien and her family battled over the trust fund in New York Surrogate Court. Marilyn's sisters contended that O'Brien abandoned her when he learned that she was dying, and that during the marriage he "neglected at all times to support her, thereby under law forfeiting all rights to her money." Judge

Bernard Sheintag finally exonerated O'Brien of those charges, ruling that the evidence against him did not merit consideration under the laws pertaining to support, since "the wife neither expected or demanded it."

In 1939, the Surrogate Court ruled that Marilyn's mother should be preferred above all other legatees, as specified in the will, but that Chet O'Brien was entitled to share in the residue under the decedent estate law. Then the Internal Revenue Service became involved, claiming that Marilyn Miller had underpaid her income tax for 1930 and 1931.

It wasn't until 1941 that the dispute was finally settled. By that time, only $16,982 remained to be divided up among O'Brien and Marilyn's relatives.

A funny thing happened in Hollywood in 1942. Marilyn Miller suddenly became a "hot property" at Warner Brothers, the very studio that had fired her ten years earlier.

Staff producer Jerry Wald had a sudden brainstorm that a musical based on Marilyn Miller's life would be a natural follow-up to the company's current blockbuster about George M. Cohan, *Yankee Doodle Dandy*. Already in development at Warner Brothers were musical biographies of two other great Broadway figures, George Gershwin and Cole Porter, so why not a third? The similarities in background and time span would mean a big saving in production costs. Many of the same sets and costumes could be used, with audiences none the wiser because the three films would be released months or even years apart.

Jack Warner, still very much in charge of production, wasn't euthusiastic about glorifying one of his former mistresses, but since Jerry Wald had recently done well with *The Man Who Came to Dinner*, he was given a chance to develop his idea. Warner cautioned him to steer clear of Marilyn's movie career. Something that neither he nor the studio were proud of, it was better left buried and forgotten.

Jerry Wald assigned the project to Bert Kalmar and Harry Ruby. A highly successful songwriting team, they had also spent much of their lives in vaudeville and the theater, which made them experts on the subject. Even more important, they'd known Marilyn Miller personally, as had Harry Ruby's wife, Eileen Percy, once a star for Charles Dillingham.

But Kalmar and Ruby were humorists at heart, having worked extensively for the Marx Brothers and written such songs as "Show Me a Rose and I'll Show You a Girl Named Sam" and "I Wanna Be Loved By You, Boop-Boop-a-Doop." Confronted with the tragic aspects of Marilyn Miller's personal life, they realized it was not the kind of story to warm the hearts and cheer the spirits of World War II audiences. Using some of the musical numbers from Marilyn's shows as a base, they concocted a rags-to-riches story that was almost pure fiction except for her bittersweet romance with Frank Carter. Her young husband's death in a car crash was sure to strike a responsive chord among a public that was losing loved ones every day in combat.

The project was shelved, however, for lack of a leading lady. Jack Warner wanted an established star, but his own studio had none under contract who suited the role. He could hardly ask Bette Davis, Ida Lupino, Olivia de Havilland, or even Ann Sheridan to play Marilyn Miller. Jerry Wald wanted to borrow Betty Grable from 20th Century-Fox, but Jack Warner wouldn't even make the attempt. It meant dealing with Darryl Zanuck, with whom he'd had too many quarrels in the past, including a few over Marilyn Miller herself.

Seven years later, in 1949, *The Marilyn Miller Story* again became viable when Warner Brothers signed June Haver to a four-picture contract. Since Haver was developed by 20th Century-Fox as a successor to Betty Grable, Jack Warner saw good reason to start her off with a property once considered for Grable. Kalmar and Ruby's treatment (Kalmar had died by that time) was turned over to the husband-and-wife writing team of Henry and Phoebe

Ephron. The end result was a screenplay titled after the song most closely identified with Marilyn Miller, "Look for the Silver Lining."

The other main roles were Frank Carter, portrayed by Gordon MacRae, and Marilyn's great dance partner, Jack Donahue, played by Ray Bolger. To avoid a hassle with MGM, which had staked a claim on the name Ziegfeld with two other films after *The Great Ziegfeld*, the most influential person in Marilyn Miller's life wasn't depicted or even mentioned. Neither were husbands two and three, Jack Pickford and Chet O'Brien, who were replaced by a fictional secondary character named Henry Doran, a millionaire who helps her to forget her grief over Frank Carter. Caro Miller, played by Charles Ruggles, became lovable "Pop" Miller, fobbed off as Marilyn's actual father.

Although a reviewer later said that *Look for the Silver Lining* deserved an Oscar for the most inaccurate movie biography ever made, Jack Warner was delighted with Henry and Phoebe Ephron's script. He predicted it would be Warner Brothers' best musical since *Night and Day*, the Cole Porter story with Cary Grant, which was heavily criticized for its factual distortions, but was a box-office smash nonetheless.

But there was one thing in *Look for the Silver Lining* that Jack Warner strongly objected to—the ending. "Marilyn Miller cannot die!" he insisted.

The Ephrons argued that was the whole point of the film—a great star dying at the height of her career. It was the one fact of Marilyn Miller's life that couldn't be altered. She had been dead for thirteen years.

But Jack Warner was adamant and the ending had to be changed. Instead of a deathbed scene, Marilyn Miller got one more big musical number. After a doctor tells her that she's a very sick woman and doesn't have long to live, she courageously goes out on stage in a revival of *Sally* and performs a rousing version of Kern's "Wild Rose."

Watching from the wings is Ray Bolger as Jack Donahue (who

in reality died six years before Marilyn). While her singing and dancing continues to fill the screen, he says in a voiceover: "Marilyn Miller will go on forever."

As long as there are Marilyns, maybe she will.

ACKNOWLEDGMENTS

I am extremely grateful to the people who contributed information and a frame of reference for this book. Listed alphabetically, they include: Peggy Cornell Benline, Irving Caesar, Agnes DeMille, Doris Eaton, Charles Eaton, Joe Eaton, Ruth Gordon, Elinora Hayes, Selena Wallace Joiner, John Kenley, Maurice Lapue, Lorraine Sobel Lee, James Morcom, Chester O'Brien, Eleanor Dana O'Connell, Margaret Sauer, the late Hans Spialek, Blanche Sweet, Rose Marie Mariella Vulcano, Jerome Zerbe, the late Ruth Taylor Zuckerman.

Much of my research was done at the Billy Rose Theater Collection of the Performing Arts Library at Lincoln Center, New York, which has a superb collection of Marilyn Miller material, including many of her own family scrapbooks and photo albums. I thank curator Dorothy Swerdlove and her knowledgeable staff for their cooperation.

Thanks also go to the following for their splendid assistance: Camille Dee, Theater Collection, Museum of the City of New York; Judith Hanefeldt, Evansville-Vanderburgh County Public Library, Evansville, Indiana; and Barbara Flanary, Memphis-Shelby County Public Library, Memphis, Tennessee. I am indebted to Mary Ann Jensen of the Princeton University Library, Princeton, New Jersey, and to Leith Adams of the University of Southern California Library, Los Angeles, for permitting me access to their Warner Brothers–First National Pictures archives.

A special note of appreciation is due the Ziegfeld Club, whose members work so diligently at keeping Flo Ziegfeld's memory and tradition alive.

235

For their encouragement and good cheer, my thanks go to George Bester, Bob Christie, Norman Flicker, Owen Laster, Barry McGoffin, Derek Pyper, Rodger Robinson, Nen Roeterdink, Ron Samuels, Dorothy Sawyer, Rick Tutoni, Bob Ullman, Jay Watnick and Jerry Weitzman, Yaffa Weitzman, and Christopher Weitzman. And, of course, Russ, Stella and Lisa, plus all the Martoranas.

Special thanks to Eva Franklin, who contributed so much to this book and kept me smiling; to Evelyn Seeff, who has been so supportive over the years; and to Jerry Silverstein, who assisted in the research for this project as well as *Gable and Lombard*.

For helping me through the most crucial and difficult moments in so many ways, I am particularly grateful to Barry Conley.

STAGE AND FILM CHRONOLOGY

THEATER

The Passing Show of 1914, Winter Garden Theatre, New York, opened June 10, 1914. Cast: José Collins, Marilyn Miller, Bernard Granville, Ethel Amorita Kelly, George Monroe, Frances Demarest, T. Roy Barnes, Lew Brice, Robert Emmett Keane. Dialogue and lyrics by Harold Atteridge. Music by Sigmund Romberg and Harry Carroll. A Shubert production, staged by J. C. Huffman. Ran 133 performances.

The Passing Show of 1915, Winter Garden Theatre, New York, May 29, 1915. Cast: Marilyn Miller, Frances Demarest, John Charles Thomas, Daphne Pollard, Willie and Eugene Howard, George Monroe, Theodore Kosloff, Maria Baldina, Sam Hearn, John Boyle, Juliette Lippe, Irene West's Royal Hawaiian Sextet. Dialogue and lyrics by Harold Atteridge. Music by Leo Edwards, William F. Peters, and J. Leubrie Hill. A Shubert production, staged by J. C. Huffman. Ran 145 performances.

Show of Wonders, Winter Garden Theatre, New York, October 26, 1916. Cast: Marilyn Miller, John T. Murray, Eugene and Willie Howard, Grace Fisher, Daisie Irving, George Monroe, Doris Lloyd, James A. Watts, George Baldwin, Sidney Phillips, Alexis Kosloff, Lew Clayton, Marie Lavarre, Eleanor Brown, Sam White. Dialogue and lyrics by Harold Atteridge. Music by Sigmund Romberg, Otto Motzan, and Herman Timberg. A Shubert production, staged by J. C. Huffman. Ran 209 performances.

Fancy Free, Astor Theatre, New York, April 11, 1918. Cast: Clifton Crawford, Marilyn Miller, Marjorie Gateson, Ray Raymond, Harry Conor, Charles

Brown. Book by Dorothy Donnelly and Edgar Smith. Music and lyrics by Augustus Barratt. A Shubert production, staged by J. C. Huffman. Ran 116 performances (MM replaced after first 26 by Ada Weeks).

Ziegfeld Follies of 1918, New Amsterdam Theatre, New York, June 18, 1918. Cast: Marilyn Miller, Will Rogers, Lillian Lorraine, Harry Kelly, Eddie Cantor, Frank Carter, Ann Pennington, W. C. Fields, Bee Palmer, the Fairbanks Twins, Gus Minton, Allyn King, Dolores, Kay Laurell, Savoy and Brennan, Joe Frisco. Book and lyrics by Rennold Wolf and Gene Buck. Music by Irving Berlin, Louis Hirsch, Victor Jacobi, and Dave Stamper. Staged by Ned Wayburn. Ran 151 performances.

Ziegfeld Follies of 1919, New Amsterdam Theatre, New York, June 23, 1919. Cast: Marilyn Miller, Eddie Cantor, Bert Williams, Eddie Dowling, Johnny and Ray Dooley, George LeMaire, Mary Hay, Phyl Dwyer, Van and Schenck, John Steel, the Fairbanks Twins, DeLyle Alda. Book and lyrics by Gene Buck, Dave Stamper, and Rennold Wolf. Music by Irving Berlin, Victor Herbert, Harry Tierney, and Joseph J. McCarthy. Staged by Ned Wayburn. Ran 171 performances.

Sally, New Amsterdam Theatre, New York, December 21, 1920. Cast: Marilyn Miller, Leon Errol, Walter Catlett, Irving Fisher, Dolores, Mary Hay, Stanley Ridges, Alta King, Betty Williams, Vivian Vernon, Barbara Dean, Gladys Montgomery, Frank Kingdon, Jacques Rebiroff. Book by Guy Bolton. Lyrics by Clifford Grey, B. G. DeSylva, P. G. Wodehouse, and Anne Caldwell. Music by Jerome Kern. Butterfly Ballet music by Victor Herbert. A Ziegfeld production, staged by Edward Royce. Ran 570 performances.

Peter Pan, Knickerbocker Theatre, New York, November 6, 1924. Cast: Marilyn Miller, Leslie Banks, Violet Kemble Cooper, Dorothy Hope, Charles Eaton, Wilfred Seagram, Victor Tandy, Edward Rigby, William Dean, Anne Delafield, Eugene Weber. Written by James M. Barrie. Produced by Charles B. Dillingham. Directed by Basil Dean. Ran 125 performances.

Sunny, New Amsterdam Theatre, New York, September 22, 1925. Cast: Marilyn Miller, Jack Donahue, Clifton Webb, Mary Hay, Paul Frawley, Joseph Cawthorn, Esther Howard, Cliff Edwards, Pert Kelton, George Olsen and His Music. Book and lyrics by Otto Harbach and Oscar Hammerstein II. Music by Jerome Kern. Produced by Charles B. Dillingham. Staged by Hassard Short. Ran 517 performances.

Rosalie, New Amsterdam Theatre, New York, January 10, 1928. Cast: Marilyn Miller, Jack Donahue, Frank Morgan, Oliver McLennan, Margaret Dale,

Claudia Dell, Gladys Glad, Hazel Forbes, Katherine Burke, Jack Bruns. Book by William Anthony McGuire and Guy Bolton. Lyrics by Ira Gershwin and P. G. Wodehouse. Music by George Gershwin and Sigmund Romberg. A Ziegfeld production, staged by William Anthony McGuire and Seymour Felix. Ran 335 performances.

Smiles, Ziegfeld Theatre, New York, November 18, 1930. Cast: Marilyn Miller, Fred and Adele Astaire, Paul Gregory, Tom Howard, Eddie Foy, Jr., Larry Adler, Jean Ackerman, Clare Dodd, Georgia Caine, Virginia Bruce, Aber Twins, Kathryn Hereford, Bob Hope. Book by William Anthony McGuire. Lyrics by Clifford Grey, Harold Adamson, and Ring Lardner. Music by Vincent Youmans. A Ziegfeld production, staged by Ned Wayburn and William Anthony McGuire. Ran 63 performances.

As Thousands Cheer, Music Box Theatre, New York, September 30, 1933. Cast: Marilyn Miller, Clifton Webb, Helen Broderick, Ethel Waters, Leslie Adams, Jerome Cowan, Thomas Hamilton, Peggy Cornell, Hal Forde, Harry Stockwell, Hamtree Harrington, Harold Murray, José Limón, Letitia Ide, the Charles Weidman Dancers. Book by Moss Hart and Irving Berlin. Music and lyrics by Irving Berlin. Produced by Sam H. Harris. Staged by Hassard Short. Ran 400 performances (MM replaced by Dorothy Stone for last 80).

FILMS

Sally, a First National Picture in Vitaphone and Technicolor. Cast: Marilyn Miller, Alexander Gray, Joe E. Brown, T. Roy Barnes, Pert Kelton, Ford Sterling, Maude Turner Gordon, Nora Lane, E. J. Ratcliffe, Jack Duffy. Based on the Ziegfeld stage production, screen version by Waldemar Young. Featured some of the original Jerome Kern score, plus new songs by Al Dubin and Joe Burke. Directed by John Francis Dillon. Running time, 103 minutes. Released, January 1930.

Sunny, a First National Picture in Vitaphone and black and white. Cast: Marilyn Miller, Lawrence Gray, Joe Donahue, Mackenzie Ward, O. P. Heggie, Inez Courtney, Barbara Bedford, Judith Vosselli, Clyde Cook, Harry Allen, William Davidson, Ben Hendricks, Jr. Based on the Dillingham stage production, screen version by Humphrey Pearson and Henry McCarty. Lyrics by Otto Harbach and Oscar Hammerstein II. Music by Jerome Kern. Directed by William A. Seiter. Running time, 77 minutes. Released, December 1930.

Her Majesty Love, a First National Picture in Vitaphone and black and white. Cast: Marilyn Miller, Ben Lyon, W. C. Fields, Ford Sterling, Leon

Errol, Chester Conklin, Harry Stubbs, Maude Eburne, Harry Holman, Ruth Hall, William Irving, Mae Madison. Based on a play by R. Bernauer and R. Oesterreicher, screen adaptation by Robert Lord and Arthur Caesar. Lyrics by Al Dubin. Music by Walter Jurmann. Directed by William Dieterle. Running time, 75 minutes. Released, December 1931.

BIBLIOGRAPHY

Astaire, Fred. *Steps in Time*. New York: Harper & Brothers, 1959.

Baral, Robert. *Revue*. New York: Fleet Publishing, 1962.

Bordman, Gerald. *American Musical Theater*. New York: Oxford University Press, 1978.

Burke, Billie, with Cameron Shipp. *With a Feather on My Nose*. New York: Appleton-Century-Crofts, 1949.

Cantor, Eddie. *Take My Life*. New York: Doubleday & Co., 1957.

———. *Ziegfeld—The Great Glorifier*. New York: Alfred H. King, 1934.

Carrera, Liane. *Anna Held and Florenz Ziegfeld*. Hicksville: Exposition Press, 1979.

Ephron, Henry. *We Thought We Could Do Anything*. New York: W.W. Norton & Co., 1977.

Ewen, David. *Complete Book of the American Musical Theater*. Henry Holt & Co., 1958.

Farnsworth, Marjorie. *Ziegfeld Follies*. New York: G.P. Putnam's Sons, 1956.

Finney, Ben. *Feet First*. New York: Crown Publishers, 1971.

Gordon, Ruth. *Myself Among Others*. New York: Atheneum Publishers, 1971.

Green, Abel, and Joe Laurie Jr. *Show Biz—From Vaude to Video*. New York: Henry Holt & Co., 1951.

Guiles, Fred Laurence. *Marion Davies*. New York: McGraw-Hill Book Co., 1972.

Hecht, Ben. *A Child of the Century*. New York: Simon & Schuster, 1954.

Higham, Charles. *Ziegeld*. Chicago: Henry Regnery Co., 1973.

Kreuger, Miles, ed. *The Movie Musical: From Vitaphone of "42nd Street."* New York: Dover Publications, 1975.

Loos, Anita. *A Girl Like I*. New York: The Viking Press, 1966.

Pickford, Mary. *Sunshine and Shadow*. New York: Doubleday & Co., 1955.

St. Johns, Adela Rogers, *Love, Laughter and Tears*. New York: Doubleday & Co., 1978.

Sillman, Leonard. *Here Lies Leonard Sillman, Straightened Out At Last*. New York: Citadel Press, 1959.

Sobel, Bernard. *Broadway Heartbeat*. New York: Hermitage House, 1953.

Sobel, Louis. *The Longest Street*. New York: Crown Publishers, 1968.

Wallis, Hal, with Charles Higham. *Starmaker*. New York: Macmillian Publishing Co., 1980.

Warner, Jack L., with Dean Jennings. *My Hundred Years in Hollywood*. New York: Random House, 1964.

Waters, Ethel, with Charles Samuels. *His Eye is On the Sparrow*. New York: Doubleday & Co., 1951.

Wodehouse, P.G. and Guy Bolton. *Bring on the Girls*. New York: Simon & Schuster, 1953.

Ziegfeld, Patricia. *The Ziegfelds' Girl*. Boston: Little, Brown & Co., 1964.

INDEX

243